CERTIFICATION MARKS

AUSTRALIA
Law Book Co.—Sydney

CANADA and USA
Carswell—Toronto

HONG KONG
Sweet & Maxwell Asia

NEW ZEALAND
Brookers—Wellington

SINGAPORE and MALAYSIA
Sweet & Maxwell Asia
Singapore and Kuala Lumpur

SPECIAL REPORT

CERTIFICATION MARKS

JEFFREY BELSON, PH.D.

LONDON
SWEET & MAXWELL
2002

Published in 2002 by Sweet & Maxwell Limited of
100 Avenue Road,
London, NW3 3PF
Typeset by LBJ Typesetting Ltd
of Kingsclere
Printed in Great Britain by Bookcraft (Bath) Ltd

No natural forests were destroyed to make this product; only farmed timber was used and replanted.

A CIP catalogue record for this book is available from the British Library

ISBN 0421 75820 1

ISBN 0-421-758-201

9 780421 758209

To my wife Margalit, and to my children, Susannah and Sharon.

About the Author

Dr Jeffrey Belson is manager of intellectual property and regulatory affairs for the Indigo group of companies in Rehovot, Israel.

He is a long-standing member of the International Trademark Association (INTA) and past member of the INTA Board of Directors. Dr Belson is also an active member of the Unfair Competition—Trade Identity Committee of the American Bar Association's Intellectual Property Law section.

Preface

This book presents, in a single text, a description of the current law and practice of certification marks while putting the subject into wide legal, historical and commercial context. The book is directed towards trade mark practitioners and legal professionals, regulators, certification and accreditation bodies and policy-makers who deal with matters involving certification marks. Besides trade mark law, other areas of the law that can significantly affect the proprietorship, regulation and use of certification marks are treated as well.

The use of certification marks alongside ordinary trade marks for products and services is likely to increase in importance. The last decades of the twentieth century witnessed dramatic growth in public and governmental attention to environmental, health and safety, and product quality issues. Governments have gradually expanded their control over land use and created agencies with regulatory rationales, such as environmental protection, occupational safety and health, and consumer product safety. As part of this growth in control and regulation, certification and certification-like marks are being exploited increasingly by government regulators, within the purported scope of their regulatory authority.

This book takes the position that certification marks can play a greater role in promoting commercial trust and protection of the trading community, including purchasers as well as manufacturers. Despite their versatility, modern channels of trade are often anonymous and less conducive than traditional channels to the formation of trust embedded in personal relationships. In particular, trust in electronic commerce rests more upon technological and legal safeguards and less upon knowledge that people gain about each other through personal discourse. Certification marks are one form of legal safeguard which mitigates the negative effects of a reduced role for interpersonal trust.

Given the changing patterns of commerce and regulation, the development of wider certification mark use in connection with trade mark use, both off-line and on the internet, is intriguing. This book aims to inform and contribute to the debate that will accompany such development.

Jeffrey Belson
Petah Tikva, Israel
December 2001

Acknowledgments

It is a pleasure to acknowledge the assistance of a number of colleagues and official sources during the writing of this book.

I am especially indebted to Dr Neil J. Wilkof (Tel Aviv) for kindling my interest in writing a book of this type, reviewing much of the manuscript and providing constructive criticism, advice and support.

Special thanks are due also to Rochelle D. Alpert (San Francisco), Belinda Isaac (London), Karen Orlin (Boston) and Stephen C. Tupper (London) for their sustained interest, reviewing various chapters and making helpful suggestions. I am grateful also for the assistance of the following individuals: Hubert Best (London), Dr Joop Elzas (Amsterdam), Clive Gordon (London), Dr A. Michael Klier (London), Dinah Nissen (London), Professor Jeremy Phillips (London), Howard Poliner (Jerusalem), Catherine Mary Still (Sydney), Gustaaf Vandegaer (Brussels), Donna G. White (Ottawa) and John Yelencich (Chicago).

I wish to acknowledge helpful discussions with the staff of the trade mark registries of the United Kingdom, Australia and the Office for Harmonisation in the Internal Market, and with the staff of the United Kingdom Department of Trade and Industry, Consumer Affairs Directorate. The kind assistance provided by James R. Sewell, City Archivist, and the staff of the Guildhall Library, Corporation of London, is much appreciated.

The editorial staff of Sweet and Maxwell have been unstinting in their active support and co-operation from inception of the book until its publication.

Needless to say, the mistakes are all mine.

J.B.

Contents

Appendix

Table of Cases

Table of United Kingdom Legislation

Statutes

Statutory Instruments

Table of European Legislation

Directives

Regulations

Treaties

Table of International Legislation

Conventions, Agreements and Treaties

Statutes

Australia

Benelux

Israel

United States

1

INTRODUCTION

What is a Certification Mark?

A certification mark is a mark which indicates that certain characteristics of goods or services, in connection with which the mark is used, are certified. Whereas the legal perception of ordinary trade marks is primarily one of individual source designation, certification marks are upheld as indicia of conformity of goods or services to particular standards which are stipulated by the proprietor. Thus a certification mark is a guarantee that goods or services, in connection with which the mark is used, conform to certain standards (one example being the BSI Kitemark). Certification marks, in one form or another, have been registrable in the United Kingdom and other countries for nearly a hundred years. However, relatively few certification marks are added to the register each year. **1–01**

About the Book

This book presents the principles of certification mark law and related issues of law and policy that seem set to play a significant role in the future. The approach taken is to put certification marks into wide historical, legal and commercial context. Thus the ensuing chapters deal with the historical development of certification marks, pertinent trade mark law and practice, certifiers' liability, commercial considerations, regulations and standards, electronic certification and authentication of digital products. **1–02**

It is hoped that this contextual approach will assist lawyers and policy-makers in considering the pros and cons of certification mark law reform. It is suggested that such consideration is needed, if only to remedy the under-utilisation of the registered certification mark system. It is unfortunate that a corpus of law and practice as worthy as that of the United Kingdom certification mark system yields only a few registrations each year. Certification marks, it is submitted, are highly beneficial to industry, regulators and the purchasing public alike, and it is time to seek ways for them to be exploited by a wider constituency of potential proprietors and users. **1–03**

Overview of Contents

Chapter 2 traces the historical development of certification marks from medieval times, when the craftsman's mark was used by the guilds to police standards of workmanship and assure the genuineness of goods. Craftsmen's marks, such as those of the London **1–04**

Coopers, shown in Appendix A, were registered by the guilds in order to provide traceability and accountability of the craftsman for his work. The mark of the guild appeared on his goods as well, attesting to his affiliation and to true guild workmanship. With gradual emancipation of the trades from the guild system the liability marks of the craftsmen evolved into trade marks, or personal symbols of goodwill. Regulatory law was displaced by trade mark law as the means of protecting the public from deception.

1–05 Chapter 2 goes on to describe how, as industrialisation gathered pace, a need was identified to protect marks used by members of trade associations of the modern kind. The United Kingdom adopted the approach according to which members of associations could use an "association mark", provided that their goods met the proprietor-association's standards for certification. Registration of association marks, or certification marks as they became known, was first introduced under the Trade Marks Act 1905.[1] The Act initiated the practice of integrating the registration of certification marks into the statutory framework for registration of ordinary trade marks, subject to special provisions.

1–06 Chapter 3 presents a description of the current statutory framework specific to certification marks and the laws and treaties upon which the protection of certification and collective marks is based in the Anglo-American system. A distinction is made in the treatment between marks that certify geographical origin and other attributes—such as material, mode of manufacture of goods or performance of services, quality, accuracy and the like. Other issues considered in Chapter 3 include what is required of the mark and its proprietor before registration can be granted, the notion of the proprietor's "competence to certify", proprietors' regulations, exclusion of the proprietor from use and openness of access for all qualified products. Protection of a certification mark through the right to sue for infringement, the likening of users to trade mark licensees in certain matters and the regulation of assignment of a registered certification mark are also addressed.

1–07 Chapter 4 deals with questions of liability attaching to certification mark proprietors in the context of product liability claims. Following an outline of the history of liability rules in general, the principles of product liability impacting product certifiers are considered under different legal theories and policy objectives. The problems in delineating the boundary of certifiers' liability are illustrated by reference to certification not only of chattels, but also real property and shipping. Because product liability rules have widened considerably over recent years, especially in United States law, this chapter pays particular attention to United States perceptions of certifiers' liability, which can extend to trade associations that set standards and certify.

1–08 Chapter 5 examines the legal and commercial significance of certification marks under United Kingdom law. In particular, the legal status of the "guarantee" function of a certification mark is addressed in light of the commercial circumstances of particular transactions. Suggestions are offered as to how trust in certification marks may be enhanced, including the adoption of a more directly consumer-oriented model of a certification mark. Such a model might emerge under the stimulus of competing means of protecting geographical indications under European Union (E.U.) regulations, and published United Kingdom government proposals requiring more informative marking and greater accountability of certifiers.

1–09 Chapter 6 describes the developing international framework for promulgation and implementation of the technical standards that underpin the use of certification marks, especially in the regulatory sphere. Included is an outline of the principles behind

[1] Trade Marks Act 1905, s.62.

mutual recognition of product conformity assessment procedures, of which certification is but one. The presentation is according to world economic groupings, in "top-down" order. Thus standard-setting frameworks and processes are described first in the context of the world trade system. Then institutions responsible for regulation and standardisation within the E.U. and the United Kingdom are described.

Chapter 7 deals specifically with certification of the authenticity of digital products, **1–10** such as digital books, videos, music, films and software, all of which may be delivered on tangible carriers such as CDs or DVDs, or via electronic communications channels such as the internet, satellite or cable. It is proposed that a legally protectible authentication right, manifest in use of an "authentication mark" is associable with digital products. The proposition builds on the notion that an authentic digital product is distinguished from an unauthentic product by virtue of it having been reproduced or distributed with legitimate authority or approval. The digital watermarks and digital signatures currently used in digital products are, it is suggested, forms of authentication mark.

Chapter 7 also draws attention to recent United Kingdom, E.U. and United States **1–11** legislation that appears to comport with the idea of a digital authentication right. Of particular relevance is recent legislation granting full legal recognition to digital signatures, and treaty-based E.U. and United States laws that outlaw unauthorised circumvention of access control and copyright protection devices, trafficking in devices that facilitate circumvention, and interference with rights management information.

Emerging Issues and Debates

Besides setting forth the essential black letter law relating to certification marks this book **1–12** also identifies emerging issues of law and policy. Emerging issues are sooner or later surrounded by debate and an attempt has been made in this book to convey the essence of the debate to the reader. In this connection it is submitted that a debate is in order on the value of continuing to deny the right of user to the owner of a certification mark. Inflexible adherence to the principle may be thought by some to limit the inherent versatility and potential usefulness of certification marks. Consideration should be given as to whether in fact the disadvantages in lost applicability outweigh the purported public interest in maintaining certifier "independence" or "detachment". For example, there can be no self-certification of one's own products through use of a registered certification mark. Yet self-certification is a cornerstone of E.U. regulatory policy, impacting a large number of product categories.

There are other issues that attach to exclusion of the proprietor from use as well. **1–13** Consider a computer product that is a *per se* or consensus industry standard with the brand name or logo "licensed" on the internet by many thousands of users around the world. Is that really a trade mark licence,[2] or is it closer to a certification mark? If it is closer to a certification mark and the owner is excluded from use there is a basic conceptual problem, since in practise the mark will be used by the owner.

Problems associated with exclusion of the proprietor from use also affect other **1–14** countries which follow the principle, such as the United States, and yet advocate implementation of TRIPS protection of "geographical indications" through their certification mark registration provisions. Such an approach may violate treaty obligations

---

[2] N.J. Wilkof, *Trade Mark Licensing*, (Sweet & Maxwell, London, 1995).

because the prohibition on use by the registrant does not appear to hold with regard to either TRIPS "geographical indications" or Lisbon "appellations of origin".

1–15 Another area of debate focuses on the corporate status of the proprietor of a certification mark, particularly where the mark certifies health and safety-related characteristics of a product. Should the proprietor be required to have non-profit status, which in the United Kingdom, at least, has been considered traditionally to be more compatible with the public interest? It seems now that the United Kingdom registry may be changing its policy in this regard and opening up registration of certification marks to for-profit applicants. As a final example of debatable areas for present purposes, there is the question of the nature and extent of liability that should properly attach to certification mark proprietors when products which they certify are found to be defective and cause physical injury or economic damage.

Summary

1–16 This book is intended to assist practitioners and policy-makers to gain an appreciation of the current state of the law and practice of certification marks and various topical issues associated with the subject. The book places the subject in wide context, based on the belief that there is a need to consider reform of the certification mark system and that reform would be best accomplished where the historical, legal and commercial significance of the system are all accorded their due weight. The research for this work has drawn from a large base of research materials and numerous sources, all of which are cited in copious footnotes. Consequently, it is hoped that the work will also be of value as a reference source for further work.

2

HISTORICAL DEVELOPMENT OF CERTIFICATION MARKS

Introduction

2–01 This chapter outlines the medieval and later history that led to the modern form of certification mark. Medieval product marking was closely controlled by societies of craftsmen, or guilds, as part of the regulation and supervision of their trades. By controlling the marking of products, the guilds aimed to assure compliance with prevailing standards of product quality and fair dealing. The personal mark of the medieval craftsman served as an instrument of control for the regulator rather than a source-identification emblem for purchasers.

Post-medieval history indicates that the old order began to change from the sixteenth century onward. As the trades were emancipated from the restrictions of the guild system, regulatory marks gave way to marks that were perceived by purchasers as identifiers of product source and attestations of quality. Traders assumed personal responsibility for their marks and trade mark law developed to replace regulatory law as the means of preventing unauthorised use of such marks.

In the wake of widespread industrialisation and dramatic growth in domestic and international trade, certification marking acquired renewed importance in the early part of the twentieth century. Ownership of certification marks by trade associations, some having their roots, at the local level at least, in the guild system, re-emerged as an effective means of controlling industry standards and maintaining the quality or other attributes of goods or services.

What is Certification?

2–02 Certification is vouching for the truth of certain information. To certify is to proclaim certain, to declare, attest or assure about something by formal or legal certificate.[1] A certificate is evidence or probative matter providing assurance that some act has or has not been done, or some event occurred, or some legal formality has been complied with.[2] A certification mark is statutorily defined as an indication that goods, or services, in

---

[1] *Shorter Oxford Dictionary on Historical Principles* (C.T. Onions ed., 3rd ed., Clarendon Press, 1962), pp. 285 and 286.

[2] Henry Campbell Black, *Black's Law Dictionary* (4th ed., St Paul: West Publishing Co., 1968), p. 285.

connection with which the mark is used, are certified by the proprietor in respect of origin, material, mode of manufacture of goods or performance of services, quality, accuracy or other characteristics.[3]

What is Regulation?

2–03 This chapter will show how the history of certification marks is founded on regulation. The term "regulation", as used here, means the process by which governments impose requirements on enterprises, citizens, and government itself, including laws, orders and other rules. The objectives of regulation typically are to protect values such as the quality and quantities of goods, environmental quality, public health and safety. Requirements for protecting these values have, throughout history, been issued by a range of governmental levels and by bodies to which governments have delegated regulatory powers.[4] This chapter will consider how product marking developed as an interplay with regulation to become part of the apparatus for meeting these requirements.

Regulatory Origins of Marking: The Guilds

2–04 One of the characteristic institutions of social and economic life in Britain, particularly between the eleventh and sixteenth centuries, was the guild.[5] The earliest guilds appear to have been religious or social associations. Later other forms of guild were formed to control specific trades, thereby protecting and advancing their members' trading interests.[6] The guild as such did not carry on a trade. That was left to the individual members, acting independently and subject to the by-laws of the guild.[7] By controlling, among other things, the use of markings on products, the guilds controlled, policed and enforced standards of workmanship, the quality of merchandise, and weights and measures.[8] Thus, the marks used by the individual craftsmen have been described as liability marks, police marks or regulatory marks.[9]

Means of enforcing the marking rules included searching for and seizing non-compliant or non-guild produced wares and the right to punish offenders following trial, often in the guild's own court of justice.

---

[3] Trade Marks Act 1994 (TMA 1994), s.50.

[4] For a discussion of the international dimension of modern regulation see *The OECD Report on Regulatory Reform*, published by OECD, May 1997.

[5] Like the *collegia* or *corpora* of ancient Rome and Constantinople, the guilds were geographically localised confraternities or societies that provided mutual support for their members. They were secured by statutory authority and deliberately exploited by the state to maintain public authority and social order. The oldest chartered craft in the City of London, the weavers, received charters from King Henry I (1100–1135) and Henry II (1154–1189), the goldsmiths were incorporated in 1327, mercers in 1373, haberdashers in 1407, and the fishmongers in 1433.

[6] The ubiquity of the guilds may be gauged from Richard II's 1388 Inquisition [*sic*] into the state of the social and craft guilds. From the returns, one can infer the existence of about 40,000 guilds throughout England at the time. They ranged in membership from a few to about 15,000 persons. See W. Carew Hazlitt, *The Livery Companies of the City of London* (Swann Sonnenschein & Co., London, 1892), p. 66.

[7] William F. Walsh, *Outlines of the History of English and American Law* (New York University Press, New York, 1924), p. 463.

[8] Because they are of central importance to trade, coinage, weights and measures were regulated from early times by the legislature. The guild's role in controlling such areas would have been specific to their crafts and sub-ordinate to the legislature's role. See W.S. Holdsworth, *A History of English Law* (Methuen & Co., London, 1923), Vol. II, p. 467.

[9] Frank I. Schechter, *The Historical Foundations of the Law Relating to Trade-Marks* (Columbia University Press, New York, 1925), pp. 47–48.

Whereas the craftsman's mark might provide a control and regulatory trace to an offending craftsman, the guild's mark would provide assurance that goods were the result of true guild workmanship. The guild mark was the mark of the association as a whole. As such it bore resemblance to a modern collective mark, that is owned by and symbolises an association of producers, the members of which use the mark under the control of the association, to distinguish the goods of members from those of other undertakings.[10]

Compulsory Trading Standards

Because of the wealth of historical information available and the general prominence of their trade, it is instructive to consider the development of goldsmiths' markings in particular. Throughout the fourteenth and fifteenth centuries the craft was subject to much regulating legislation.[11] Under the legislation, those who could be held liable for unauthorised marking and selling of wares included craftsmen, dealers, assayers and wardens of the craft. Thus members of the craft at all levels were held legally responsible and subject to forfeitures and other penalties for failing to make, mark and deal in compliant goods and to enforce the relevant standards. 2–05

Marking, inspection, testing and legal sanctions were, and remain today, the primary tools for assuring compliance with the required standards of fineness for gold and silver wares. The first statute regulating the standard of silver and gold was enacted in 1300, when a statute of King Edward I provided that no silver or gold ware could be sold until it had been tested at the Guild of Goldsmiths for the proportion of precious to base metal in the mixture.[12] Then, if approved, the article was to be struck with the Leopard's Head, the so-called "King's Mark", as a guarantee of quality.[13] The King's Mark bore resemblance to a modern certification mark; it attested to verification of products against a standard. Later, in 1363, a statute of King Edward III provided for each goldsmith to have his own mark, for which he would answer, to be struck next to the King's Mark.[14]

Enforcement of Trading Standards

The Guild of Goldsmiths regularly searched shops and workplaces for non-compliant goods and use of counterfeit marks.[15] Suspect goods were seized for further investigation and the wardens, sitting as a court of justice, would fine purveyors of substandard products and counterfeiters. They would even mete out prison sentences.[16] Nevertheless, unscrupulous dealers still found it profitable to sell substandard silver and run the risk of being caught. Increased efforts were made to curb such practices by extending 2–06

[10] No member can own the mark individually, instead the collective organisation holds the title to the collective mark for the benefit of all members.

[11] For some of the more important statutes see nn. 12, 14, 18 and 20, below.

[12] 28 Edw. 2, c.20 (1300). See also, John Bly, *Discovering Hall Marks on English Silver* (4th ed., Shire Publications, Aylesbury, 1979), pp. 6–7 and J.S. Forbes, *Hallmark: A History of the London Assay Office* (Unicorn Press, London, 1999), pp. 16–24.

[13] *ibid.*

[14] 37 Edw. 3, c.7 (1363).

[15] Many other London companies such as the Girdlers, Skinners, Cutlers and Coopers also exercised rights of search for, and seizure of, substandard and counterfeit goods.

[16] Forbes, *op. cit.*, describes a 1468 case in which Deryk Knyff and Thomas Gomercy were imprisoned for 5 days and fined 20 shillings for manufacturing substandard silver spoons bearing imitation Leopard's Head marks, found on the premises of a John Fabian in Coggeshall, Essex.

liability. In particular, liability was extended by statute in 1423 to a keeper of the touch[17] who marked or "touched" substandard wares.[18] Later, under a 1478 statute, an additional mark, known as the assay mark, was introduced in order to identify the assayer responsible.[19] This statute held the goldsmiths' company liable and subject to a fine if substandard silver was found marked.

Another well-documented practice of compulsory marking is that of the London Coopers' trade. The objective was suppression of the sale of oil and soap barrels to brewers for holding ale and the use of inferior materials such as unseasoned wood. A decree of the Court of Aldermen[20] required all coopers to bring their goods into the Chamber of London to be marked, and as a means of verifying the maker, a duplicate of his mark was recorded against his name. Faced with continual disregard of such regulations, they were renewed in 1420, 1428 and 1440. An additional form of enforcement was the inspection of places of business, so that all unapproved vessels might be seized, and the holders fined.[21]

Significance of Guild Marks Compared to Modern Marks

2–07 Figures 1 and 2 of Appendix A show selections of Coopers' marks which were registered with their users' names at the London Guildhall in 1420[22] following an ordinance issued by the Mayor, Richard Whittington, and the Court of Aldermen, that every cooper within the Liberty of London should have his own iron mark or sign for marking barrels and kilderkins and have the same entered on record. Pursuant to the ordinance coopers residing within the franchise of the City were to present their marks, made of iron, to the Court within 14 days, to be there recorded.

Figure 1 shows the first 12 marks. Many of the recorded marks exhibit certain common elements such as circles and crosses or modifications of them. Figure 2 shows three groups of marks, including marks not shown in Figure 1, selected to illustrate additional similarities. Such similarities among makers' marks would not have been considered undesirable. Indeed, guilds repressed the adaptation of individuals' marks to render them distinctive in form and size.[23] Whereas a guild's mark might serve to symbolise the good name of the guild to purchasers, the individuality of a craftsman's mark had merely to be adequate to enable the regulator to trace its owner. A craftsman's mark was not a designator of personal identity for the benefit of purchasers. Geographical proximity of all the players in the medieval trading environment, coupled with

---

[17] Assaying and marking or "assay and touch" as it was known, was the duty of the wardens, assisted by another member of the company where necessary. See Forbes, *op. cit.*, p. 24.

[18] 2 Hen. 6, c.14 (1423). See also, Forbes, *op. cit.*, p. 32.

[19] See Bly, *op. cit.*, at p. 8. The assay mark was struck next to the King's mark and the maker's mark and changed every year with the change of wardens of the guild.

[20] 9 Hen. 4 (1407–8).

[21] Hazlitt, *op. cit.*, pp. 433 and 435 recounts a 1413 case in which the Coopers discovered, seized and burned 260 barrels and firkins of unsatisfactory wood, "sawn from the middle and of untrue measure", clandestinely constructed by a fishmonger.

[22] A selection of these coopers' marks also appears at the frontispiece of Schechter, *op. cit.*, and in Hazlitt, *op. cit.*, at p. 436.

[23] Schechter, *op. cit.*, pp. 44–77.

widespread shady trading practices, and persistent disregard of the regulatory ordinances provided the context for the liability or "policing" function of the craftsman's mark.[24]

Post-Medieval Regulation

From the sixteenth century onward, the power and influence of the guild system began to decline. The monarchy and later parliament directly intervened in guild affairs to the point of taking outright control.[25] In place of guild-centred regulation, a new administrative system arose that was more suited to large-scale expansion of internal and external trade. Autonomous, localised regulation at the scale of the community, ward or borough gave way to geographically more extensive regulation. The new system, based on bureaucratic departments and officers of the state,[26] permitted more uniform regulation of trade and industry throughout the realm.[27] **2–08**

Legal Protection of Marks: Regulatory Law Displaced by Trade Mark Law

The legal framework for product marking as described above was one of regulatory law and not trade mark law. This is logical because the law that governed marks used in medieval trade was essentially regulatory in nature; it was not law of a kind that addressed unfair competition among makers, personal trade mark protection, rights of merchandising, distribution, advertising and so on. However, with the transfer of the power to control trade from the guilds to central government and the advent of the industrial revolution, a climate of economic liberalism developed, encouraged by the emergence of the entrepreneurial class.[28] This new climate was conducive to the ascendancy first of a passing off right[29] and later, towards the end of the nineteenth century, a registration right[30] in trade marks. **2–09**

Previously, the trade mark right had been merely an inchoate right, held in check by the guild system. Now, with the gradual[31] emancipation of the trades from guild control, trade mark use was to become more widespread and trade mark law began to evolve to replace regulatory law as the means of protecting such marks against unauthorised use.

---

[24] In the cloth trade, Britain's most important trade, the marks which became most significant were the collective marks of the centres of the cloth industry. Similarly, the records of the London Barber-Surgeons and the Pewterers show that individual marking initiatives were strongly repressed. Nevertheless, other crafts, notably cutlery, showed evidence of more rapid evolution of the individual craftsman's mark from a liability mark to an emblem of goodwill.

[25] As early as 1503, a statute of Henry VII's reign (19 Hen. 7, c.7) required all ordinances of crafts, mysteries, guilds, or fraternities to receive the assent of the chancellor, treasurer, the chief justices or three of them, or by both the justices of assize for the county in which the ordinance had been made.

[26] See Geoffrey K. Fry, "The Development of the Civil Service", paper prepared for presentation at Civil Service Systems in Comparative Perspective, School of Public and Environmental Affairs, Indiana University, Bloomington, Indiana, April 5–8, 1997, at www.indiana.edu/csrc/fry1.html.

[27] See Holdsworth, *op. cit.*, p. 322.

[28] For a historical view of the concept of entrepreneurship see Robert Ronstadt, *Entrepreneurship, Text, Cases and Notes* (Lord Publishing, Dover, 1985), pp. 6–9.

[29] See para. 2–10, below.

[30] See paras 2–12 to 2–14, below.

[31] In some cases, the process of emancipation was *very* gradual and guild control of members' rights of self-advertisement persisted for centuries after the general demise of the guild system. Thus, the question of whether or not the Pewterers of London would allow members' names to appear on their products was finally settled in their favour only in 1747, See Schechter, *op. cit.*, p. 45. See also n. 24, above.

An important aspect of this evolution was that traders had to take personal responsibility for protection of their marks.[32]

The Passing Off Right

2–10 Traders would protect their marks through the tort that became known in the nineteenth century as 'passing off'.[33] The tort was originally concerned with misrepresentations (representations calculated to deceive) that the goods, services or business of the defendant were those of the plaintiff. Later, the scope of the tort was expanded to include misrepresentations as to the quality or nature of the goods or services concerned. The vehicle for such misrepresentation was, and still is, usually a name, mark or trade dress deceptively similar to that of the plaintiff. Passing off was expressly based on fraud, even as late as the end of the nineteenth century, but it is now independent of whether or not the defendant intended to deceive.

The earliest known English case involving misrepresentation as to the source of goods is believed to be *Sandforth's Case* (1584)[34] in which a high-quality cloth maker's mark was allegedly used without authorisation by a maker of lower quality cloth. The high-quality maker's mark had a reputation that allegedly extended beyond the area (possibly Gloucestershire) in which he made the cloth, over England and Wales and "in various other places in parts beyond the seas".[35]

Thereafter, in the case of *Blanchard v. Hill*,[36] Hardwicke L.C. conceded that "every particular trader has some particular mark or stamp". Nevertheless Hardwicke denied a merchant's motion to enjoin another's misappropriation of his Great Mogul stamp on playing cards.[37] Hardwicke alluded to *Sandforth's Case*[38] and acknowledged that an injunction might issue in the right circumstances, in other words, where customers might be drawn away from the plaintiff with "fraudulent design".

Later in the eighteenth century, under Lord Mansfield, a judge noted for his intolerance of passing off, juries commonly awarded large amounts in damages.

2–11 However, in *Singleton v. Bolton*,[39] the plaintiff was nonsuited, with Mansfield holding that both plaintiff and defendant were using a mark of a third party. Had the defendant been selling his own medicine under the plaintiff's mark an action for fraud would lie.

[32] Noteworthy in this context is the case known as *Sandforth's Case*, Cory's Entries, BL MS Hargrave 123, folio 168 (1584), which was tried in the reign of Elizabeth I. See Keith M. Stolte, "How Early Did Anglo-American Trademark Law Begin? An Answer to Schechter's Conundrum" (1998) 88 T.M.R. 564.

[33] The term first appears to have been used in *Perry v.Truefitt* (1842) 49 E.R. 749. For a carefully traced history of the tort see Christopher Wadlow, *The Law of Passing-Off* (2nd ed., Sweet & Maxwell, London 1995), pp. 9–31.

[34] See n. 32, above.

[35] *ibid.* This case was heard during a boom in English litigation that took place between 1560 and 1640 (particularly marked in the reign of Elizabeth I). See W.A. Champion, "Litigation in the Boroughs: The Shrewsbury Curia Parva 1480–1730", 15 Legal History 1994, pp. 201–222. See also M. Smuts, "Rituals of Power and National Identities in Seventeenth-Century Britain" at web.gsuc.cuny.edu/renaissancestudies/geograph/smuts.htm. According to Smuts, Elizabethan operation of the common law extended at the expense of local tribunals like manorial courts and cruder forms of seigniorial power backed by physical coercion. He suggests that whereas in most of Europe the expansion of state power in the sixteenth century led to a proliferation of paid royal officials, in England it brought instead a swelling volume of litigation and a many-fold growth in the number of country attorneys. "Being English" he writes, "meant, among other things, possessing a set of legal rituals with which to defend one's rights and harass one's neighbors."

[36] (1742) 26 E.R. 692.

[37] Wadlow, *op. cit.*, p. 14, suggests that, owing to the background to the case—the outlawed and hated monopoly over playing cards—the outcome to the plaintiff's claim to exclusive use of the Great Mogul on playing cards by virtue of the charter granted to the Cardmakers Company by Charles I, could not have been otherwise.

[38] See n. 32, above.

[39] (1783) 3 Dougl. 293.

There was no evidence of the defendant selling goods as if prepared by the plaintiff. Significantly, Douglas's report mentions another reason for the decision against the plaintiff, namely that he could not show any property interest in a name or mark that was invaded.[40] Thus in the late eighteenth century there was already a sign of judicial appreciation of the notion of property in a trade mark.

By the end of the eighteenth century, it was accepted that fraudulent misrepresentation causing damage to a trader gave a cause of action.[41] Furthermore, it was deemed not necessary that the defendant be "benefited by the deceit, or that he should collude with the person who is."[42] This principle opened the way to prevention, by injunction, of the fraudulent use of another's mark to sell one's own goods. The next major development is associated with the landmark case of *Millington v. Fox* where Lord Chancellor Cottenham enjoined a defendant who had acted in ignorance and without fraudulent intent, stating that he had

> [C]ome to the conclusion that there was sufficient in the case to shew that the Plaintiffs *had a title* to the marks in question; and they undoubtedly had a right to the assistance of a Court of Equity to *enforce that title*. At the same time, the case is very different from the cases of this kind which usually occur, where there has been a fraudulent use, by one person, of the trade marks or names used by another trader. [emphasis added][43]

Thus the court, in equity, was now prepared to enjoin a defendant's misuse of another's trade mark on the basis of the plaintiff's "title" to the mark and without requiring fraudulent intent on the part of the defendant. At common law however, fraud remained the basis for a cause of action until law and equity were fused under the Judicature Acts of 1873–1875.

Introduction of the Registration Right

The need for plaintiffs in passing off cases to establish their reputation in the marks that 2–12
they sought to protect constituted a heavy burden. Furthermore, they had to face the expense and inconvenience of re-establishing their rights in subsequent actions. Trade mark registration was instituted partly to remedy this situation.

Registration of trade marks and their proprietors in the United Kingdom dates from the Trade Marks Registration Act 1875. The Act defined a trade mark as consisting of the name or signature of an individual or firm, or a "distinctive device, mark heading, label or ticket" to which may be added "any letters, words or figures or combinations of letters, words or figures".[44] There was no entitlement to institute proceedings for infringement of a trade mark until and unless such mark was registered pursuant to the Act.[45] Registration of a person as first proprietor of a mark was prima facie evidence of a registrant's right to exclusive use of the mark. After five years on the register, registration was considered conclusive evidence of the proprietor's right to the exclusive

[40] James Oldham, *The Mansfield Manuscripts and the Growth of English Law in the Eighteenth Century* (University of North Carolina Press, Chapel Hill & London, 1992), Vol. 1, pp. 769 and 770.
[41] *Pasley and Another v. Freeman* (1789) 3 Term Rep. 51.
[42] *ibid.*
[43] *Millington v. Fox* (1838) 3 My. and Cr. 338 at 352.
[44] Trade Marks Registration Act 1875, s.10.
[45] Trade Marks Registration Act 1875, s.1.

use of such trade mark[46] provided the proprietor remained the owner of the goodwill of the business to which the mark attached.[47]

In addition to improving the registration proceeding, a new Act, in 1905, defined a trade mark as a mark

> [U]sed or proposed to be used upon or in connexion with goods for the purpose of indicating that they are the goods of the proprietor of such trade mark by virtue of manufacture, selection, certification, dealing with or offering for sale.[48]

Although the definition included certification, it was held in *Prorace Ltd v. Le Brasseur*[49] that if the only function performed by the registered proprietor was certification, the mark could only be registered under section 62, which dealt specifically with certification marks.[50]

2–13 The Trade Marks Act 1938 consolidated the Acts of 1905, 1919 and 1937, and brought the law into line with changes in trading practices that had occurred since the instituting of registration in 1875. A trade mark was defined as indicating a connection in the course of trade between goods and a person entitled to use the mark. Among the most important provisions of the 1938 Act were those permitting licences and assignments of trade marks without goodwill. Licensing of a registered trade mark was treated as valid if the licensee was a registered user.[51]

The Trade Marks Act 1994 (TMA 1994), which superseded the 1938 Act, takes account of drastically changed trading practices in the intervening 56 years. Furthermore, the Act implements Directive 89/104 to harmonise the laws of the Member States relating to trade marks. The requirement for a mark to indicate a connection in the course of trade is eschewed. A mark need only be "capable of distinguishing goods or services of one undertaking from those of other undertakings".[52]

2–14 In the United States, the first Federal Trademark Act was enacted in 1870 at a time of recovery and rapid economic growth following the Civil War. This Act and the Act of 1876, designed to punish counterfeiting of trade marked goods, and the sale or dealing in, of counterfeit goods were declared unconstitutional by the United States Supreme Court in 1879.[53] A comprehensive new trade mark law was enacted in 1905, but unlike the original 1870 Act, or the United Kingdom Trade Marks Act of 1905, it did not provide for applications to register based on proposed use. In fact, intent-to-use applications were only re-introduced into the United States statute in 1989, as a result of an amendment to the Trademark Act of 1946 (The Lanham Act).[54]

---

[46] Trade Marks Registration Act 1875, s.3.

[47] Decoupling of a trade mark from the goodwill of the business using it was regarded by the judiciary of the time as deception and contrary to public policy. This position was based on the notion that a trade mark always indicates to purchasers that goods bearing a mark emanate from a single business. Thus the granting of licenses to use trade marks, or their assignment without assignment of the relevant goodwill, was not acceptable.

[48] Trade Marks Act 1905, s.3.

[49] 44 R.P.C. 73; [1927] 1 Ch. 589.

[50] See paras 2–15 to 2–19, below.

[51] Trade Marks Act 1938, s.28.

[52] TMA 1994, s.1.

[53] *United States v. Steffens, et al.* 100 U.S. 82. The Supreme Court upset convictions against the defendants who were charged, *inter alia*, with counterfeiting trade marks in violation of the 1876 Act, on the ground that Congress had no power to regulate *intrastate* commerce as it had done in both the 1870 and 1876 Acts. The court refused the Attorney General's suggestion that the Acts be held valid at least as to *interstate* commerce.

[54] Trademark Law Revision Act of 1988, Pub. L. 100–667, 102 Stat. 3935.

Until the passage of the Lanham Act perhaps the only significant benefit deriving from registration had been the right to sue in Federal Court. The lack of any strong incentive to register may explain the relatively small registered fraction of all trade marks at the time. Thus, the register was only of very limited use when selecting a new mark that was not confusingly similar to a mark already in use somewhere in the United States.[55]

The Lanham Act defines a trademark as follows:

> The term "trademark" includes any word, name, symbol, or device or any combination thereof adopted and used by a manufacturer or merchant to identify his goods and distinguish them from those manufactured or sold by others.[56]

Important substantive rights are accorded to a registrant under sections 15 and 33(b) of the Act. Together, they provide for exclusive use of a registered mark in interstate commerce and, subject to certain qualifications, for such a right to become "incontestable".[57] Incontestability under the Act is contingent upon the filing of an affidavit by the registrant at the end of any five years subsequent to registration declaring that the mark had been in use for such a five-year period.

In dealing with trade mark licensing, the Lanham Act adopts the concept of a "related company". A related company is any person whose use of a mark is controlled by the owner of the mark with respect to the nature and quality of the goods or services on or in connection with which the mark is used.[58] Use of a registered trade mark, or one sought to be registered, inures to the benefit of the registrant, or applicant, without vitiating the validity of the mark, or its registration, provided such mark is not used in a manner to deceive the public.[59]

Re-emergence of the Certification Right

The re-emergence of the certification right may be said to date from the late nineteenth century, at a time when the courts were presented with a large number of cases concerning the adoption of geographical names on products and commodities originating from particular geographical locations. Use of the name of the city or location in which goods originated to indicate their provenance is open to all traders in that city or location. In some instances, over the course of time, the geographical name, adopted as a mark might even become a synonym for superior quality. The geographical name in effect certifies the origin of the goods, and the goodwill and reputation in the name deemed deserving of protection under the common law principle of passing off.[60] In such cases, persons 2–15

---

[55] For such reasons, the original Lanham Bill, H.R. 9041, of January 19, 1938, proposed, in s.32, that "It shall be unlawful to use any mark in commerce unless and until such mark has been deposited in accordance with this section." This rather extreme proposal was dropped from the next trade mark bill.

[56] Lanham Act 1946, s.45, 15 U.S.C. 1127.

[57] The notion of incontestability is reminiscent of s.13 of the Trade Marks Act 1938, which stated that, after seven years, a mark registered in Part A of the register, was to be "taken to be valid in all respects" unless the registration was obtained by fraud or offended against s.13 which made unlawful registration of a mark likely to deceive or cause confusion.

[58] Lanham Act 1946, s.45.

[59] Lanham Act 1946, s.5.

[60] See Annotation: Unfair competition in use of geographical tradename by persons carrying on business elsewhere, 174 American Law Reports, Annotated pp. 496 *et seq.*

> [r]esiding at other places [would] not be permitted to use the geographical name so adopted as a brand or label for similar goods for the mere purpose by fraud and false representation of appropriating the good will and business . . . rightfully built up."[61]

The courts distinguished between a trade mark proper which indicated an exclusive right and the use of a geographical name where no exclusive property can be had.[62] However, when a defendant company that had no connection with the plaintiff's locality used a geographical name that was used by the plaintiff and in so doing diverted the plaintiff's trade by practices that were designed to mislead its customers, such as simulating labels or representing its product as the plaintiff's, the defendant would be enjoined against passing off.

2–16 A significant case recognising common law certification of origin as described above is *Pillsbury-Washburn Flour Mills Co. v Eagle*,[63] in which the marks "Minneapolis", "Minneapolis Minn.", "Minnesota", and "Minnesota Patent", used by a group of Minneapolis traders, in effect represented a certification of the origin of their flour. The court enjoined a Chicago dealer who had been obtaining an inferior grade of flour from Milwaukee, Wis. mills, labelling it as "Best Minnesota Patent, Minneapolis, Minn.," and advertising it as made at Minneapolis, Minn. The notion of certification in this case is reinforced by the fact that the Minnesota mills' products were systematically inspected and graded by State of Minnesota-appointed inspectors.[64] The case is important because the misapplication of a certification mark *per se* does not immediately constitute a deception of the public as to the individual source of the goods, which had been the classical basis for an action for passing off.

In addition to upholding rights in geographical names effectively certifying location of origin, the courts protected names used to designate merchandise selected by firms in the course of their business, on the basis of the merchandise being of a particular standard or uniformity of quality. A leading case in this regard is the United States Supreme Court case of *Menendez v. Holt*.[65] Although the brand name used by Holt did not indicate by whom the flour was manufactured, it did indicate the origin of its selection and classification. The court took the view that the brand was equivalent to the signature of Holt & Co. to a certificate that the flour was the genuine article, which had been determined by them to possess a certain degree of excellence. Nevertheless mere symbols affixed by a manufacturer to denote class, grade or quality only, were held not to be capable of protection for exclusive use as a trade mark, as in *Amoskeag Manufacturing Co. v. Trainer*[66] and in *Lawrence Manufacturing Company v. Tennessee Manufacturing Co.*[67]

---

[61] *Pillsbury-Washburn Flour Mills Co. et al. v. Eagle* [1898] 86 Fed.Rep. 608 at 618.

[62] "Their nature [*i.e.* geographical names, designating districts of country] is such that they cannot point to the origin (personal origin) or ownership of the articles of trade to which they may be applied. They point only at the place of production, not to the producer, and could they be appropriated exclusively, the appropriation would result in mischievous monopolies. Could such phrases, as 'Pennsylvania wheat', 'Kentucky hemp', 'Virginia tobacco', or 'Sea Island cotton', be protected as trademarks . . . it would greatly embarrass trade, and secure exclusive rights to individuals in that which is the common right of many." *Per* Strong J., in *Canal Co. v. Strong*, 13. Wall. 311 at 320; (1871) U.S. Sup. Ct.

[63] See n. 61, above.

[64] See n. 61, above, at p. 611.

[65] 128 U.S. 514.

[66] 101 U.S. 51.

[67] 138 U.S. 537. More than 20 years after *Lawrence*, the Missouri Supreme Court, in *Sessinghaus Milling Co. v. Hanebrink*, 247 Mo. 212; 152 SW 354, held that a miller's quality marks could be protected where the respondent knowingly and willfully sold an inferior grade of product as and for appellant's higher and finer grades.

The *registrable* certification mark was established in the first decades of the twentieth century. A treatment of all of the industrial, social and legal factors that may have influenced its establishment is beyond the scope of this work. It is nevertheless noteworthy that the period was marked by a significant rise in domestic and international trade and competition. Furthermore, collective marks were required to be registrable pursuant to the 1911 Washington meeting of the Paris Convention.[68] Industries could therefore be expected to take collective action to protect their reputations and prevent infiltration of inferior goods into their markets. 2–17

In view of the above, it is perhaps not surprising that trade associations have figured prominently among applicants for certification mark registration. The roots of trade associations can be traced back, on the local level at least, to the craft guilds. In their modern form, trade associations date from the 1880s and, until World War I, were concerned with control of competition and problems of international trade. During and after World War I, the trade associations proliferated and assumed greater importance as they moved into a more consultative mode, in which they worked closely with government on standard-setting and scientific, technological and production matters.[69] An association's registered certification mark would provide assurance to the trade and consumers alike that goods bearing the mark met a certain quality standard, had a certain geographical origin, or possessed other particular attributes. Furthermore, ownership by a trade association of certification marks underpinned by industry standards would protect association members against goods passed off as having the certified attributes.

Section 62 of the Trade Mark Act 1905 provided for the registration of certification marks, referred to as standardisation marks. Under section 62, any association or person that undertook the examination and certification of any goods in respect of origin, material, mode of manufacture, quality, accuracy, or other characteristic, could be permitted to register such mark as a trade mark, subject to approval of the Board of Trade. The 1911 Washington Conference of the International Convention for the Protection of Industrial Property[70] introduced Article *7bis*, providing for the filing of collective marks belonging to associations "even if such associations do not possess an industrial or commercial establishment." Thus, from 1905, there was already a provision in the United Kingdom trade mark statute that met the requirements of Article 7bis provided that the associations in question undertook examination and certification of some attribute of the goods. 2–18

From the outset, the registration procedure for certification marks was integrated into the statutory framework for registration of ordinary trade marks, subject to special provisions. These special provisions were refined to include the signs of which a certification mark may consist, the nature of the proprietor's business, the filing and approval of regulations governing use of the mark, regulation of alienation, and grounds for cancellation. Additionally, an applicant for a certification mark has always been

---

[68] See n. 70 below, Article *7bis*. Consider a traders' association that requires conformity of members' goods or services with certain standards or conditions as a condition for membership and admits all traders whose goods meet such standards or conditions. In such cases, there may, in practice, be little to differentiate between the collective mark and a certification mark.

[69] For an account of the development and characteristics of trade associations in the U.S., see David B. Truman, *The Governmental Process: Political Interests and Public Opinion* (Alfred A. Knopf, New York, 1958), Chap. 4.

[70] Paris Convention for the Protection of Industrial Property of March 20, 1883, as revised at Brussels on December 14, 1900, at Washington on June 2, 1911, at the Hague on November 6, 1925, at London on June 2, 1934, at Lisbon on October 31, 1958, and at Stockholm on July 14, 1967, and as amended on October 2, 1979.

required to file regulations governing use of the mark which comprise the standard that has to be met for certification.

2–19 A notable feature of a certification mark is that permission to affix the mark may not be refused to anybody who complies with the required standards. This feature distinguishes a certification mark from a collective mark, to which access is limited to, for example, members of an association or co-operative that owns the mark.[71]

Another principle fundamental to the concept of a certification mark in most, but not all, Anglo-American jurisdictions, and others as well, is that the owner of the certification mark is precluded from using the mark for the certified goods, or services where covered. This rule was followed even under the 1905 Act, on public interest grounds, although there was no written provision for it. Under the 1938 Act, a certification mark was not registrable in the name of a person who carried on a trade in goods of the kind certified.[72] The 1994 Act contains a similar provision.[73]

Under the United Kingdom and United States statutes, a certification mark is subject to cancellation if the registrant engages in the production or marketing of any goods or services to which the certification mark is applied.[74] This goes to the heart of the nature of a certification mark as conceptualised in most Anglo-American jurisdictions. The owner may not use the mark. The owner's function is to exercise control over use of the mark by others, thereby ensuring that their products meet his required standards.

Summary

2–20 Compulsory marking was widely used by the medieval guilds to control and enforce standards of workmanship and assure the genuineness of goods generally. The craftsman's mark served a liability or regulatory function and was used on all manner of goods from gold and silverware, to cloths, pewter wares, ale barrels, cutlery and bread. The marking regulations were backed by powers of search, seizure and destruction of substandard and counterfeit goods, the levying of fines and sentencing to imprisonment. In addition to the craftsman's mark, the guild mark appeared on goods to attest to the fact that they were the result of true guild workmanship.

As the power of the guilds waned, from the sixteenth century onwards a personal trade mark right began to evolve. The erstwhile regulatory mark used by the individual craftsman came to be perceived as his trade mark, representing a transformation from a liability to an asset mark, a symbol of goodwill to be valued by its owner. As trade mark use developed so did a body of law that protected trade marks against unauthorised use. The law afforded traders remedies against passing off and, towards the end of the nineteenth century, against infringement of a registered trade mark.

2–21 In the late nineteenth and early twentieth centuries, trade associations, in some respects the latter day guilds, emerged to assume an important role in an increasingly industrialised society. Needs developed for marks that could be used by association members, on their goods, to indicate membership as well as conformity of their products to approved standards, developed and administered by the trade associations. The approach adopted in the United Kingdom was that members could benefit from the

[71] But see n. 68, above.
[72] Trade Marks Act 1938, s.37(1).
[73] TMA 1994, Sched. 2, para. 4. An interesting departure from this principle is embodied in the Australian Trade Marks Act 1995, s.169, under which the goods or services certified can be those of any person, including the owner of the certification mark.
[74] Lanham Act 1946, s.14(5).

collective goodwill of an association through use of an association mark provided that their goods met the proprietor-association's requirements for certification.

Provision was made for registration of association marks, or certification marks as they became known, under the Trade Marks Act 1905,[75] subject to special provisions. An association's registered certification mark would provide assurance to the trade and purchasers that goods bearing the certification mark met a certain quality standard, had a certain geographical origin, or possessed other particular attributes. Over the past century, the principles underpinning the scheme governing registration of certification marks have not changed significantly. However, the current trade marks statute, the Trade Marks Act 1994, allows applications for registration of not only certification marks[76] but also collective marks.[77] Furthermore such marks may now be registered in respect of services as well as goods.[78] Collective marks are intended to distinguish the goods or services of members of an association which is the proprietor of the mark from those of other undertakings, without any requirement, under the Act, for certification of the goods or services.[79]

---

75 Trade Marks Act 1905, s.62.
76 TMA 1994, s.50.
77 TMA 1994, s.49.
78 See Appendix C, below.
79 TMA 1994, s.49.

3

CERTIFICATION AND COLLECTIVE MARKS: ELEMENTS OF STATUTORY PROTECTION

Introduction

Part 1 of this chapter provides an overview of the functions of certification marks and collective marks, and the laws and treaties upon which their protection is based in the Anglo-American system. 3–01

Part 2 considers the statutory framework specific to certification marks. A distinction is made between certification marks that indicate certification of geographical origin and those that indicate certification of other attributes of goods and services, including material, mode of manufacture of goods or performance of services, quality, accuracy and the like. The requirement that the proprietor of a certification mark be "competent" to certify is considered in light of successive trade mark statutes and the one or two cases that have interpreted the requirement. Other issues which are considered include the proprietor's regulations, financial terms and conditions for certification, the distinctiveness standard for registration, exclusion of the proprietor from use and openness of access to the certification mark for all qualified products. Infringement, the status of authorised users, their likening to trade mark licensees in certain matters and the regulation of assignment of a registered certification mark are also addressed.

Part 3 of the chapter focuses on the functions and protection of collective marks in the context of the statutory scheme and treaty obligations. Like certification marks, collective marks may, or may not, constitute indications of geographical origin. Among the topics included are whether the corporate status and conditions of incorporation of an association impact eligibility for ownership of a collective mark, the statutory requirement for regulations governing use of the mark, grounds for revocation, infringement, and likening of an authorised user to a trade mark licensee in certain matters. Similarities and differences are pointed out between the United Kingdom and United States systems for registration of collective marks.

Finally, the conflation of certification marks and collective marks is treated as emanating from the correlation between association and standardisation. It is submitted that varying degrees of conflation are likely, such that the usefulness and specificity of the information conveyed by a collective mark may at times be closer to that of a traditional certification mark and at other times less so.

1 OVERVIEW OF CERTIFICATION AND COLLECTIVE MARKS

Basic Significance

Certification Marks

3–02 Whereas ordinary trade marks serve to distinguish the goods or services of one individual source from another, certification marks have a different significance. Certification marks are principally indicia of conformity of goods or services to particular standards, stipulated by the proprietor of the mark. Such marks are for the use of multiple sources,[1] provided that their goods or services meet the proprietor's required standard. Certification may be in respect of geographical origin, material, mode of manufacture of goods or performance of services, quality or accuracy, but is not limited to such characteristics.[2] The mark signifies that its proprietor vouches for the conformity of the goods or services to approved and often quantitative standards. To the extent that the standard goes to quality, the certification mark attests to attainment of an *absolute* level of quality. By way of contrast, an ordinary trade mark's quality is considered to be an assurance to the consumer of a *consistent* level of quality in the product as a whole.[3]

Collective Marks

3–03 A collective mark is a mark owned by an association or "collectivité"[4] for the use of its members. The United Kingdom perception of a collective mark is that it is for use in connection with goods and services to indicate that they are goods and services of members of an association which is the proprietor of the mark. Protection of collective marks is expressly provided for under the international framework founded on the Paris Convention.[5]

The TMA 1994 does not make registration of a collective mark contingent upon the goods' or services' conformity to standards.[6] However, the proprietor-association is required to file with the registrar regulations governing use of the mark, specify the persons authorised to use the mark, the conditions of membership of the association, and any conditions for use of the mark and sanctions against misuse.[7] Other jurisdictions as well, including the United States, require an applicant for registration of a collective mark to file with the registry regulations governing use of the mark. In effect the

[1] Which may not necessarily be individual sources. For an example of a case involving use of a certification mark by a syndicate of associations see, *Re Union Nationale Inter-Syndicates des Marques Collectives' Application* [1922] 39 R.P.C. 97.
[2] TMA 1994, s.50.
[3] See N.J. Wilkof, *Trade Mark Licensing* (Sweet and Maxwell, London, 1995), Chap. 2, pp. 28 *et seq.*
[4] See para. 3–06, below.
[5] See n.18, below.
[6] TMA 1994, s.49.
[7] TMA 1994, Sched. 1, para. 5.

regulations specify not only conditions of membership of the association but also, where appropriate, provisions for ensuring correct use of the association's name, marks, professional designations and any other manifestations of collective goodwill.

In the United States collective marks have been registrable to foreign and domestic associations since 1936 and 1938, respectively.[8] Under the United States Trademark Act of 1946 (the "Lanham Trademark Act" or "Lanham Act"), registration of collective and certification marks is open to "[p]ersons, and nations, States, municipalities, and the like, exercising legitimate control over the use of the marks sought to be registered, even though not possessing an industrial or commercial establishment".[9] Such wording follows the wording of Article 7bis of the Paris Convention.[10] The United States concept of a collective mark embraces both marks used in commerce by members of an association and marks that indicate membership without "use" in the trade mark sense.[11] Registration is permitted of a form of collective mark which merely serves to indicate, on pins or lapel badges for example, membership in an association without use, in the trade mark sense, on goods or services. Such marks are known as collective membership marks.[12]

A Collective Mark Can Denote Certification

Collective marks are also used to certify, particularly in countries that do not provide for registration of certification marks, and there is widespread use of "collective mark" to denote certification marks, including geographical indications of origin.[13] Perhaps that is why the word "association", or an equivalent word, is not always present in the language used to describe a collective mark. Consider the statement of section 19 of the Benelux Trade Marks Act 1996: 3–04

> [A]s collective marks shall be considered all signs that are thus indicated upon their application and that serve to distinguish one or more characteristics of goods originating from different enterprises applying the mark under the supervision of the proprietor.

Firth observes that the language used in the World Intellectual Property Organisation's (WIPO) training manual, which describes a collective mark as a mark that

---

[8] See also para. 3–39, below. On June 20, 1936, the U.S. trade mark law was amended to provide for registration of collective marks to associations located in foreign countries, in order to implement treaty obligations. However the Commissioner refused to register collective marks owned by domestic associations until legislation provided for such registrations. In April 1938, the Committee on Patents of the House of Representatives reported that "[U]nder existing laws, and in keeping with international conventions, foreign trade-marks of a collective character enjoy a protection in the United States not now afforded to domestic users of collective trade-marks." See "Registration of Collective Marks" 75th Congress, 3d session, Senate, Report No. 1770, (1938). Bill H.R. 9966, authorising the registration of collective trade marks was introduced on March 23, 1938. From this bill emanated Public Law 586, approved June 10, 1938, which afforded registration to foreign and domestic associations alike.

[9] Lanham Act 1946, 15 U.S.C. 1054.

[10] See para. 3–06, below.

[11] s.45 of the Lanham Act 1946, 15 U.S.C. 1127, provides *inter alia*: The term "collective mark" means a trademark or service mark—(1) used by the members of a co-operative, an association, or other collective group or organisation, or (2) which such co-operative, association, or other collective group or organisation has a bona fide intention to use in commerce and applies to register on the principal register established by this Act, and includes marks indicating membership in a union, an association, or other organisation.

[12] *Trademark Manual of Examining Procedure*, §1304.09: "Examination of Collective Membership Mark Applications," See website of United States Department of Commerce, Patent and Trademark Office, www.uspto.gov.

[13] A. Firth, "Collectivity, control and joint adventure—observations on marks in multiple use.", in *Perspectives on Intellectual Property: Trade Marks Retrospective* (Sweet & Maxwell, London, 2000), Vol. 7, p. 178.

> does not distinguish between different concerns, but serves to distinguish goods or services with common characteristics from goods or services without those characteristics.[14]

seems more to describe a certification mark than an association mark. It is submitted that the description of collective marks on the WIPO website as marks

> owned by an association whose members use them to identify themselves with a level of quality and other requirements set by the association[15]

is also quasi-certification language.

3–05 Even where a jurisdiction admits registration of both certification and collective marks, a collective mark may still be used to certify. The United Kingdom Registry, in response to inquiries, acknowledges that a collective mark can serve a certification function in relation to the products of the members of the proprietor association where the association chooses to set standards which its members must meet when using the mark. But, unlike a certification mark, the proprietor does not *have* to set any such standards as a condition of registration. Noteworthy also is the expressly declared certifying function in the particular registration of a collective mark in the United States to show that "The mark certifies that persons belonging to the International Association of Machinists and Aerospace Workers performed the work or labor on the above-identified goods."[16] There appears to be no material difference between the message conveyed by that mark and by the certification mark owned by the same union, comprising a similar design, words and letters, which "[C]ertifies that the work or labor on the goods was performed by members of the applicant."[17]

Treaty Influences on Certification and Collective Mark Legislation

The Paris Convention

3–06 The Paris Convention is the basis of the mutual obligation among nations to accept for filing and to protect marks owned by associations.[18] In pertinent part, the relevant article of the Convention, Article 7*bis*, relates to "collective marks belonging to associations". Discussions on the protection of association marks (the term used to denote an association in the French language draft of Article 7*bis* was "une collectivité") took place at the Madrid and Brussels Conferences for the Revision of the Convention of 1883, in 1890 and 1900 respectively, but without any promulgation.[19] At the Washington

[14] Geneva, 1997, World Intellectual Property Organisation, para. 2.5.

[15] WIPO, "What kinds of trade marks can be registered?" See www.wipo.org/about-ip/en/index.html.

[16] Registration No. 1133886, registered April 22, 1980.

[17] Registration No. 0646221, registered May 28, 1957.

[18] Paris Convention for the Protection of Industrial Property of March 20, 1883, as revised at Brussels on December 14, 1900, at Washington on June 2, 1911, at The Hague on November 6, 1925, at London on June 2, 1934, at Lisbon on October 31, 1958, and at Stockholm on July 14, 1967, and as amended on October 2, 1979. The Convention laid the foundations for international collaboration in the field of protection and commercialisation of industrial inventions, trade marks, and other forms of industrial property, set forth in Art. 1 of the Convention. The substantive provisions of the Convention may be summarised as comprising national treatment for foreign applicants, priority rights and common rules. The total number of Contracting States on December 31, 1998, was 151.

[19] See Stephen P. Ladas, *Patents, Trademarks and Related Rights* (Harvard University Press, Cambridge, 1975), Vol. II, pp. 1289–90. Nevertheless, the U.K., in s.62 of the Trade Marks Act 1905, put in place a basis for meeting the obligations of future Art. 7bis, which was promulgated at the Washington Conference of 1911, see N. Dawson, *Certification Trade Marks Law and Practice* (Intellectual Property Publishing, Ltd., London, 1988), p. 15.

Conference of the Convention, in 1911, Article *7bis* was adopted. This Article requires the countries of the Union to accept for filing and to protect collective marks belonging to associations the existence of which is not contrary to the law of the country of origin, "even if such associations do not possess an industrial or commercial establishment." This latter qualifying expression implies that it was considered "normal" for associations to have a commercial establishment and the expression was a compromise, made in deference to countries, notably Britain, that did not favour ownership of collective marks by commercially based associations. However, pursuant to paragraph 3 of Article *7bis*, each country is to be the judge of the particular conditions under which a collective mark is to be protected and may refuse protection if the mark is contrary to the public interest.[20]

The approach taken at the time by the United Kingdom to protection of association marks is apparent from section 62 of the United Kingdom Trade Marks Act 1905. This section introduced into the law the *examination* and *certification* of the result of such examination of goods in respect of characteristics such as origin, material, mode of manufacture, and the like. Any association or person certifying the results of such examination by mark used upon or in connection with the goods would be eligible to apply for registration of the mark. The 1905 Act referred to these marks as standardisation marks.[21] Because they were intended to serve as a warranty or certificate, they became more generally known as certification or association marks.

Eventually, in 1934, a Board of Trade report, the Goschen Committee Report, recommended to Parliament that "Certification Trade Marks" would be a more appropriate name.[22]

The TRIPS Agreement

Certification and collective marks can also be indications of geographical origin. The TRIPS Agreement of 1994[23] places an obligation on Members[24] to protect "geographical indications", which are defined in TRIPS as **3–07**

> [I]ndications which identify a good as originating in the territory of a member, or a region or locality in that territory, where a given quality, reputation or other characteristic of the good is essentially attributable to its geographical origin.[25]

TRIPS incorporates by reference a number of Articles of the Paris Convention, including Article *7bis*.[26] Therefore, protection of collective marks belonging to associations and serving as geographical indications is included under TRIPS. Producers of

[20] At the London Conference of the Convention, in 1934, the British delegation declared that it interpreted the reservation of public interest as meaning that protection may be refused to an association transacting ordinary commercial business. Other delegations had pointed out the need for syndicates, particularly agricultural syndicates, to own collective marks and yet be engaged in commercial activities, particularly purchase and sale of products. See Ladas, *op. cit.*, p. 1295.

[21] The Trade Marks Act 1905 was entitled "An Act to consolidate and amend the Law relating to Trade Marks". Section 62 appears under the heading "Special Marks" and in the margin against the text of s.62 appear the words "Standardisation &c., trade marks."

[22] "Report of the Departmental Committee on the Law and Practice relating to Trade Marks" (Cmd. 4568 (1934), para. 229(i)).

[23] Agreement on Trade-Related Aspects of Intellectual Property Rights, Including Trade in Counterfeit Goods (TRIPS), Section 3, Geographical Indications. For a succinct review of the topic of geographical indications, see Barbara E. Cookson, "Geographical Indications, Made in France and Exported Worldwide", INTA Bulletin, August 15, 2000, Vol.55, No.15, pp.4–5.

[24] Members of the World Trade Organisation, successor to the General Agreement on Tariffs and Trade, to which TRIPS forms Annex 1C.

[25] TRIPS, Art. 22(1).

[26] TRIPS, Art. 2(1) requires compliance with Arts 1 through 12, and Art. 19 of the Paris Convention 1967.

agricultural and food products, in particular, are often organised into associations or co-operatives on the basis of their common geographical location. The goods of these association's members may not just originate from the same place; they may also have attributes which are physically connected with the location, other than the fact that the factory is situated there. The collective marks that identify the goods of such associations as originating in that location and as having characteristics attributable to that location are required to be protected under the TRIPS geographical indications provision.

Under TRIPS, legal means must be provided for interested parties to prevent designation or presentation of a good suggesting origin of the good in a geographical area other than the true place of origin in a manner which misleads the public as to the geographical origin of the good.[27] Furthermore, an interested party is entitled to refuse or invalidate the registration of a trade mark which contains or consists of a geographical indication with respect to goods not originating in the territory indicated if use of the indication is "such as to mislead the public."[28]

3–08 One class of goods accorded special attention in TRIPS is wines and spirits.[29] Members are required to provide additional protection to prevent use of a geographical indication identifying wines or spirits for wines or spirits not originating in the place indicated by the geographical indication in question, even where the true origin of the goods is indicated or the geographical indication is used in translation or accompanied by expressions such as "kind", "type", "style", "imitation" or the like.[30] Furthermore, registrations of trade marks for wines which contain or consist of a geographical indication identifying spirits are to be refused or invalidated *ex officio* if a Member's legislation so permits or at the request of an interested party, with respect to such wines and spirits not having this origin.[31]

The TRIPS provisions in respect of geographical indications, particularly those relating to refusal and invalidation of registration, are controversial and must be viewed against the traditional contention in international economic relations over the protection of geographical indications. Producers of a good that has characteristics attributable to the place of origin naturally wish to defend their goodwill in the geographical indication. On the other hand, producers elsewhere may have long used the geographical name without any dishonest intentions and accrued goodwill in it or prior to the name of the place having become a "geographical indication".

Before TRIPS was concluded, the E.U. mandated by Regulation[32] the treatment of Geographical Indications (GIs) as a registrable right; but they do not appear to be viewed as an intellectual property right.[33] GIs are treated as though they are part of agricultural law. Thus in the United Kingdom, administration of GI registration is the responsibility of the Department for Environment, Food and Rural Affairs. This may be thought inconsistent with the fact that the underlying *ratio* for TRIPS and the Paris Convention, which TRIPS incorporates, is the protection of intellectual property. The United States in particular is strongly opposed to the E.U.'s position, believing that the obligations of TRIPS with respect to geographical indications can be satisfied by existing genres of intellectual property, such as certification marks.

---

[27] TRIPS, Art. 22(2)(a).
[28] TRIPS, Art. 22(3).
[29] TRIPS, Art. 23.
[30] TRIPS, Art. 23(1).
[31] TRIPS, Art. 23(2).
[32] Council Reg. 2081/92 of July 14, 1992.
[33] For further discussion of Geographical Indications and the as yet unresolved World Trade Organisation dispute between the U.S. and the E.U. concerning them, see Chap. 5, para. 5–19, n. 92, below.

The European Community Collective Trade Mark

The Council Regulation on the Community Trade Mark (CTM) provides for registration of collective marks but not certification marks.[34] The Regulation was published in 1994. Provision is made for registration of a CTM as a single registration covering all Member states of the E.U. A CTM registration does not replace national registrations; instead it can coexist with them in a duel system. A proprietor of a CTM is accorded exclusive rights to use of its trade mark throughout the European Community. Furthermore, the proprietor may prevent registration of a mark that is identical to its mark and is for identical goods or services. Likewise, a proprietor of an existing CTM may prevent registration where the marks and the goods or services are similar and there is a likelihood of confusion. Where the goods or services are dissimilar to those for which there is an existing similar CTM, the CTM may be protected against use of a sign where the CTM has a reputation in the E.U. and where use of the sign without due cause takes unfair advantage of, or is detrimental to, the distinctive character or repute of the CTM. **3–09**

In the United Kingdom, implementation of the Regulation is reflected in section 49 and Schedule 1 to the TMA 1994. A Community collective mark must be capable of distinguishing the goods or services of the members of the association that is the proprietor of the mark from those of other undertakings. Registration is open to associations of manufacturers, producers, suppliers of services, or traders and legal persons governed by public law.[35] In derogation of Article 7(1)(c) of the Regulation, signs or indications designating the geographical origin of the goods or services may be registered as Community collective marks.

It appears that a CTM-registered collective mark may coexist on the United Kingdom register with a United Kingdom domestic registration of the same mark as a certification mark. Thus, if the certification mark HALLOUMI, applied for in the United Kingdom and published[36] in respect of "[C]heese made from sheep's and/or goat's milk; cheese made from blends of cow's milk; all included in Class 29", is registered, it will coexist with the CTM collective mark HALLOUMI[37] for "Cheese".

2 CERTIFICATION MARKS

Geographical Name Certification Marks

A certification mark may comprise the geographical name of the place from where the product originates. The desirability, for traders, of using geographical place names as certification marks may derive from valuable public association of the place names with special traditional skills or particular geographical features. However, the TMA 1994 provides that registration of such a mark does not allow its proprietor to prevent bona fide use of a geographical name in the course of trade by a person whose goods or services originate in the area concerned.[38] **3–10**

---

[34] Council Reg. No. 40/94 of December 20, 1993, [1994] O.J. L11/1, Art. 64.
[35] Council Reg. No. 40/94, Art. 64(1).
[36] Filed December 22, 1990, No. 1451888, published July 5, 2000. The applicant is the Cyprus Ministry of Commerce & Industry, Nicosia, Cyprus.
[37] Filed February 22, 1999, No. 1082965, registered July 14, 2000. The proprietor association is Organismos Kypriakis Galaktokomikis Viomichanias, Lefkosia, Cyprus.
[38] TMA 1994, Sched. 2, para. 3(2).

Illustrative of registration of a geographical name for goods is the Irish Linen Guild's word and device certification mark IRISH LINEN.[39] Another example is the registration of the word and device certification mark DANISH for "[M]ilk, cheese, butter and dairy products (for food)."[40] In some cases it is a condition of registration that the words "Certification Trade Mark" or "Certification Mark" are used in conjunction with the mark as registered. In other cases the words form an integral part of the mark, as in STILTON CERTIFICATION TRADE MARK.[41] Furthermore, language that constitutes a guarantee may form an integral part of a certification mark. Such an example is the United Kingdom-registered ROQUEFORT GARANTI D'ORIGINE ET DE QUALITÉ[42] for "Roquefort cheese".

Non-Geographical Certification Marks

3–11 A large percentage of certification mark registrations are of a non-geographical nature. Actual control of the use of such marks may be vested in private bodies, or public bodies, such as government agencies or departments. A typical example is CERTIFICATION TRADE MARK BASEC,[43] which is owned by the British Approvals Service for Cables (BASEC) and is registered for "Electric cables and electric insulated wires." BASEC is a group comprising cable manufacturers, cable users and the British Standards Institution. It is a non-profit, government-nominated body, which examines manufacturers' production processes and controls, and tests cable and wire products for compliance with recognised safety and quality standards.[44]

Certification marks may be owned outright by government agencies.[45] Thus, the FLP[46] mark is registered to the United Kingdom Health and Safety Executive (HSE) in respect of flameproof enclosures for electrical apparatus; but not including goods for domestic use. The registration is subject to the disclaimer that the mark shall give no right to the exclusive use of the letters "F.L.P." Additional examples of government agency-owned certification marks are the HSE Electrical Equipment Certification Service's series of MEX[47] and EX[48] stylised word marks. Formed in 1990, HSE's Electrical Equipment Certification Service (EECS) operates on a commercial basis to provide testing and certification services primarily related to equipment and systems intended for use in potentially explosive atmospheres. Its marks are used to certify electrical and electronic apparatus and instruments for use in hazardous environments.[49] Registration of EECS's

[39] Filed May 15, 1962, No. 834734. A disclaimer to the registration states "Registration of this mark shall give no right to the exclusive use of the words 'Irish Linen'".

[40] Filed August 6, 1985, No.1247723. The proprietor is Mejeriforeningen Danish Dairy Board.

[41] Filed February 28, 1962, No. 831407. The proprietor is the Stilton Cheese Makers' Association, a U.K. association which also holds U.K. registrations of the word and device certification marks STILTON and STILTON CHEESE.

[42] Word and device, filed July 13, 1994, No.1578049. The registration gives no right to the exclusive use, separately, of the word "Roquefort".

[43] Filed March 14, 1974, No. 1026532.

[44] See BASEC website at www.basec.org.uk.

[45] Early drafts of Art. 7bis of the Paris Convention, such as proposed at the Brussels Conference of 1900, expressly included protection of marks belonging to public administrations, such as state, district, region or community. See *Actes de la Conference de Bruxelles* (1901), p.69.

[46] Filed April 21, 1934, No. 550563.

[47] Filed May 1, 1990, Nos 1426550 and 1426551.

[48] Filed May 1, 1990, Nos 1426552 and 1426553.

[49] See EECS home page at www.hse.gov.uk./eecs/abouteec.httm. The Department for the Environment, Transport and the Regions collected fees amounting to £2.4M and £2.5M payable to EECS for the years 1997–98 and 1998–99, respectively. See written answer of Beverly Hughes M.P., Under Secretary of State, to parliamentary question, *House of Commons Hansard*, "Written Answers for 31 January, 2000", Pt(1), cols 398W and 399W. Ms Hughes pointed out that such fees can be used "to offset relevant expenditure".

MEX and EX certification marks is subject to the disclaimer of the right to exclusive use of the letter "X". Furthermore it is a condition of registration of these marks "[T]hat the mark shall not be used in any printed advertisements or printed publicity matter . . . without indicating that it is a Certification Trade Mark".

A certification mark that is frequently used to guarantee compliance to safety standards is the Underwriters Laboratories' certification mark consisting of the familiar "UL" and Design, which started to appear on products in the United States in 1937. The mark is registered as UL CERTIFICATION TRADE MARK in the United Kingdom since 1998.[50] In the United States the UL certification mark was registered in 1964[51] and is described as used "[B]y persons authorised by applicant to indicate that representative samplings of the products conform to the safety requirements used by the applicant." The older certification mark, UNDERWRITERS LABORATORIES INC.,[52] was first used in 1906 and registered in the United States in 1978 to certify that "[R]epresentative samplings of the goods conform to the requirements used by the applicant." Underwriters also owns other certification marks, such as its Recognised Component mark (logo) which is for use on components.[53] **3–12**

Underwriters Laboratory, Inc. is a Nationally Recognised Testing Laboratory (NRTL) for a large number of product safety standards. Under the NRTL programme, the United States Occupational Safety and Health Administration (OSHA) accredits suitable inspection and testing laboratories to certify, for OSHA's mandatory certification scheme, electrical equipment for use in the workplace. An NRTL's mark provides information to the regulator as well as assurance to a purchaser that a product has undergone safety evaluation for approval and that its manufacture is being periodically monitored to sustain that approval. Permission to affix an NRTL's mark is granted only if the product complies with the certifier's standards.

United States Trades Unions' Marks

In the United States, against a history of denied protection, labels attached by union members to goods they produce[54] are expressly accorded protection as certification marks or collective marks. The Lanham Act expressly provides for registration of certification marks owned by trades unions, to certify that "[t]he work or labor on the goods or services was performed by members of a union or other organization."[55] Typical of such marks is the FARMWORKERS AFL-CIO UNION LABEL.[56] The mark **3–13**

[50] Filed June 25, 1962, No.1177428, for all goods in Classes 1,2,6,7,8,9,10, 11, 17,19 and 21, for motor vehicles and parts and fittings therefor in Class 12, clocks and watches in Class 14 , and office machines included in Class 16 and photographic prints.

[51] Registered December 29, 1964, No. 078259, for a wide range of products including among other things Electrical Equipment; Building Materials and Equipment; Fire Fighting and Fire Prevention Equipment; Chemicals, Hydraulic Equipment; Equipment for the Handling and Utilisation of Hazardous Liquids and Gases, Safety Appliances and Air Ducts.

[52] Registered December 26, 1978, No. 1110289. The term "INC." is disclaimed apart from the mark as shown.

[53] Registered July 24, 1979, No. 1123070. The record states that "[T]he mark represents samplings of the goods conform to the safety standards which include design, construction features and performance capabilities established by the applicant." Information about the various marks of Underwriters Laboratories, Inc., is given at their website, www.ul.com.

[54] Typically, state courts in the 19th and early 20th centuries held that union labels were not trade marks since they did not indicate the persons making (or trading in) the goods, but merely that the goods were made by members of a union.

[55] Lanham Act 1946, 15 U.S.C. 1127. The same section of the Act also provides for collective marks, "indicating membership in a union, an association, or other organisation."

[56] Registered March 9, 1971, No. 0909835. Rights are disclaimed to exclusive use of the terms "Union Label" and "AFL-CIO" apart from the mark as a whole.

certifies that "[t]he labor involved in producing and harvesting the goods was performed by members of applicant". Several union marks consist of an expression or a series of expressions detailing the union's name and the recognition accorded by certification.[57].

Competence to Certify

3–14 What are the nature and extent of the duties of the proprietor of a certification mark under the statute? The proprietor of the certification mark is responsible ultimately for controlling its use. However, as a practical matter, in many cases it is physically impossible for the proprietor, or his agents, to inspect and certify every article, or even batch of articles, emanating from a production line. Some certifiers, such as the British Standards Institution and Underwriters Laboratories authorise thousands of manufacturers to use their marks on numerous product lines. Continuous real-time quality control of the merchandise of the manufacturer who affixes the mark is not the aim or the responsibility of the proprietor. His function is to control use of the mark and to ensure that his authorisation to affix the mark is not abused by use on non-compliant goods. Thus, in summary, his function is to certify goods that are representative of production and conform to his requirements. Clearly an important aspect in assuring ongoing conformity is the conducting of periodic, unannounced inspections to assure compliance of output with his requirements.

The impracticality of personal certification of 100 per cent of an authorised user's production was recognised early in the statutory and case law development of certification marks. The United Kingdom Trade Marks Act of 1919 altered the requirement for a proprietor to undertake to examine goods and to certify the result of such examination, to an undertaking to certify, with the requirement that the Board of Trade should be satisfied that the association was competent to certify. This competence criterion was interpreted by the court in *Re the Matter of an Application by Union Nationale Inter-Syndicale des Marques Collectives to register Trade Marks*.[58] Access to registration was seen as extending

> [T]o all associations which, while not directly examining every parcel of goods upon which the Mark is to be affixed, exercises [*sic*] a sufficient supervision and control over the affixing of Marks upon goods by means of subordinate associations or branches or by the careful selection and control of the members of the Association or other persons who are permitted to affix the Mark.[59]

A similar view was expressed in *Sea Island Cotton Certification Trade Marks*,[60] in which the Board of Trade held that competence to certify under paragraph 4(i)(a) of the 1938 Act did not place any obligation to carry out any examination. Rather, it meant that the proprietor must have the legal and practical ability to certify.[61]

---

[57] For example, the word and design mark HOTEL EMPLOYEES & RESTAURANT EMPLOYEES INTERNATIONAL UNION AFFILIATED WITH AFL-CIO RECOGNIZES THIS BAR AS A UNION BAR AND WORTHY OF SUPPORT OF ORGANIZED LABOR ORGANIZED 1891. Registered April 12, 1988, No. 1484832, the certification mark, as used by persons authorised by the certifier, certifies that the labour used in rendering the services was labour performed by members of the certifying union.

[58] [1922] R.P.C. 97.

[59] [1922] R.P.C. 97 at 102.

[60] [1989] R.P.C. 87.

[61] [1989] R.P.C. 87 at 102.

Statutory Definition of Certification Mark

The treatment of a certification mark in any given jurisdiction must depend upon the statutory definition. Though there is no uniform definition of a certification mark, the present United Kingdom and United States trade mark statutes and those of some other countries conceive of certification marks in similar fashion. The United Kingdom TMA 1994 defines a certification mark as a **3–15**

> [m]ark indicating that the goods or services in connection with which it is used are certified by the proprietor of the mark in respect of origin, material, mode of manufacture of goods or performance of services, quality, accuracy or other characteristics.[62]

The United Kingdom Trade Marks Registry, in the current issue of the Work Manual chapter dealing with certification marks, states that "[A] certification mark *denotes* independent certification. . ."[63] [emphasis added] This is different from the previous version, which stated that a "certification mark is a mark which *certifies* a characteristic of the goods or services on which it is used". [emphasis added] The previous version implied that the presence of the mark on the product went beyond being a mere *indication* of certification; rather, it was to be viewed as an *instrument* of certification. The Registry's position in this respect had been close to that of the section 62 definitions in the United Kingdom Trade Mark Acts of 1905 and 1919, where the operative term was "certification . . . by mark". This position was also close to the definition of a certification mark in the United States Trademark Act of 1946 as a mark used in commerce

> [t]o *certify* regional or other origin, material, mode of manufacture, quality, accuracy, or other characteristics of such person's goods or services or that the work or labor on the goods or services was performed by members of a union or other organization.[64] [emphasis added]

Certification Mark Registration under the Trade Mark Act 1994 is Regulated by Schedule 2

Certification mark registration in the United Kingdom is regulated by Schedule 2 to the TMA 1994. Besides prohibiting registration of a certification mark unless the applicant is competent to certify[65] the goods or services, Schedule 2 addresses, among other things, the signs of which a certification mark may consist,[66] the nature of the proprietor's business,[67] the filing and approval of regulations governing the use of the mark,[68] regulation of alienation,[69] and grounds for revocation.[70] The standard that has to be met **3–16**

---

[62] TMA 1994, s.50.

[63] *Trade Marks Registry Work Manual*, Chap. 12, *Certification Marks*, July 2001, §1.3. *cf.* §2 of the previous version of Chap. 12, dated June 1996.

[64] Lanham Act 1946, s.45, 15 U.S.C. 1127.

[65] TMA 1994, Sched. 2, para. 7(1)(b).

[66] Under Sched. 2, para. 2, a certification mark's capability to distinguish goods or services is construed as distinguishing goods or services which are certified from those which are not.

[67] Sched. 2, para. 4, prohibits the proprietor from carrying on a business involving the supply of goods or services of the kind certified.

[68] Sched. 2, para. 6, requires that the regulations indicate *inter alia* the characteristics to be certified and how the certifying body, which is not constrained to be the proprietor, is to test those characteristics and supervise the use of the mark.

[69] Sched. 2, para. 12.

[70] Sched. 2, para. 15.

for certification must be set forth by the applicant as part of the regulations governing use. Schedule 2 prohibits registration if the public is liable to be misled as to the character or significance of the mark, in particular if it is likely to be taken to be something other than a certification mark.[71] Accordingly, the registrar may require that a mark be used with some indication that it is a certification mark.[72]

The Proprietor's Regulations Determine the Significance of a Certification Mark

3–17 The essence of what a certification mark's signifies, for all interested parties, including the public and government regulators, is embodied in the proprietor's regulations that govern its use. Authorisation to use the mark depends on compliance with the regulations. In a United Kingdom application for registration, the applicant files, for examination by the registrar, draft regulations, which must indicate who is authorised to use the mark, the characteristics to be certified, how the certifying body is to test those characteristics, and to supervise use of the mark.[73] Once approved, the regulations must not be altered without the Registrar's consent.[74] Furthermore, the regulations are open to public inspection.[75]

In the United States as well, an applicant for registration of a certification mark must submit the standards established to determine whether others may use the certification mark on their goods and/or in connection with their services.[76] The standards need not be original with the applicant. They may be standards established by another party, such as specifications promulgated by a government agency or standards developed through research of a private research organisation.[77] For an intent-to-use application, under section 1(b) of the Lanham Act 1946,[78] the standards are submitted with the amendment to allege use or the statement of use.

Distinctiveness Standard for Certification Marks

3–18 Is the distinctiveness standard for certification marks lower than for ordinary trade marks? The statement in paragraph 2 of Schedule 2 to the TMA 1994, that the distinguishing function of a certification mark is to be construed as distinguishing goods

---

[71] Sched. 2, para. 5(1).

[72] Sched. 2. para. 5(2). Notwithstanding the discretionary tone of expression of para. 5(2), namely "*may* accordingly require some indication that it is a certification mark", §2.4.4 of the *Trade Marks Registry Work Manual*, Chap. 12, *Certification Marks*, July 2001, states that "The overriding obligation is not to register the mark if the public is likely to be misled as regards the character or significance of the mark. This would appear to mean that the public should be aware, or made aware, that the mark is a certification mark." The Work Manual goes on to say that in practice awareness may be achieved by indicating on the mark *as registered* [original emphasis] that it is a certification mark, or by indicating in the usage of the mark that it is not being used as an ordinary trade mark through words such as "accredited to a particular standard [*sic*]", "certified by", "certification number" and the like, or "member of. . ." a particular trade body. Alternatively, "[T]he regulations may stipulate that *in use* the mark will always be used with an indication of its status" [original emphasis]. For example it may be acceptable for the regulations to establish the condition that "[T]he mark shall not be used in any printed advertisements or printed publicity matter directed primarily to the market in the United Kingdom and in the Isle of Man or in retail point of sale display cards distributed by the Registered Proprietor for use within the United Kingdom and in the Isle of Man without indicating that it is a certification mark."

[73] Sched. 2, para. 6(2).

[74] The Trade Marks Rules 1994, S.I. 1994 No. 2583. Rule 23 requires an application for the amendment of the regulations of a collective or certification mark to be filed on Form TM36.

[75] Sched. 2, para. 10.

[76] 37 C.F.R. §2.61(b).

[77] *Trademark Manual of Examining Procedure*, §1306.04, at USPTO website at www.uspto.gov.

[78] 15 U.S.C. 1051(b).

or services which are certified from those which are not, does not, in itself, make for a lower standard. Historically, the standard was judicially regarded as lower and was treated as such by the Registry.[79] But the reasoning for such a position does not appear to have been explained adequately. Nevertheless, some jurisdictions do expressly provide for a lower standard of distinctiveness for certification marks in their statutes.[80]

Objections based on lack of distinctiveness grounds were raised by the Registrar in a 1996 application for registration of LEGAL AID in respect of "legal services; conciliation services".[81] The applicant, The Legal Aid Board, was held not to be in a position to have educated the public that the term "legal aid" had acquired a distinctive character as a mark which certifies the quality of legal and conciliation services provided to the public because they appeared to have no effective control of a significant number of users of the mark. Further, there was no evidence that the relevant public, being the users of legal services, had been educated to the perception that the words said anything more than state funded financial aid for legal services. On appeal it was held that the mark had acquired a distinctive character through use, and there was no reason not to infer that the public understood the nature of the Legal Aid scheme operated by the Board. The mark was deemed capable of registration as a certification mark.[82]

Disclaimers and Other Restrictions on the Certification Right

If the standard of distinctiveness for certification marks is lower, then disclaimers should **3–19** be less important in relation to certification marks than to ordinary marks. A disclaimer renounces any claim to an exclusive right to use matter (such as one or more letters, words or devices) that is common to the trade[83] or otherwise of a non-distinctive character, in a mark that is distinctive as a whole, except in the mark as registered. Disclaimers were used quite frequently in registrations of certification marks under the 1938 Act. Under the TMA 1994, a disclaimer may only be entered voluntarily by the applicant[84] but not insisted upon by the Registrar. Marks which would have been accepted under the 1938 Act provided specific elements were disclaimed at the Registrar's insistence are now accepted without disclaimer. Where the applicant does decide to volunteer a disclaimer, it is up to him to provide the necessary wording, which is accepted without editing.

Limitations and Conditions on Registration

Under section 13(b) of the TMA 1994, an applicant may agree to a specific territorial or **3–20** other limitation, such as limitation to particular colours, to the rights conferred by the registration. A further restriction of the powers of the Registrar is evident in the fact that conditions can no longer be requested on the TMA applications. Thus, conditions of the

[79] *Re an Application by the British Motor Cycle Manufacturers' and Traders' Union Limited for a Trade Mark* [1923] R.P.C. 226. See also N. Dawson, *op. cit.*, p. 25.
[80] See, for example, the Israel Trade Marks Ordinance 1972, s.14(b).
[81] *In the Matter of Application No. 2114581 by the Legal Aid Board to Register a Certification Mark in Class 42*, January 27, 2000.
[82] *Kerly's Law of Trade Marks and Trade Names* (D. Kitchin, D. Llewelyn, J. Mellor, R. Meade and T. Moody-Stuart eds 13th ed., Sweet & Maxwell, London, 2001), p. 321.
[83] Meaning either "in common use in the trade" or "open to the trade to use". See T.A. Blanco White and R. Jacob, in *Kerly's Law of Trade Marks and Trade Names* (11th ed., Sweet and Maxwell, London, 1983) pp. 130.
[84] See *Trade Marks Registry Work Manual*, Chap. 6, *Examination and Practice*, pp. 154–5, August 1998.

type "It is a condition of registration that the mark shall be used in relation only to goods the produce of Denmark" in the registration of DANISH[85] are no longer appropriate. Furthermore, conditions requested in relation to previous registrations of the same mark (under the 1938 Act) cannot be used as precedents for requesting a condition under the TMA 1994.

The Proprietor is Excluded from Use

3–21 A principle fundamental to the concept of a certification mark in most, but not all, Anglo-American jurisdictions, and others as well, is that the owner of the certification mark is precluded from using the mark for the certified goods, or services where covered. This principle derives from the notion that it would not be in the public interest for a non-independent person, that is a person carrying on a trade in the goods or services certified, to act as certifier. Thus, according to the TMA 1994:

> A certification mark shall not be registered if the proprietor carries on a business involving the supply of goods or services of the kind certified.[86]

Indeed, registration of a certification mark is subject to revocation if the proprietor has begun to carry on a business involving the supply of goods or services of the kind certified. In the United States as well, a certification mark is subject to cancellation if the registrant engages in the production or marketing of any goods or services to which the certification mark is applied.[87] A certification mark registration, as conceptualised in most Anglo-American jurisdictions, requires the owner not to use the mark. The owner's function is to *control* use of the mark by those he authorises, thereby ensuring that their products meet his required standards.

Openness of Access: Certification Must not be Refused to any Qualified Goods or Services

3–22 Yet another notable feature of a certification mark in the Anglo-American system is that certification may not be refused to anybody who complies with the required standards. Indeed, a certification mark is subject to cancellation if, in the language of the United States law, the registrant

> discriminately refuses to certify or to continue to certify the goods or services of any person who maintains the standards or conditions which such mark certifies.[88]

The Board of Trade, when responsible under earlier United Kingdom Trade Marks Acts for reviewing and approving the proprietor's regulations governing use of his certification mark, traditionally required such regulations to include the right of any trader in goods meeting the proprietor's standard for certification to have them so certified. The United Kingdom Trade Mark Registry, which, under the TMA 1994, assumed the foregoing responsibility from the Board of Trade, states:

> It is not a statutory requirement that a certification mark shall be open for use by any person who is competent to produce goods of the required standard but in practice this "open door" policy is invariably

---

[85] See para. 3–10, above.
[86] TMA 1994, Sched. 2, para. 4.
[87] Lanham Act 1946, s.14, 15 U.S.C. 1064.
[88] Lanham Act 1946, s.14, 15 U.S.C. 1064–5(D).

> pursued. The undertaking that the applicant gives that use of the mark will be permitted to anyone who complies with the regulations and produces goods which have the certified characteristic is intended to prevent a scheme of certification becoming a restrictive trade practice (Restrictive Trade Practices Act 1976, Schedule 3, Paragraph 4(1)).[89]

This very openness of access to certification marks distinguishes them from collective marks, to which access is limited to members of an association.

It is submitted that complete openness gives rise to uncertainty as to whether a certification mark can constitute property. Theories of property and ownership rest heavily on the cornerstone of exclusive control. If a party has neither the right to exclusive control over use of a mark, nor the right to exclude others from such use, then may there not be a conceptual problem in regarding the mark as property?

Regulation of Certification Fees

Until recently, the United Kingdom registry's position was that a certification mark scheme had to be run on a non-profit making basis.[90] However, current policy places greater emphasis on the financial terms and conditions appertaining to certification from the authorised users', or potential authorised users', viewpoint, rather than ascertaining precisely whether or not the scheme itself makes a profit. The proposed fees to be paid in connection with the operation of the mark must be stated by the applicant and approved by the registry.[91] Furthermore fee changes, once the mark is registered, are subject to scrutiny by the registry. Since the fees form part of the regulations, any inordinately large proposed increase in charges to authorised users may have to be explained by the proprietor and could trigger publication for opposition or observations, where the Registrar considers it expedient. **3–23**

Regarding income from certification fees, to the extent that certifiers may also be trade associations, they may find themselves caught between a need to be financially sound, on one hand, and a need to make certification affordable to all qualified traders, large and small, alike. Certifying associations may therefore find it helpful to bear in mind the criteria set forth in the Department of Trade and Industry's Model Trade Association best practice guide. The guide recommends as a Key Characteristic, that the association be "properly resourced". Furthermore, the association should be "successful both in generating income from members' subscriptions and from sales of services to members and to others."[92] To the extent that product certification impacts consumer safety, the current public debate in the United Kingdom concerning the corporate structures of bodies that bear responsibility for public safety is relevant to the present work. Whether such bodies should be profit-making or non-profit-making is a prominent aspect of the debate.[93]

---

[89] *Trade Mark Registry Work Manual*, Chap. 12, *Certification Marks*, July 2001, at §3.3.1.

[90] *Trade Mark Registry Work Manual*, Chap. 12, *Certification Marks*, June 1996, p. 19.

[91] TMA 1994, Sched. 2, para. 6(2).

[92] See www.dti.gov.uk/EAM/MTA/MTAkey.html.

[93] Notwithstanding an unsatisfactory safety record in the privatised rail transportation sector the U.K. Government announced in June 1998 that 51% of National Air Traffic Services (NATS)—the U.K.'s air traffic control system, which is part of the Civil Aviation Authority—was to be sold off. The Government wishes to have a "public-private partnership" (PPP) run NATS. This move is controversial. On one hand, the airlines support a "much more flexible and robust approach to investment that only the private sector can provide"; on the other hand there are claims that "[T]here is bound to be an increased risk to safety, however small and albeit with stringent regulation, where private profit is a prime consideration." See speech of Lord Clinton-

Infringement of a Certification Mark

3–24 What types of act constitute infringement of a registered certification mark? The acts amounting to infringement of a registered trade mark, if done without the consent of the proprietor, are specified in the TMA 1994, s.10. By virtue of section 1(2), references in the TMA 1994 to a trade mark include, unless the context requires otherwise, references to a certification mark, subject to the provisions of Schedule 2. Applying firstly section 10(1) to certification marks, one can conclude that if a person uses in the course of trade a sign identical to a registered certification mark in relation to goods or services for which it is registered, such use constitutes infringement. In addition, according to subsection 10(2), infringement of a certification mark includes use in the course of trade, of a sign identical to the registered mark in relation to similar goods or services, or a similar sign on identical goods or services, to cause a likelihood of confusion, which includes the likelihood of association with the certification mark.[94]

For the purposes of the statutory provisions concerning infringement, section 10(4) enumerates as "use" of a sign the affixing of the sign to the goods or their packaging, offering or exposing goods for sale, putting them on the market or stocking them under the sign, offering or supplying services under the sign, importing or exporting under the sign, or using the sign on business papers or in advertising.

In infringement proceedings brought by the proprietor of a registered certification mark any loss suffered or likely to be suffered by authorised users is to be taken into account. Furthermore, the court has discretion to give such directions as it thinks fit as to the extent to which the plaintiff is to hold the proceeds of any pecuniary remedy on behalf of authorised users.[95]

Authorised User of Certification Mark Likened to Licensee in Certain Matters

3–25 In certain matters an authorised user of a certification mark is treated by the TMA 1994, as a licensee in the sense applied to an ordinary trade mark. Specifically, in case of infringement, the TMA 1994 Sched.2, para.13, likens an authorised user to a licensee in regard to his rights where there is (a) unauthorised application of the mark to labelling,

---

Davis, *House of Lords Hansard*, June 5, 2000, Col. 956, and speech of Lord Hoyle, at Col. 977, supporting the non-profit-making trust system as putting "safety foremost", endorsed by Lord Smith of Clifton as follows: "The advantage of the public trust model is that it is a not-for-profit body and thus can concentrate on safety." *House of Lords Hansard*, July 6, 2000, Col. 1640. The government announced on March 27, 2001 that a consortium of seven airlines had been chosen as the strategic partner in the NATS PPP. Contracts were due to be completed by the end of 2001.

[94] The concept of "likelihood of association" is derived from Benelux jurisprudence. Neither the U.K. courts not the European Court of Justice (ECJ) have accepted the concept as sufficient by itself to constitute a likelihood of confusion. The concept was analysed by the ECJ in *Sabel B.V. v. Puma AG*, Case C–251/95 [1998] E.T.M.R. 1. The ECJ saw likelihood of association, where a sign is similar to a mark, as embracing situations where the public perceives a connection between the proprietor of a sign and that of a trade mark and confuses them; or, more directly, where the public considers the sign to be similar to the mark, calling to mind the memory of the mark, although the public is not confused by this calling to mind. In *Wagamama Ltd. v. City Centre Restaurants Plc* [1995] F.S.R. 713, ChD, Laddie J. held that the Benelux philosophy was tantamount to introduction of a new kind of monopoly for which he was unable to discern any clear legislative intent. For opposing views as to the proper place of likelihood of association in relation to likelihood of confusion, see A. Kamperman Sanders, "Back to the Dark Ages of Trade Mark Law", [1996] EIPR 3 and P. Prescott, "Think Before You Waga Finger" [1996] EIPR 317.

[95] TMA 1994, Sched. 2, para. 14.

packaging, advertising and other materials[96]; (b) consideration by the court of the adequacy of other remedies to compensate, in relation to an order for disposal of infringing goods, materials or other articles[97]; and (c) a request to the Commissioners of Customs and Excise concerning prohibition of infringing imports.[98]

However, although the matter is not completely settled, it is unlikely that the broader proposition, that an authorised user of a certification mark is a licensee, is generally applicable.[99]

Assignment of a Registered Certification Mark Must Assure Continuity of its Significance

The United Kingdom registry attaches considerable importance to continuity of what a certification mark signifies. If there is to be a new proprietor, then the mark in his hands must continue to signify precisely what it did prior to the transfer. Furthermore, the new proprietor-certifier must show that he has the necessary competence, which is usually a question of the new proprietor's ability to exercise sufficient monitoring and control over use of the mark by the authorised users. If the new proprietor-certifier is a trade body, the Registry would want to be satisfied that the body is strongly representative of the trade concerned in the goods or services being certified. In fact the Registry states that a competent body is one having "a well-known status in the trade concerned."[1] Thus, unlike the assignment of an ordinary trade mark or a collective mark, an assignment or other transmission of a certification mark is not effective unless the consent of the Registrar is given.[2] **3–26**

3 COLLECTIVE MARKS

Statutory Definition of Collective Mark

Until the TMA 1994 came into force collective marks were not registrable in the United Kingdom. The TMA 1994 conceives of a collective mark as a mark indicating a connection in trade to the proprietor organisation. Thus it is defined in section 49(1) as a mark **3–27**

> distinguishing the goods or services of members of the association which is the proprietor of the mark from those of other undertakings.

Rights in the mark are acquired through use by the association's members on their goods or in connection with their services. There is no obvious provision for rights to accrue through mere sporting of the mark on the accoutrements of membership such as membership pins, lapel badges and the like.

Proprietorship of Collective Marks

A collective mark is for use by the individual members of an association in the course of trade but is registered to the association as a whole, as distinct from its members. The collective holds title to the mark for the benefit of all members. However, a conceptual **3–28**

---

[96] TMA 1994, s.10(5).
[97] TMA 1994, s.19(2).
[98] TMA 1994, s.89.
[99] See Wilkof, *op. cit.*, Chap.12, p.162.
[1] *Trade Marks Registry Work Manual*, Chap.12 *Certification Marks*, July 2001, at §§5 and 3.5. See also *UNIS* and *Sea Island Cotton* cases for judicial interpretation of "competence to certify", para. 3–14, above.
[2] TMA 1994, Sched. 2, para. 12.

problem may arise where an association is unincorporated because an unincorporated association does not have legal personality and so cannot normally own property itself.[3] The association's name may be entered as the proprietor on the register but ownership of the goodwill in the mark would appear to be owned collectively by the members, subject to the contractual terms and conditions of their membership of the association.[4]

For-Profit Organisations Not Excluded from Ownership of Collective Marks

3–29 Inquiries to the United Kingdom registry indicate that there is no requirement that the scheme of authorisation to use a collective mark must be administered on a non-profit basis. This position agrees with that of the E.U. in relation to collective CTM registrations. The European Community Regulation[5] does not contain a non-profit requirement in relation to collective marks and inquiries to OHIM indicate that there is no such requirement.

Parallel Use as Collective Mark and Ordinary Trade Mark

3–30 A collective mark is not for use by the owner association on an equal footing with, and in the same manner as, the individual members. However, the owner association may use the collective mark to identify itself as the representative of its members on business papers and publications. Consider an association, as distinct from its members, that produces and distributes goods, or performs services for others and uses a mark to distinguish such goods or services. The mark is in fact being used as an ordinary trade mark (or service mark), not as a collective trade mark. The policy of the United Kingdom trade mark registry is that one and the same mark may not be used as both the collective mark of the association and an ordinary trade mark of the owner, for the same goods or services. This policy is intended to assure compliance with the requirement that the mark not be misleading as to its character or significance.[6] Use of the collective mark in a manner likely to mislead the public is grounds for revocation.[7]

In this regard, United States policy appears to be different from United Kingdom policy. The Trademark Law Revision Act of 1988 amended the Lanham Act[8] in a way that appears to except collective marks from the statutory prohibition against use of a collective mark in the way that the proprietor of a certification mark is prohibited.[9] Thus

---

[3] See Christopher Wadlow, *The Law of Passing-Off*, (2nd ed., Sweet & Maxwell, London, 1995), pp. 53–56.

[4] See, Firth, *op. cit.*, pp. 173 and 174. Note that Art. 64(1) of the Community Regulation 40/94 on the Community Trade Mark, states, regarding collective marks, "Associations of manufacturers, producers, suppliers of services, or traders which, under the terms of the law governing them, have the capacity in their own name to have rights and obligations of all kinds, to make contracts or accomplish other legal acts and to sue and be sued, as well as legal persons governed by public law, may apply for Community collective marks.

[5] See n.35, above.

[6] TMA 1994, Sched. 1, para.4(1). See also Appendix B, below.

[7] TMA 1994, Sched. 1, para.13(a).

[8] Lanham Act 1946, s.4, 15 U.S.C. 1054.

[9] Trademark Law Revision Act of 1988. Pub.L. No.100–667, See legislative history, Senate Report No.100–515, May 12, 1988, Cong. Record Vol.134 (1988), in which the Committee on the Judiciary states "Section s.6(2) [of the bill, S. 1883] contains an amendment which clarifies the difference between collective and certification marks, the former of which, by definition, can be used to represent that their owners (that is unions, associations or other organisations) make or sell the goods or perform the services on or in connection with which the mark is used." Amended s.4 of the Lanham Act allows for collective and certification marks to be registrable and entitled to protection "except in the case of certification marks when used so as to represent falsely that the owner or a user thereof makes or sells the goods or performs the services on or in connection with which such mark is used."

use of a collective mark by an owner-user, notwithstanding use by the members of the collective, is possible under the United States legislation.[10]

Collective Mark Registrants

Association by Trade or Profession

Applicants for registration of collective marks are typically incorporated trade associations or professional organisations. The Chartered Institute of Patent Agents mark, C.P.A, is an example of a collective mark registered to a professional association under the TMA 1994. The mark is used in connection with professional business, commerce and legal advisory services.[11] Another example is the collective word mark MEMBER OF THE SOCIETY OF TECHNICIANS IN INSURANCE[12] registered to The Chartered Insurance Institute. The registration covers insurance and financial services and professional advice and consultation relating to insurance and finance. Professional bodies such as these sometimes need to apply for a series of marks covering various grades of membership, such as "Fellow", "Member" or "Associate Member". In such circumstances the Registry does not treat the membership qualifier as a material part of the mark. An example of a professional organisation's series of collective marks, registered under the TMA 1994, is the Institute of Trade Mark Attorneys marks denoting the grades of Fellow and Member of ITMA (or I.T.M.A.) for professional consultancy services relating to industrial and intellectual property.[13] **3–31**

Both the newer and the traditional trade organisations are registering their collective marks under the TMA 1994. The word mark SCOTTISH GLASS ASSOCIATION S.G.A. COLLECTIVE MARK[14] is registered to the Scottish Building Employers Federation for building repair and installation services connected with window frames, double glazing and the like. The mark NACS[15] is registered to the National Association of Chimney Sweeps, for chimney sweeping services, repair, maintenance and servicing of fuel appliances and so on. Collective marks are also registered to associations of manufacturers, importers or distributors in order to distinguish their members' offerings from those of other undertakings. An example is the word and device mark ASSOCIATION OF PHARMACEUTICAL IMPORTERS[16], registered to The British Association of European Pharmaceutical Distributors in respect of "Pharmaceutical preparations". This association claims to represent almost all those companies engaged in the parallel pharmaceutical distribution industry within the United Kingdom.

Because they often comprise and represent a major percentage of all firms in a given commercial sector, such associations can expect to be listened to attentively, by government and the public, when speaking on trade-related policy, including trade

---

[10] *Roush Bakery Products Co. v. F.R. Lepage Bakery Inc.*, 4 U.S.P.Q.2d 1401 (TTAB 1987), *aff'd,* 851 F.2d 351, 7 U.S.P.Q.2d 1395 (Fed. Cir. 1988), *withdrawn, vacated and remanded,* 863 F.2d 43, 9 U.S.P.Q.2d 1335 (Fed. Cir. 1988), *vacated and modified,* 13 U.S.P.Q.2d 1045 (TTAB 1989).

[11] Filed August 9, 1995, No.2029755.

[12] Filed February 17, 1995, No.2011419A.

[13] Filed October 31, 1994, No.2001536.

[14] Filed March 18, 1997, No. 2127035.

[15] Filed March 3, 1998, No.2159791. NACS claims to be the only trade association in the U.K. to represent Chimney Sweeps. Members work strictly to a Code of Practice and British Standards 6461 Part 1 and BS7566 for the cleaning of chimneys. See NACS website at www.chimneyworks.co.uk. A prestigious credential for chimney sweeping is the City and Guilds 7641 certificate. See Guild of Master Sweeps website at www.guild-of-master-sweeps.co.uk/7641.html.

[16] Filed January 20, 1999, No. 2186632.

mark issues. For example, in 1999, collective mark owners mentioned in the foregoing examples provided, with other industry associations, evidence on trade and trade mark matters to the House of Commons Select Committee on Trade and Industry.[17]

Association by Trade and Geographical Name

3–32 An example of a geographical collective mark is the word and device SCOTLAND'S TOMATOES,[18] registered to Scotland's Tomatoes, Ltd., for "Tomato seed; tomato plants; tomatoes." The TMA 1994 provides that a collective mark may be registered which consists of signs or indications that designate in trade the geographical origin of the goods or services,[19] even though registration of such a sign or indication as an ordinary trade mark is prohibited under section 3(1)(c) unless it has acquired "a distinctive character as a result of the use made of it." However, Schedule 1, paragraph 3 also states that the proprietor is not entitled to prohibit the use of such signs or indications in accordance with honest practices in industrial or commercial matters (in particular, by a person who is entitled to use a geographical name). Thus, registration of a geographical name as part of a collective mark, does not give the association which owns the registration the right to prevent one manufacturing goods in that place from stating on the goods that they are produced in that place.

Churches and Charities

3–33 The common law has historically taken a very broad view of "trade" and "goodwill", extending the terms to include churches, charities, schools and the like. In addition to seeking donations, churches and charities often resort to trade as a means of raising funds. Such organisations, whether incorporated or not, have standing as traders to bring passing-off actions in the same way as any other business, regardless of whether defendants are bodies of a similar nature or not.[20] With the advent of statutory protection of collective marks, such bodies are well-placed to benefit from this additional means of protection afforded by the TMA 1994.

A charitable organisation that trades may apply to register its collective mark and a registration provides the possibility of resorting to action for infringement where its mark is used without authorisation with concomitant likelihood of confusion. Thus, the Association of Vineyard Churches has registered the mark VINEYARD[21] for a wide range of audio and video apparatus and recording products, printed matter, clothing, and the provision of education and training, services and counselling, relating to religion, philosophy and theology. Recently, the Association of Charity Shops, whose member shops offer household and domestic goods, clothing and charitable fund raising services has filed for a collective mark[22].

Regulations Governing Use of a Collective Mark

3–34 Because there is no requirement for the regulations to stipulate objective standards for the goods or services bearing the collective mark, the Registry conducts no substantive examination of the regulations. This policy was stated in the Department of Trade and

[17] See House of Commons, minutes of evidence taken before the Trade and Industry Committee, May 11, 1999, at www.parliament.the-stationery-office.co.uk/pa/cm199899.htm.

[18] Filed October 31, 1994, No. 1553454.

[19] TMA 1994, Sched. 1, para. 3.

[20] See Wadlow, *op. cit.*, p.60.

[21] Filed August 17, 1995, No. 2030852. See www.vineyard.co.uk.

[22] MAKING THE MOST OF YOUR DONATIONS ASSOCIATION OF CHARITY SHOPS, filed February 22, 2000, No. 2223210. See www.charityshops.org.uk.

Industry White Paper on Intellectual Property and Innovation[23] that preceded enactment of the TMA 1994. Nevertheless, it is through the regulations that control of use of the mark is effected by the proprietor-association. Such control is a *quid pro quo* for the protection that is to be accorded to the registered mark. Therefore, among other things, Schedule 1 to the TMA 1994, addresses the filing of regulations governing the use of the mark.[24]

The products of member companies of an industry or trade association will normally need to meet certain professional or industry standards as a pre-requisite for membership. The regulations are published and notice of opposition may be given and observations made, relating to persons authorised to use the mark, conditions of membership of the association, any conditions of use of the mark and any sanctions against misuse.[25]

Grounds for Revocation

Prominent among the grounds for revocation of a collective mark under the TMA 1994 is **3–35** that the mark is used in a manner likely to mislead the public, particularly if it is likely to be taken to be something other than a collective mark.[26] Other grounds for revocation are failure, on the part of the proprietor to observe, or secure the observance of, the regulations governing use of the mark[27]; amendment of the regulations that results in non-compliance with the statutory requirements and any further conditions imposed by rules; or amendment of the regulations so that they are contrary to public policy or to accepted principles of morality.[28]

Infringement of a Collective Mark

Acts constituting infringement of a registered trade mark are set out in the TMA 1994, **3–36** s.10, which, by virtue of section 1(2), applies to collective marks as well, subject to the provisions of Schedule 1. Subsection 10(1) may therefore be read as applying to infringement by virtue of use of a sign identical to a registered collective mark in relation to goods or services which are identical with those for which the collective mark is registered. Subsection 10(2) may be applied to infringement of a collective mark by virtue of use in the course of trade, of the identical mark in relation to similar goods or services, or a similar mark on identical goods or services, to cause a likelihood of confusion, which includes the likelihood of association with the collective mark[29].

Therefore, infringement proceedings might be taken where a person uses a sign identical with or similar to a registered collective mark without authorisation in the course of trade to represent that he is a member of the proprietor association, or that he holds a particular title or degree awarded by the association. Another possible scenario is one in which a competing association, holds itself out as the plaintiff association or claims the right to use the collective mark. Such a scenario can develop as the result of schism of an association with an ensuing dispute over rights to the mark.[30]

---

[23] Cm. 9712 at para. 5.03.
[24] TMA 1994, Sched. 1, para. 5.
[25] TMA 1994, Sched. 1, para. 8.
[26] TMA 1994, Sched. 1, para. 13(a).
[27] TMA 1994, Sched. 1, para. 13(b).
[28] TMA 1994, Sched. 1, para. 13(c).
[29] See n. 94, above.
[30] For a recent example in the context of passing-off, see *Artistic Upholstery Limited v. Art Form Limited* [1999] 4 All E.R. 227. See also, *Certification in Occupational Therapy, Inc. v. American Occupational Therapy Association, et al.*, Civ.No.AMD 97–767 (U.S. District Court for the District of Maryland) (1998).

Authorised User of Collective Mark Likened to Licensee in Certain Matters

3–37 In certain matters the user of a collective mark is treated by the TMA 1994 as a licensee in the sense applied to an ordinary trade mark. However it is unclear to what extent the treatment as a licensee is valid beyond the matters specifically recited in the Act. Nevertheless, in case of infringement, the TMA 1994, Sched.1, para.11, accords an authorised user of a collective mark certain rights as in relation to a licensee and likens him to a licensee. In particular this applies where there is (a) unauthorised application of the mark to labelling, packaging, advertising and other materials[31]; (b) consideration by the court of the adequacy of other remedies to compensate, in relation to an order for disposal of infringing goods, materials or other articles[32]; and (c) a request to the Commissioners of Customs and Excise concerning prohibition of infringing imports.[33]

Infringement Proceedings Taken at Authorised User's Request

3–38 An authorised user of a collective mark has the right to require the proprietor to take infringement proceedings, where his interests are at stake. Subject to any agreement to the contrary between an authorised user and the proprietor of a collective mark, the authorised user is entitled to call on the proprietor to take infringement proceedings in respect of any matter which affects his interests.[34] If the proprietor (a) refuses to do so, or (b) fails to do so within two months after being called upon, the authorised user may bring the proceeding in his own name as if he were the proprietor.[35] However, in such a case, the authorised user may not, without the leave of the court, proceed with the action unless the proprietor is either joined as a plaintiff or added as a defendant.[36] This does not affect the granting of interlocutory relief on an application by an authorised user alone.[37]

Where infringement proceedings are brought by the proprietor of a registered collective mark any loss suffered or likely to be suffered by authorised users must be taken into account; and the court may give such directions as it thinks fit as to the extent to which the plaintiff is to hold the proceeds of any pecuniary remedy on behalf of such users.[38]

Collective Mark Registration in the United States

3–39 Development of the concept of the collective mark and provisions for its registration followed a different course in the United States. The United States Trademarks Act of 1905 specifically provided for registration of trade marks owned by associations. Nevertheless, for many years the Commissioner of Patents denied registration of these marks of a collective nature, taking the position that he was not obliged to recognise the international obligation imposed by the Paris Convention unless and until Congress

[31] TMA 1994, s.10(5).
[32] TMA 1994, s.19(2).
[33] TMA 1994, s.89.
[34] TMA 1994, Sched. 1, para. 12(2).
[35] TMA 1994, Sched. 1, para. 12(3).
[36] TMA 1994, Sched. 1, para. 12(4).
[37] *ibid.*
[38] TMA 1994, Sched. 1, para. 12(6).

enacted enabling legislation. This position should be viewed against the historical backdrop of trade mark law in the early part of the twentieth century. At that time there was no established basis for according trade mark rights in marks that their "owners" did not use in a trade mark sense and affix to their goods. Moreover, licensed use of a mark by others had not yet gained general judicial acceptance.

However, certain professional bodies, such as accountants' and doctors' associations were deemed to have goodwill with respect to their members that could be protected by the association's bringing of a passing-off action. An action of that type might be justified where, for example, there was unauthorised use of its professional titles. Such unauthorised use, if not prevented, could simply eviscerate the association. By 1936, international pressure resulted in an amendment to the United States statute to permit registration of marks of associations located in foreign countries. Domestic associations were still precluded from registering their marks until 1938, when the law was amended to provide for registration of domestic and foreign associations' collective marks alike.

Collective marks may be registered under the Lanham Act,[39] which provides a broader concept of a collective mark than the United Kingdom statute, since it extends registration to membership collective marks as well.[40] These are marks that members use, on a badge for example, as mere indicia of their membership in the group or collective. The Lanham Act defines a collective mark as "[A] trademark or service mark (1) used by the members of a cooperative, an association, or other collective group or organisation, or (2) which such cooperative, association, or other collective group or organisation has a bona fide intention to use in commerce and applies to register on the principal register established by this Act, and includes marks indicating membership in a union, an association, or other organisation."[41]

Person and nations, States, municipalities and the like, exercising legitimate control over the use of the marks sought to be registered, even though not possessing an industrial or commercial establishment, are eligible to seek registration of collective (and certification) marks.[42]

Conflation of Certification and Collective Marks

It was pointed out earlier in this chapter that collective marks are sometimes used to certify attributes of goods or services.[43] Commentators, particularly in the United States at the time of enactment of the Lanham Act, have discussed inconsistencies in registrations of collective marks and certification marks.[44] The uncertainty as to which mark is appropriate for a particular use has even led to consideration whether both types of mark are needed.[45] The United Kingdom approach seems to make a clear distinction between these two apparently different forms of mark. The certification mark indicates certification of one or more characteristics of goods or services, whereas the collective mark distinguishes the goods or services of the proprietor undertaking (namely, the "association") from those of other undertakings. One might take the **3–40**

[39] Lanham Trademark Act 1946, §4, 15 U.S.C. 1054.
[40] Lanham Act 1946, §45, 15 U.S.C. 1127.
[41] *ibid.*
[42] Lanham Act 1946, §4, 15 U.S.C. 1054.
[43] See paras. 3–04 to 3–05, above.
[44] W. Derenberg, *Preparing for the New Trade-Mark Law* (Research Institute of America, 1946); Breitenfeld, "Collective Marks—Should They Be Abolished?" (1957) 47 T.M.R. 1.
[45] Breitenfeld, *op. cit.*

position, therefore, that there is a watertight separation of certification and collective marks. Before questioning such a position, it is well to set forth clearly the point to be made hereunder—that collective marks and certification marks are different facets of the correlation between association and standardisation.

3–41 Association implies standardisation. The goods or services of persons who belong to an association, either voluntarily or in order to operate legitimately, *e.g.* to protect the public against unqualified professionals or to legally market their goods, are normally required to meet certain standards. An association of lawyers has definite qualification requirements for membership; those requirements constitute the standard. An association of churches will have certain rules and regulations for membership which constitute the standard. The process of forming an association, even if membership requirements are not onerous, constitutes conformity to a standard.

To the extent that traders whose products are certified as conforming to standards wish to protect themselves against traders whose goods are not certified or are substandard, they tend to belong to trade associations. Therefore, the inverse proposition, that standardisation implies association commonly holds as well. The group exists to protect its standardised membership from the uncertified, non-standardised, outside.

Conflation of certification and collective marks has been tacitly recognised by commentators and in the U.S. case law.[46] It is brought into clear relief by situations where the same mark may become a CTM collective mark and a United Kingdom domestically-registered certification mark,[47] or where the purpose of a United States registered collective mark is declared as being to certify.[48] However, varying degrees of conflation are likely, such that the usefulness and specificity of the information conveyed by a collective mark may at time be closer to that of a traditional certification mark and at other times less so. At the subjective level, consumers may feel that a certification mark provides them with more specific standards and more reliable information and assurances than does a collective mark. For example, they may feel more assurance when seeing WOOLMARK on a garment than seeing a wool producers' association mark. Though it could be that the sense of assurance from the WOOLMARK derives from long term familiarity with that mark and a collective mark might ultimately win a consumer's trust as well.

Conclusion

3–42 This chapter has reviewed the basic elements of the statutory framework for registration and protection of certification and collective marks. The United Kingdom, United States and like trade mark statutes assimilate certification and collective marks to ordinary marks for the purposes of examination and registration. The impetus for integrating the registration and protection of these special marks into the trade mark statutes derives from the Paris Convention. Under Article 7*bis*(2) of the Convention, each country is entitled to be the judge of the particular conditions under which a collective mark should be protected.

An important difference, in the United Kingdom framework at least, between certification and collective marks and ordinary or "individual" trade marks is that they are intended for use in the trade mark sense by parties other than the proprietor. The

[46] *Opticians Association of America v. Independent Opticians of America*, 920 F.2d 187 (1990).
[47] See HALLOUMI example, para. 3–09 and nn. 36 and 37, above.
[48] See paras 3–04 to 3–05 and nn. 16 and 17, above.

function of the proprietor, or his agents, is a control function. It is his responsibility to exercise lawful control of use of the mark, thereby ensuring that such use is in accordance with his requirements, conditions, or regulations. A prime function of the registry, in this regard, is to examine the regulations as part of the process of application for registration.

It is submitted that conflation of certification and collective marks is to some extent inevitable. Leaving aside semantic difficulties, there has been some real confusion over their respective roles during the first century of the registration system. This situation may not improve because there is proliferation and growing divergence of policy and law regarding certification and collective marks, even within the group of countries still referred to as the "Anglo-American countries". The prohibition against use of a certification or a collective mark by the proprietor is no longer applied to both types of mark in all cases and in the United Kingdom there are signs of a policy shift towards acceptance of applications for registration by for-profit undertakings. Finally, it is noteworthy that geographical indications, traditionally the province of intellectual property rights exercised though certification and collective marks, are being protected by new modalities which seem closer to agricultural law than intellectual property law. This is ironic in view of the fact that protection of geographical indications is mandated by TRIPS, which may prove to be one of the most, if not the most, important of all intellectual property treaties concluded since the Paris Convention.

4

CERTIFIERS AND PRODUCT LIABILITY

Introduction

In this chapter the liability of those who certify or otherwise vouch for products that subsequently cause injury or damage is considered in the context of product liability[1] claims. Authoritative undertakings provide third-party attestations[2] of safety, quality or other product attributes to the public and regulators alike in the form of certifications, approvals, listings and "guarantees". Among such undertakings are public and private-sector inspectorates, recognised testing laboratories, professional institutions, consumer magazines and trade and industry bodies that provide guidance to their members and the public. However, today's manufacturer is required to be a certifier as well, in respect of the products that he places on the market. Consequently, it is appropriate to include manufacturers' liability with regard to the self-certification of their products in the subject matter of this chapter. 4–01

Before considering certifiers' liability in particular, the chapter firstly outlines the history of liability rules in general. Then the principles behind product liability policy and laws potentially applicable to product certifiers are considered under breach of statutory duty (strict liability), tort (negligence) and breach of contract (warranty). Statutory provisions in the United Kingdom which impose liability for defective products are addressed in the context of the laws governing the sale and supply of goods, and consumer and employee protection. This is followed by a discussion of certifiers' potential tortious liability. The problems in delineating the boundary of certifiers' liability are illustrated by reference to certification not only of chattels, but to real property and shipping.

The scope of product liability rules and the category of potential product liability respondents has widened considerably over recent years, especially in United States law. Therefore later portions of the chapter pay particular attention to United States perceptions of certifiers' liability, including issues pertaining to trade associations that

---

1 Also known as "products liability", especially in the United States. Black's Law Dictionary includes the term from the fifth edition, Henry Campbell Black, *Black's Law Dictionary* (5th ed., St. Paul: West Publishing Co., 1979).

2 Through the use, among other things, of certification or collective marks on or in connection with the product. See generally Chap. 3, above.

set standards and certify, and to proprietors of ordinary trade marks[3] who control the quality of products bearing their trade marks under license.

The Manufacturer is a Certifier

4–02 Though third-party certification of product conformity to standards is widely accepted as providing "independent" assurance, changing patterns of commerce are leading to growing reliance on the manufacturer's self-declaration. The need to trade in an increasingly segmented and fast-changing marketplace can render third-party certification incompatible with the worldwide scope and rapid pace of modern commerce. Furthermore, while product diversity and customised "solutions rather than products"[4] are important elements in many companies' strategies for success, they are elements that do not readily fit the mould of third-party certification. The costs associated with third-party certification are more readily recovered by manufacturers who produce and sell large quantities of a particular product.

In today's commercial environment, governments and industry in Europe, the United States and elsewhere, recognise the value and importance of manufacturers' self-declarations[5] of conformity to standards.[6] The National Institute of Science and Technology, the agency of the United States Department of Commerce's Technology Administration which is responsible for developing and applying technology, measurements and standards, has described United States regulatory philosophy as relying

> heavily on a manufacturer's declaration of conformity (or self-certification) wherever possible. Manufacturers' declaration of conformity is one of the oldest and simplest forms of certification. The vast majority of United States marketplace transactions involve only the buyer and the seller—without intervention by any third party, whether government or the private sector.[7]

Manufacturers in many industries are now required not only to test their products but to formally certify them. Indeed they may operate in markets that impose legal sanctions for failure to self-certify.[8] It is therefore necessary to include manufacturers as certifiers when discussing certifiers in the context of product liability.

The Term "Product" Can Include Real Property

4–03 Definition of the term "product" where inspection and certification are concerned is broad in United Kingdom and United States jurisprudence. Real property is not excluded.[9] In fact during the second half of the last century, the metes and bounds of

---

[3] As distinct from certification mark proprietors.

[4] See, for example, J.C. Anderson and J.A. Narus, "Business Marketing: Understand What Customers Value", *Harvard Business Review*, Nov.–Dec., 1998, pp. 53 and 61; Justin Martin, "Give 'Em Exactly What They Want", 136 Fortune 283 (1997); "Q&A With Intermedia's David Rutberg", Business Week, April 6, 1998; "Total Customer Solutions Key to the Future Says Boeing", P.R. Newswire May 16, 2000.

[5] See Comment No. 36 of *Community Legislation on Machinery—Comments on Directive 98/37/E.C.* (Office for Official Publications of the European Communities, Luxembourg, 1999).

[6] As to the role of regulations and standards against which certification is effected and the significance of the term "product conformity" see Chap. 6, below.

[7] Maureen A. Breitenberg, NISTIR 6077 (October 1997), "The U.S. Certification System from a Governmental Perspective" at http://ts.nist.gov/ts/htdocs/210/217/govcer.htm.

[8] Under procedures laid down in the European Union's "New Approach" directives, it is necessary and, for many product categories, sufficient, that the manufacturer or his representative in the E.U. self-certify conformity of his product to essential health and safety requirements that are set out in the directives. A manufacturer who puts a product on to the market without self-certification, evidenced by, among other means, the "CE" mark on the product, is potentially subject to criminal sanctions.

[9] See *Dutton v. Bognor Regis U.D.C.* [1972] 1 Q.B. 373, *per* Lord Denning, M.R. See also David W. Lannetti, "Towards a Revised Definition of 'Product' Under the Restatement (Third) of Torts: Products Liability", 55 The Business Lawyer 798 at 814 (2000).

inspectors' and certifiers' liability in the United Kingdom were delineated in several important appeal court decisions involving allegations of negligent inspection of real property. Therefore, a review of relevant cases of negligent inspection of buildings and their foundations is included in the present chapter.

Product Liability Distinguished From Product Safety

Product liability addresses claims for injuries or damage that are normally asserted in civil actions, brought by the injured party. The term 'product safety' will be reserved for regulatory provisions for consumer protection against unsafe goods. Failure to comply with such provisions can result in the imposition of sanctions under the criminal law. Product liability claims can arise under statutory provisions, at common law, or both. Furthermore, liability arising out of a contract, for example between a vendor and a purchaser, must be distinguished from liability in tort, such as in a claim from a person injured by a product that was purchased by another.[10] 4–04

Liability in Historical Perspective

In historical terms, the treatment of the law of claims for product-related injury or damage as a separate branch of the law is a relatively recent development.[11] According to some commentators, its roots are in the industrial revolution.[12] Whether or not that is the case, the following broad historical contours of liability and negligence may provide useful insight into the policy and law of product liability. 4–05

Early Anglo-Saxon law operated a liability system in which obligations engendered by a man's actions were discharged through monetary payments.[13] If his actions resulted in the death or injury of another, he was required to make preordained payments by way of compensation—even if the act causing the harm was accidental or done in self-defence. Forms of such compensation included *bote*[14] and *were*.[15] Failure to compensate financially, as prescribed, could result in a man's paying with his life.[16]

---

10 But there is no rule barring concurrent claims in contract and in tort. See *Henderson v. Merrett Syndicates* [1995] 2 A.C. 145.

11 The term 'products liability' was not commonly included in leading law dictionaries until the 1970s. See n. 1, above.

12 Lannetti, *op. cit.*, p. 799. See also P.H. Winfield, *The History of Negligence in Torts*, CLXVI The Law Quarterly Review 184 at 195 (1926).

13 See, for example, the laws of Ethelbert, King of Kent, 560–616 A.D. The laws detailed fixed payments for defined injuries to the various parts of the human body, including a sinew, big toe and other toes. Similarly, the Dooms of Hlothaere and Eadric of Kent, 673–686 A.D., prescribed sums payable for the slaying of men of different standing. From *The First Written Laws of the Anglo-Saxons*, www.geocities.com/others/delphi/6909/ASlaws.html.

14 Saxon word signifying composition or restitution owed for physical injury. See John S. James, *Stroud's Judicial Dictionary* (5th ed., Sweet & Maxwell, London, 1986), Vol. 3, p. 295. Except for the clergy, the bote in the tariff lists of Kings Ethelbert and Alfred is independent of social rank, see Stanley Rubin, "The Bot, or Composition in Anglo-Saxon Law: A Reassessment", 17 Legal History 145 at 148 (1996).

15 The pecuniary estimation of a man, by which the payment to the kin or family for his death were determined. The amount depended on the person's social status. The payment arrangement was contractual, in order to ensure compliance, and a surety was required to guarantee the payments. See Rubin, *op. cit.*, p. 145.

16 There is, however, evidence of some flexibility and discretion in the implementation of the compensation tariffs. By the time of Canute (1016–1035), the law differentiated between care and carelessness and allowed for clemency for the aged, the poor and the sick in the levying of amends. See Theodore F.T. Plucknett, *A Concise History of the Common Law* (5th ed., Butterworth & Co., London, 1956), p. 464. See also Rubin, *op. cit.*, p. 146.

4–06 In medieval times liability depended on whether the damage was due to conduct that was regarded by the law as wrongful.[17] In this regard, perhaps little has changed since medieval times—apart from the actual standard for wrongdoing and the way in which compensation is exacted. Consider, for example, the statement of Lord Atkin in *Donoghue v. Stevenson*[18] that "The liability for negligence, whether you style it such or treat it as in other systems as a species of 'culpa,' is no doubt based upon a general public sentiment of moral wrongdoing for which the offender must pay."

Writing in the thirteenth century, Bracton[19] expounds liability for homicide by differentiating the results of lawful acts from wrongful or unlawful acts and effectively admits the role of negligence in apportioning liability.[20] Even where a man's actions are lawful, says Bracton, unless due care is exercised liability will be attributed to him".[21] The conduct of the medieval actor who undertook, or contracted to do, something for another, and did it so badly that the other was damaged, was considered wrongful.

In order to succeed in court, a medieval plaintiff had to show that the defendant's conduct had been incommensurate with a duty not to cause damage to the plaintiff. Such conduct could be treated as trespass.[22] At first a wrong of intentional violence, trespass evolved to include situations where harm was caused without intent.[23] Once unintentional trespass was recognised, liability for damage could exist only if some degree of blameworthy remissness, or lack of care, on the part of the actor was shown.[24]

Early Strict Liability

4–07 In the context of trespass, allegations that a wrong or damage was due to a defendant's conduct were tested against proximity of consequences to the wrong. Cases turned on whether the undesirable outcome could have been avoided. For example, in *Lambert and Olliot v. Bessey*,[25] a case tried in 1681, arguments and illustrative scenarios advanced in the 1466 case known as the *Case of Thorns*[26] were used as precedent for the

---

[17] William Holdsworth, *A History of English Law* (2nd ed., Methuen & Co. Ltd., 1937 and reprinted Sweet & Maxwell, Ltd., London, 1966), Vol. 8, pp. 450 *et seq.*

[18] [1932] A.C. 562 at 580.

[19] Sir Henry de Bratten, commonly known as Bracton, c.1210–1268. See generally *Bracton, Coproduction of the Harvard Law School Library, the Ames Foundation and the Cornell Legal Information Institute*, at http://supct.law.cornell.edu/bracton/unframed/English.htm.

[20] *ibid.*, Vol. 2, p.341.

[21] *ibid.*

[22] *Bukton v. Townsend* [1348] K.B. roll. Mich. 22 Edw. 3 is believed to be the earliest known case of liability imposed on a person who undertook to do something and did it badly, causing damage to the plaintiff. Although the duty owed by the defendant to the plaintiff arose out of a contractual or quasi-contractual relation, the defendant's conduct was treated as trespass. See J.H. Baker, *An Introduction to English Legal History* (Butterworths, London, 1971), pp. 183 *et seq.*

[23] "Trespass, in its largest, and most extensive sense, signifies any transgression, or offence against the law of nature, of society, or of the country, in which we live; whether it relates to a man's person, or his property. . . . [S]o also, nonperformance of promises or undertakings, is a trespass, upon which, an action of trespass on the case in *assumpsit* is grounded: and, in general, any misfeasance, or act of one man whereby another is injuriously treated, or damnified, is a transgression, or trespass, in it's [*sic*] largest sense" William Blackstone, *Commentaries on the Laws of England* (University Press, Oxford, 1765–69), Book III, Chap. XII, p. 208.

[24] Thomas Atkins Street, *The Foundations of Legal Liability* (Edward Thompson Company, New York, 1906), Vol. 1, p. 74.

[25] [1681] Th. Raym., 421; 83 Eng. Rep. 220.

[26] [1466] Mich. 6 Edw. 4, f.7a, no. 18. The defendant cut a hedge of thorns on his land, and the cuttings fell on the adjoining land of the plaintiff. The defendant entered the land of the plaintiff and removed the cuttings, as a result of which he was sued by the plaintiff for trespass. Choke J. stated "Now when he cut the thorns and they fell on my land, that falling was not lawful. Therefore his coming to take them out was not lawful. And if it is said, in reply to this, that they fell into the close against his will, that is no sufficient defence. He must go on to say that he could not do it in any other way, or that he did all that lay in his power to keep them out of the close. And if not he must pay damages."

principle that liability attached where harm was done in the nature of a trespass, however involuntary, if it was in any way avoidable.[27] Civil liability was independent of the state of the actor's mind. Therefore, the absence of intent to do harm, or the absence of negligence, was no defence. In other words, the liability attaching to the actor was strict.

Negligence as a Separate Tort

Negligence came to be viewed as a separate tort at the time of the industrial revolution.[28] Certainly from the Norman Conquest until the early nineteenth century, there was no analysis of negligence in English legal writing.[29] By 1800, "case for negligence" was a common expression and from then on it became possible to argue that negligence was an independent tort.[30] By the mid-nineteenth century negligence was viewed as "[t]he omission to do something which a reasonable man, guided upon those considerations which ordinarily regulate the conduct of human affairs, would do, or doing something which a prudent and reasonable man would not do."[31] It became accepted that liability for negligence should be determined according as to whether or not the consequences of the defendant's actions could have been foreseen by an "ordinarily prudent man".[32] **4–08**

Causation

Where a third-party-certified product causes injury one might expect that the certifier's liability depends on whether the consequences of the certifier's actions, in adopting a particular standard and inspecting, testing and certifying the product to the standard, could be shown to have been foreseeable.[33] A different but related mode of analysis is based on causation. The notion of causation may be viewed as a requirement that the plaintiff show that the defendant owed him a duty, that the duty was breached, and that the breach caused the damage.[34] The certifier will be able to avoid liability in any given scenario to the extent that no causal link is established between the certifier's act and the damage. Alternatively, a chain of causation may have existed but was broken by the intervention of the manufacturer or another. The chain of causation is broken if an independent cause of damage, unrelated to the certifier's breach, intervenes between the breach and the damage. **4–09**

---

[27] See *Olliott v. Bessey*, n. 25, above.

[28] See T. Ellis Lewis, *Winfield on Tort* (6th ed., Sweet & Maxwell, London, 1954), p. 477, and n. 30, below.

[29] Though Comyns's *Digest*, which was published in 1762 and concerned with remedies, refers to "action upon the case for negligence".

[30] P.H. Winfield, *The History of Negligence in Torts*, Law Quarterly Review, No. CLXVI, 184 at 195 (1926). Nevertheless, the notion that negligence is a distinct tort was refuted by some distinguished common lawyers until the early twentieth century. See, for example, Street, *op. cit.*, at p. 72, "Negligence is not a specific injury, but, like fraud and malice, it is a factor which plays an important part in large groups of wrong."

[31] *Per* Alderson, B., in *Blyth v. The Birmingham Water Works Co.* (1856) 11 Ex. 781 at 784.

[32] The prudent man standard, as adopted in, but not limited to, cases of bailment, was recognised as the applicable test in *Vaughan v. Menlove* (1837) 3 Bing. (N.C.) 468.

[33] As to recent fluctuations in the fortunes of the foreseeability criterion, see R.A. Buckley, *The Modern Law of Negligence* (2nd ed., Butterworths, London, 1993), Chap. 1, p. 3.

[34] See generally Stewart W. Dunn "The Law of Damages" at www.netlaw.freeserve.co.uk/damages.htm. While there is no one single satisfactory theory of causation, see *Smith New Court Securities v. Scrimgeour* [1996] 3 W.L.R. 1051 at 1077, it does provide a framework for identifying a causal chain between factors involved and the damage that occurred.

It is settled that causation is a question of fact. Whether there is a causal connection must be ascertained by the standard of common sense of the ordinary man.[35] Causation is investigated through a two-part inquiry. The first part is the so-called "but-for" test, which is used to determine whether the claimant would not have been injured "but for" the factor under examination. If the injury would have occurred regardless of the factor then that factor cannot have caused the injury. The second part of the inquiry seeks to establish a chain of causation between selected factors and the damage. If an unbroken chain of causation exists between breach of a duty and the damage then the defendant may be found liable.

Liability for Defective Products

4–10 The foregoing brief historical outline of liability may provide a frame of reference, within which the relatively new branch of the law known as product liability can be viewed. Consider situations where the actor considered up to now is the manufacturer, designer, inspector, certifier, endorser, wholesaler, retailer or someone else in the "stream of commerce". Such an actor might be liable for compensation for physical injuries and property damage resulting from defective and unreasonably dangerous products and from the failure of a manufacturer or seller to warn the consumer of product dangers. What then are the various forms of liability that could attach to the different actors? Alternative theories of product liability may be conveniently stated as strict liability, negligence, and breach of warranty. More than one of these theories, and sometimes all three, may be pursued in a single case.[36] Examples are considered in later sections of this chapter. But first, some remarks are made about liability policy and fairness.

Strict Liability Not Normally Imposed on Third Party Certifiers

4–11 Successful purchaser claims in strict liability against third party certifiers are unusual, even in the United States, where the scope of product liability rules is perhaps wider than elsewhere. Strict liability implies that questions of negligence and reasonable conduct on the part of the actor are, broadly speaking, irrelevant. Such claims have not succeeded partly because third party certifiers neither manufacture nor sell the product.[37] Furthermore, it is usual for third party certifiers to authorise the manufacturer to affix the certifier's mark to the approved product without the certifier's intervention to inspect each and every item coming off the production line. Under these circumstances, it is not considered fair to allow purchasers or end users to proceed against the certifier in strict liability.[38]

---

[35] *Yorkshire Dale Steamship Co. v. Minister of War Transport* [1942] A.C 691 at 706, *per* Lord Wright.

[36] Recent U.S. examples are *Wilson v. Bradlees of New England, Inc.*, 96 F.3d 552 at 553 (1996), U.S. Court of Appeals for the First Circuit, cert. denied 519 U.S. 1149; 117 S.Ct. 1083; 137 L.Ed.2d 218 (1997), *Snell v. Bell Helicopter Textron*, 107 F.3d 744 at 745 (1997), U.S. Court of Appeals for the Ninth Circuit and *McKendall v. Crown Control Corp.*, 122 F.3d 803 (1997), U.S. Court of Appeals for the Ninth Circuit.

[37] *Hanberry v. Hearst*, 81 Cal. Reptr. 519, Cal.Ct.App. (1969).

[38] One mode of controlling the use of the certifier's certification mark after initial approval of the product, is for the certifier to conduct periodic checks on production items, without advanced warning to the manufacturer, to assure that they are being manufactured in compliance with the certifier's requirements. Such checks may include an audit of the manufacturer's quality control scheme.

Fairness and Utility in Strict Liability

Why would it not be fair to impose strict liability on a certifier if the certifier's act could be shown to have led directly to the injury or damage? This question should be considered perhaps in light of the policy rationales for strict liability on the one hand and community perceptions of fairness on the other. Fletcher puts the underlying dilemma as follows: 4–12

> The conflict is whether judges should look solely at the claims and interests of the parties before the court, or resolve seemingly private disputes in a way that serves the interests of the community as a whole.[39]

This dilemma appears formidable indeed when account is taken of the common law judge's traditional function as forger of links between law and morality.[40]

Rationales favouring strict liability over fault-based liability are largely instrumentalist; they purport to further social interests by optimising economic efficiency, accident deterrence, absorption and spreading of accident costs and accident liability costs.[41] It is generally accepted that the onus should be on the manufacturer to act as the optimiser. The case for strict liability, and for it to be borne by the manufacturer, was put in *Escola v. Coca-Cola Bottling Co. of Fresno*,[42] as follows:

> Even if there is no negligence, however, public policy demands that responsibility be fixed wherever it will most effectively reduce the hazards to life and health inherent in defective products that reach the market. . . . [T]he risk of injury can be insured by the manufacturer and distributed among the public as a cost of doing business. It is to the public interest to discourage the marketing of products having defects that are a menace to the public.[43]

Commentators have from time to time advocated strict liability for certifiers.[44] LaRaia, 4–13
writing in the early 1970s, suggested that deficiencies in certifiers' standards could be cured by "the specter of strict liability".[45] However, the adoption of strict liability for certifiers would remove the traditional exemption of "socially useful" risks from tort liability, a judicial position that can be traced back to the middle of the nineteenth century.[46]

From the instrumentalist standpoint, the economic sense[47] of making the certifier the cost minimiser is questionable. Manufacturers' insurance premiums normally provide coverage for indemnity and liability arising from defective products. Such premiums would be increased as increased certifiers' insurance costs were passed on to the manufacturers they serve. Absent some motivation for manufacturers to internalise the increased insurance costs, consumers would pay more for their purchases.

Focusing now on the issue of "fairness", a certification mark affixed to a product is a public attestation to existence of certain specific attributes in the product or in its

---

[39] George P. Fletcher, "Fairness and Utility in Tort Theory", 35 Harvard Law Rev. 537 at 540 (1972).

[40] R. Cotterrell, *Common Law Approaches to the Relationship Between Law and Morality*, 3 Ethical Theory and Moral Practice, 9 at 13 (2000).

[41] Proponents of strict liability argue that it is less cumbersome and costly than the fault liability system. For a thoughtful analysis of shortcomings in commonly-held perceptions of strict liability, see Daniel More, "Re-Examining Strict Products Liability's Goals and Justifications", 9 *Tel Aviv University Studies in Law* 165 (1989).

[42] 150 P.2d 436 (1944).

[43] *ibid.*, at 441, *per* Justice Traynor.

[44] R.F. LaRaia, "Torts: Product Certifiers—on the Periphery of Strict Liability", 26 Oklahoma L. Rev. 622 (1973).

[45] *ibid.*, at p. 628.

[46] See Fletcher, *op. cit.*, p. 566.

[47] Discussion of economic theories of resource allocation in relation to products liability is beyond the scope of this work. Such theories aim, among other things, to develop liability rules that reduce accident and accident liability costs to society.

conditions of manufacture. For example the raw material from which a garment is made, a fire extinguisher's conformity to a recognised safety standard, and so on. Certification marks are specific to particular attributes and do not provide a blanket guarantee of satisfactory or merchantable quality for the product as a whole. A certification mark's "guarantee" is narrower than one of overall compliance with the satisfactory quality requirement of the United Kingdom Sale of Goods Act 1979[48] or the United States Uniform Commercial Code.[49] The narrowness of the certification mark's guarantee, it is submitted, militates against its owner being held strictly liable to the consumer.

4–14 Consider next the implications for fairness of the certifier's role as defect detector rather than defect creator. If court decisions are consistent with fairness, then it is regarded as fair to distinguish between the imposition of strict liability on a manufacturer for selling an article containing a dangerous manufacturing defect that causes harm, but not on the certifier for its non-detection of the defect. The usual justification for this distinction is that the certifier approves the product for conformity to its requirements but does not inspect every item manufactured for such compliance.

It may be thought that fairness arguments ring hollow where the certifier fails to detect a serious design defect, which affects every article produced. The problem here is that the rationale for imposing strict liability on manufacturers for manufacturing defects, does not apply to design defects. It would hardly be fair to impose strict liability on the third-party certifier while refraining from imposing it on the manufacturer. Customer expectations as to product design are more difficult to discern than in the case of a manufacturing defect. Furthermore, use of even a reasonably designed product still involves some risks that cannot be designed out at reasonable cost.[50] In summary, the trend, particularly in the United States, is to differentiate between manufacturing and design defects, to reserve strict liability for manufacturing defects but to adopt a negligence form of liability for design defects.

Primary responsibility for assuring the quality and safety of a product rests with the manufacturer. The manufacturer is the party that places the product on the market and whets, maintains and satisfies the consumer's appetite for the product in order to make a profit. By way of contrast, the certifier is often a non-profit authoritative body operating in the public interest. In the United Kingdom at least, a registered certification mark scheme is required to be operated by a body that has the confidence of the trade and whose certification is likely to be accepted as authoritative.[51] In view of the foregoing, it is not clear that either the essential policy aims of strict liability or community notions of fairness would be furthered by generally enclosing certifiers in the net of strict liability.

Manufacturers are not Required to be Insurance Carriers

4–15 Although a manufacturer's liability can be strict, the causing of harm by a product does not automatically trigger liability on its part, as is the case if liability is absolute. The latter would put the manufacturer in the position of an insurance carrier.[52] The plaintiff

[48] s.14(2), as amended by the Sale and Supply of Goods Act 1994. See para. 5–10, below.

[49] *Uniform Commercial Code, Official Text with Comments* (11th ed., American Law Institute, Pennsylvania, 1989), §§ 2.312–315.

[50] *Restatement of the Law (Third) Products Liability* (St Paul: American Law Institute, 1998), pp. 16–17.

[51] *U.K. Trade Marks Registry Work Manual* (1996), Chap. 12, *Certification Trade Marks*, p. 9. Recent inquiries to the U.K. Registry indicate that this continues to be an important qualification for proprietorship of a registered certification mark.

[52] For U.S. court decisions upholding this position, see *Neal v. Toyota Motor Corp.*, 823 F.Supp. 939 (1993), *Binaknosky v. Ford Motor Co.*, 929 F.Supp. 915 (1996), aff'd in part, reversed in part, 133 F.3d 281 (1996) and *Carlson v. Bic Corp.* 840 F. Supp. 457 (1993).

in a strict liability action must still show that the product contained a defect (normally a defect that rendered the product unreasonably dangerous), which caused the injury or damage.

Manufacturer's Duty to Inspect and Test

A manufacturer that sells a product in a defective condition that is unreasonably **4–16** dangerous to the ordinary user may be liable for any resulting property damage or physical injuries. United States laws impose on manufacturers a duty to research and make such tests and inspections as reasonably necessary to make their product safe or to establish a basis for warning consumers of a product's unavoidable dangers.[53] Features that are dangerous may reside in the product design or manufacture, the container or the packaging, or the instructions or warning necessary for the product. Where injury is proved to have been caused by a product that is not of satisfactory quality, the exercise of reasonable care is no defence.

Statutory Liability in the United Kingdom

The United Kingdom Sale of Goods Act 1979

Statutory protection against defective goods sold in the course of a business is based **4–17** on the implied term of satisfactory quality[54] in section 14(2)(a) of the Sale of Goods Act 1979 as amended by the Sale and Supply of Goods Act 1994, which provides:

> For the purposes of this Act, goods are of satisfactory quality if they meet the standard that a reasonable person would regard as satisfactory, taking account of any description of the goods, the price (if relevant) and all the other relevant circumstances.

Section 14(2)(b) provides that the quality of goods includes their state and condition and also, where appropriate, fitness for all the purposes for which goods are commonly supplied, appearance and finish, freedom from minor defects, safety and durability. Section 53(2) of the Act provides that:

> The measure of damages for the seller's breach of contract is the estimated loss directly and naturally resulting, in the ordinary course of events, from the breach of warranty.

This admits the possibility of award of consequential damages in cases of personal injury and death, which can of course be much larger than the section 53(3) loss, prima facie calculated as the difference between the value of the goods at the time of delivery to the buyer and the value they would have had if they had fulfilled the warranty.[55] Liability arising under the Sale of Goods Act is contractual and so the purchaser may sue the manufacturer only where he purchased from the manufacturer.

---

[53] See *Richter v. Limax Intern. Inc.*, 45 F.3d. 1464 (1995) (KA law), *Jones v. United Metal Recyclers*, 825 F.Supp. 1288 (1993) (MI law), *Kramer v. Showa Denko*, 929 F.Supp. 733 (1996) (NY law), *San Diego Hosp. Ass'n. v. Superior Court*, 35 Cal. Reptr. 2d 489, 30 C.A. 4th 8, (1994) (CA law).

[54] The Sale and Supply of Goods Act 1994 replaced the *merchantable* quality requirement, which had been in successive Sale of Goods Acts since the original 1893 Act, by a requirement for *satisfactory* quality. As to whether a certification mark can be implicated in the breach of an implied term of the Sale of Goods Act 1997, see Chap. 5, below.

[55] For examples see Note "Measure of damages" in *Halsbury's Statutes of England and Wales* (4th ed. (reissue), Butterworths, London, 1995), Vol. 39, Sale of Goods Act, s.53, p. 116.

Whereas United States products liability law underwent a gradual shift in the twentieth century from negligence-based to strict liability-based principles,[56] the United Kingdom retained proof of negligence as the basis of product liability — until the advent of statutory strict liability, in the form of the Consumer Protection Act 1987.

The United Kingdom Consumer Protection Act 1987, Part I

4–18 Part I of the Consumer Protection Act implements into United Kingdom law the provisions of the E.C. Product Liability Directive.[57] Section 2(1) of the Act provides:

> Subject to the following provisions of this Part, where any damage is caused wholly or partly by a defect in a product, every person to whom subsection (2) below applies shall be liable for the damage.

where subsection (2) applies to—

> (a) the producer of the product;
> (b) any person who, by putting his name on the product or using a trade mark or other distinguishing mark in relation to the product, has held himself out to be the producer of the product;
> (c) any person who has imported the product into a member State from a place outside the member States in order, in the course of any business of his, to supply it to another.

Thus producers, those marketing "own brands" and importers are, for purposes of the act, considered as liable for damage caused by a defective product. However, a supplier may escape liability by identifying the person who supplied him. An "own brander" can escape liability if the product carries an identification of the product manufacturer. Thus if retailer X sells X-brand coffee actually produced by company Y, bearing a label stating "Produced and packaged for X by Y", X may escape liability under the Act.

4–19 Liability under Part I of the Consumer Protection Act 1987 is strict, but the plaintiff must carry the burden of proving that the defendant was the producer of a defective product or otherwise liable under the Act. The imposition of strict liability was not only the result of the Product Liability Directive; it was also a recommendation of the Law Commission and the Scottish Law Commission in their report "Liability for Defective Products".[58] The report came to the general conclusion that producers should be subject to strict liability in tort for death or personal injury caused by a defect in their products.

Certain defences are available to the defendant under sections 4 and 6 of the Act. Section 4 provides defences where a defect is due to compliance with any statutory requirement or rule of the E.C., the defendant did not supply the product (*e.g.* theft from the defendant's premises), or the defendant did not supply the product in the course of a business or with a view to profit. Additional defences are that the defect did not exist at

[56] The U.S. case that is frequently cited as the one that unequivocally instituted strict liability in tort for dangerously defective products is *Greenman v. Yuba Power Products, Inc.*, 27 Cal. Reptr. 697 at 701 (1962). Query whether the "repeal" of section 204A of the Restatement of Torts (Second) by the Restatement of Torts (Third): Products Liability, 1998 (see n. 50, above) signals a retreat from "total" strict liability, that is strict liability for all three of manufacturing, design and warning defects in products. Most notable in this connection is the Third Restatement's adoption, in s.2(b), of a negligence-based criterion for design defect related liability.

[57] Directive 85/374 of the Council of the European Communities, of July 25, 1985 on the approximation of the laws, regulations and administrative provisions of the member states concerning liability for defective products. For a discussion of European product liability law as background to adoption of the Directive see Caryl Cecilia Ben Basat, "Strict Products Liability in the United Kingdom", 14 *Journal of Products Liability* 351 (1992). For a pan-European review of product liability law and practice see generally, *Product Liability European Laws and Practice* (Christopher J.S. Hodges ed., Sweet and Maxwell, London, 1993).

[58] Cmnd. 6831 (1977).

the time the product was supplied by the defendant, the defect is due to the design of the larger product in which the product is included, or where the defect is attributable to instructions given by the manufacturer of the larger product. Finally, it is a defence that the defect was not discoverable at the time the defendant supplied the product because of the "state of scientific and technical knowledge at the relevant time".

Section 6(1) of the Act provides for a defence of contributory negligence, under which the defendant may show that the plaintiff failed to take reasonable care and is therefore partly responsible for the injuries he or she suffered.

The United Kingdom Consumer Protection Act 1987, Part II

Part II of the Consumer Protection Act 1987 contains consumer safety provisions under which civil and criminal liability may attach to persons who supply any consumer goods which fail to comply with the general safety requirement, offer or agree to supply, or expose or possess such goods for supply.[59] Under Part II, s.(10), goods fail to comply with the general safety requirement if they are not reasonably safe having regard to all the circumstances, including the use of any mark in relation to the goods and any instructions or warnings with respect to the keeping, use or consumption of the goods.[60] "Having regard to all the circumstances" includes any published standards for goods of a description which applies to the goods in question.[61] A defendant may claim due diligence as a defence in proceedings under section 10. However, before suppliers can avail themselves of this protection they "can often expect to prove that before supplying the goods they have had the goods tested by a competent person".[62] 4–20

Thus, it is an offence for a trader to supply consumer goods that fail to comply with the general safety requirement. Furthermore, consumers are entitled to sue a trader, including a manufacturer, for damages where damage or loss is suffered as the result of an infringement of safety regulations. This applies even where the plaintiff did not purchase the goods from the manufacturer. Civil liability cannot be excluded or restricted by any exemption or exclusion clause. Liability under Part II is strict; there is no requirement for the plaintiff to establish negligence on the part of the manufacturer.

United Kingdom Employer's Liability (Defective Equipment) Act 1969

Where defective equipment causes personal injuries to employees in the course of their employment, employers are liable. The term "equipment" includes any plant and machinery, vehicle, aircraft and clothing.[63] The defect must be attributable, wholly or partly, to the fault of a third party, whether identified or not. Liability is strict. If all these elements are proved or admitted, the employer is liable regardless of fault. 4–21

Tortious Liability

In broad terms, product-related torts that are based on negligence or fault liability theory concern failure to exercise reasonable care to avoid injury to others or their property.[64] Fault liability theory allows any injured purchaser, or reasonably close user, of a 4–22

---

[59] Consumer Protection Act 1978, s.10(1).
[60] Consumer Protection Act 1978, s.10(2).
[61] *ibid.*
[62] See General Note in *Halsbury's Statutes of England and Wales* (4th ed. (reissue), Butterworths, London, 1995), Vol. 39, p. 162.
[63] Employer's Liability (Defective Equipment) Act 1969, s.1(3).
[64] See generally R. A. Buckley, *The Modern Law of Negligence* (2nd ed., Butterworths, London, 1993).

defective product, to sue any person in the chain of supply, including the manufacturer. From the consumer-plaintiff's standpoint, the disadvantage of suing under a negligence theory is that he carries the burden of proof. This may be a difficult burden to carry, since he may not be sufficiently acquainted with the manufacturing process and potential breaches of good manufacturing practice.

The Privity Bar

4–23 Although a contract or its performance can affect a third party, the doctrine of privity traditionally confined rights arising under the contract to the contracting parties.[65] A "privity bar" existed, which prevented an injured purchaser from seeking redress from anyone except the person from whom the product was purchased. The rationale was that the only duty of care was that imposed by the contract.[66] In the sale of goods, there is a contractual relationship between the purchaser and the seller, often the retailer, but there is normally no contractual relationship between the purchaser and the manufacturer, the manufacturer's trade association, third party certifier or, indeed anyone else who may be standing behind the product. There were two recognised exceptions to the privity bar, namely where (1) an article was dangerous in and of itself; or (2) an article not in itself dangerous was in fact dangerous by reason of some defect or for any other reason and this was known to the manufacturer. Otherwise the purchaser would be barred from suing the manufacturer.[67]

Abolition of the Privity Bar

4–24 *Donoghue v. Stevenson*,[68] decided by the House of Lords in 1932, marked the abolition of the privity bar to actions in tort for negligence against non-contracting parties. The plaintiff allegedly became severely ill after drinking some of the contents of an opaque bottle of ginger-beer before finding it to contain a decomposed snail. The court held that the manufacturer of an article of food, medicine or the like, selling to a consumer in circumstances preventing detection of a defect, owes a duty of care to the consumer. Thus emerged a new category of plaintiffs to whom a manufacturer would be liable for harm caused by his product, notwithstanding lack of privity.

Doctrine of *res ipsa loquitur*

4–25 *Donoghue* did not eliminate the need for a plaintiff to show fault or negligence on the part of the defendant in a privity-free action. In order not to render the plaintiff's (sometimes highly technical) burden intolerable, courts have adopted the rebuttable principle[69] of *res ipsa loquitur*. For example, in *Grant v. Australian Knitting Mills, Ltd*,[70]

---

[65] The classic case is *Winterbottom v. Wright* (1842) 10 M & W 109; 152 E.R. 402, in which a passenger who was injured when a coach collapsed was not able to recover against the person responsible for keeping the coach in good repair. There was no contract between the parties. The privity doctrine appears to have become entrenched in English law with *Tweddle v. Atkinson* (1861) 1 B. & S. 393; 121 E.R. 762.

[66] *Per* Lord Denning M.R., in *Dutton v. Bognor Regis U.D.C.* [1972] 1 Q.B. 373 at 392.

[67] For examples of cases in which such exceptions were acknowledged see *Longmeid v. Holliday* (1851) 6 Ex. 761 at 767 and *Dominion Natural Gas Co., Ltd. v. Collins & Perkins* [1909] A.C. 640, PC.

[68] [1932] A.C. 562.

[69] See *Daniels v. R. White & Sons, Ltd. and Tabard* [1938] 4 All E.R. 258, in which a soft drinks manufacturer was exonerated from liability for the presence of carbolic acid in its lemonade because of its "fool-proof" bottling operation.

[70] [1936] A.C. 85; [1935] All E.R. 209, PC.

where the plaintiff alleged that underclothing he had purchased caused him serious dermatitis but was unable to identify the responsible person in the supply chain, the retailers and the manufacturers were held liable in contract and negligent tort, respectively. The case of *Carroll v. Fearon*[71] is a more recent example of the application of *res ipsa loquitur*. Referring to the *Donoghue* and *Grant* cases, the court held that where a car tyre might have failed for any one of a number of reasons, it was open to the judge to hold that on a balance of probabilities, the fault was caused by the manufacturer's negligence.

Demise of the Privity Bar in the United States

Immunity of manufacturers against non-contracting purchasers' claims in respect of defective products began to break down in the United States earlier than in the United Kingdom, commencing with *MacPherson v. Buick Motor Co.*[72] The plaintiff was injured when driving a car purchased from a retail dealer. The car suddenly collapsed due to a defective wheel. There was evidence that the defect could have been discovered by inspection, but there had been no inspection. The New York Court of Appeals rejected the rule of *Winterbottom v. Wright*[73] in favour of a higher standard of responsibility for the manufacturer towards the user. It was thus deemed unacceptable that the duty to safeguard life and limb, when the consequences of negligence are foreseeable, should grow out of contract and nothing else. **4–26**

After *MacPherson*, United States courts imposed higher standards of liability on suppliers. Liability was imposed even where suppliers had exercised all reasonable care in the preparation and sale of their products. These decisions heralded the advent of strict product liability. In 1960, a landmark decision in *Henningsen v. Bloomfield Motors*[74] held a car dealer strictly liable for injuries suffered by the wife of the purchaser of a car that she was driving when it crashed into a wall because of a defective steering mechanism. The plaintiff was unable to prove that the dealer had been negligent, but liability was imposed nevertheless, under breach of implied warranty. The wife had not been in a contractual relationship with the dealer, neither was she able to prove negligence on his part, but she was awarded damages.

Expansion of Tort Claims to Economic Loss

The scope of tortious negligence has continued to expand. Together with foreseeability,[75] other important requirements are applied as means of controlling the expansion, which reached pure economic loss in some cases.[76] These requirements are that (1) there be sufficiently close proximity of the defendant to the plaintiff and (2) it would be fair, just and reasonable to impose liability.[77] By such means, attempts are made to allow the momentum of change created by the early cases to be maintained but without undue augmentation. During the last decade in particular there has been a noticeable **4–27**

[71] [1998] P.I.Q.R. P416.
[72] 217 N.Y. 382, 111 N.E. 1050 (1916).
[73] See n. 65, above.
[74] 32 N.J. 358, 161 A.2d 69 (1960).
[75] The foreseeability criterion has suffered varying fortunes in the English courts, see n. 33, above.
[76] For examples of claims for economic loss see *Rutherford v. Attorney-General* [1976] 1 N.Z.L.R. 401, *White v. Jones* [1995] 2 A.C. 207, and *LondonWaste Ltd v. Amec Civil Engineering, Ltd*, 53 Con. L.R. 66 (1997).
[77] *Murphy v. Brentwood D.C.* [1991] 1 A.C. 398; [1990] 2 All E.R. 908; [1990] 3 W.L.R. 414, HL.

clarification of the distinction between cases of direct physical damage and indirect physical or economic loss. Thus in *LondonWaste Ltd. v. Amec Civil Engineering, Ltd,*[78] it was stated that there was a clearly established but limited head of recoverable economic loss consisting of that which is consequential upon any physical damage caused to the plaintiff's property. In *Hamble Fisheries, Ltd. v. L. Gardner & Sons, Ltd., (The Rebecca Elaine)*[79] the Court of Appeals upheld a decision that no common law duty of care was owed for economic loss caused by a vessel having defective engine components where the parties had no dealings with each other and no responsibility had been voluntarily assumed to warn the plaintiff of the danger. In *Stock v. London Underground Ltd,*[80] in which Stock's commercial premises were damaged (structurally and economically) as a result of tunnelling, the Appeal Court held that the principle applicable in personal injury cases that varied heads of claim did not create several causes of action applied also to building disputes

Inspectors' and Certifiers' Duty of Care

4–28 Various categories of professionals may be held to owe a duty of care.[81] Inspectors, certification and testing engineers are potentially liable if the purchaser, or another party in sufficiently close proximity, relies on their certification or endorsement. Whether or not the defendant failed to show reasonable care is a question of fact. A professional is required to meet the standard of the ordinary skilled man exercising and professing to have the special skill in question. Because there may have been an error of judgment it does not necessarily follow that the defendant was negligent unless a reasonably competent professional with the standard and type of skill of the defendant would not have committed the error.

Professionals serving as safety or inspecting engineers pursuant to provisions of statutes and regulations have been held to owe a duty of care to third parties affected by their negligent conduct. In a United Kingdom case involving personal injury, namely *Driver v. William Willett (Contractors), Ltd,*[82] consulting safety and inspecting engineers contracted to advise a building firm on safety requirements and building regulations. The consultants thereby assumed the position of a safety officer under the regulations. An employee of the building firm was seriously injured in an accident on a building site under the consultants' supervision. The consultants were held liable since they should have reasonably foreseen that the employee was in the class of persons who would be injured for a breach of a duty of care, owed to the plaintiff as a result of the contract between the employer and the consultants.[83]

In the United States case of *Buszta v. Souther,*[84] a car had been inspected as required under the law of Rhode Island and certified as roadworthy. the plaintiff was involved in a collision while driving the car, which belonged to her employer. The defendant's service station was authorised by the state to make such inspections and issue certificates of approval. The plaintiff alleged she had relied upon the inspection certificate and that the defendant was negligent in not finding that the brakes were

[78] See n. 76, above.
[79] [1999] C.L.Y. 3960.
[80] *The Times,* August 13, 1999; [1999] C.L.Y. 3944.
[81] See *Halsbury's Laws of England* (4th ed. (reissue), Butterworths, London, 1997), Vol. 33, para. 623.
[82] [1969] 1 All E.R. 665.
[83] The plaintiff also sued the employer in negligence and in breach of statutory duty in the usual way.
[84] 232 A.2d 396 (R.I. 1967).

defective. Overruling the lower court's dismissal of the claim, due to a lack of duty of care to the plaintiff since she was not party to the agreement with the service station, the Supreme Court of Rhode Island held there was a duty of care owing, as there would be on the part of a repairer.

Negligent Inspection of Real Property

Although something of a judicial pendulum, courts have recognised the application of the principle of *Donoghue v. Stevenson* to defects in real property that are overlooked by negligent inspectors. In *Dutton v. Bognor Regis U.D.C.*[85] The plaintiff moved into a house that she bought from an owner-occupier to whom it had been sold by the builder. Soon serious defects became apparent in the structure. It was found to have inadequate foundations, having been built on a one-time rubbish tip. The local authority's inspector had inspected the foundations when they were laid and had given his approval. His inspection was deemed by the court to have been negligent by failing to observe that the foundations were inadequate. Liability was imposed on the local authority for its construction inspector's failure to observe that the foundations for a house were inadequate. Lord Denning M.R. took the view that 4–29

> [T]he distinction between chattels and real property is quite unsustainable. If the manufacturer of an article is liable to a person injured by his negligence, so should the builder of a house be liable.[86]

Eventually, the extension of common law liability to the foregoing scenario, which is customarily considered as contract-governed, received the blessing of the House of Lords in *Anns and others v. London Borough of Merton*.[87] *Anns* was concerned directly with the liability in negligence of a local authority in respect of its inspection functions in securing compliance with building byelaws and regulations. However, as stated by Lord Keith in *Department of the Environment v. Thomas Bates & Son*,[88] a case similar to *Anns*:

> It has been generally accepted that similar principles govern the liability both of the local authority and of the builder.[89]

The pendulum swung back thirteen years later, in *Murphy v. Brentwood District Council*,[90] when the lords overruled both *Dutton* and *Anns*. Their Lordships held that the builder of a defective building is not liable to the occupier in negligence for pure economic loss. The overruling appears to have stemmed partly from the traditional fear of opening the floodgates to an overwhelming number of claims. If the earlier decisions were to be accepted as good law, it was argued, the door would be open to a mass of product liability claims which the law has not previously entertained.[91] A similar rationale was offered by the court for not allowing the plaintiff's claim in the 1842 case of *Winterbottom v. Wright*.[92]

---

[85] [1972] 1 Q.B. 373.
[86] [1972] 1 Q.B. 373 at 393. This particular proposition still stands notwithstanding the overruling of the decision on the case by the House of Lords in *Murphy v. Brentwood District Council* [1990] 2 All E.R. 908.
[87] [1978] A.C. 728; [1977] 2 All E.R. 492.
[88] [1990] 2 All E.R. 943.
[89] [1990] 2 All E.R. 943 at 946.
[90] [1991] 1 A.C. 398; [1990] 2 All E.R. 908.
[91] *ibid.*, at last page.
[92] [1842] 152 E.R. 402 at 405. "If we were to hold that the plaintiff could sue in such a case there is no point at which such actions would stop. The only safe rule is to confine the right to recover to those who enter into the contract: if we go one step beyond that, there is no reason why we should not go fifty.", *per* Alderson, B.

Shipping Inspection—Classification Societies

4–30 Organisations that promote public health and safety or the collective welfare have not often been held liable for negligence in fulfilling inspection and certification functions. Classification societies are one such type of organisation. They are old-established institutions that inspect and certify merchant ships for compliance with their seaworthiness standards.[93] They are charitable, non-profit-making organisations. "[B]ut why", in the words of Lord Lloyd (dissenting) in *Marc Rich & Co. v. Bishop Rock Marine*[94] "should this make any difference? Remedies in the law of tort are not discretionary."

To insure their vessels or secure a charterer, ship owners have no practical alternative to contracting with a classification society to obtain and maintain a classification. The aura of immunity surrounding classification societies was not dispelled by the *Marc Rich* decision. There was sufficient proximity for a duty of care to the owner of the cargo that was lost with the ship that underwent only temporary repairs at the society inspector's recommendation. However, the lords held that it would be unfair, unjust and unreasonable to impose a duty of care on a classification society.

Negligent Certification

4–31 Certifiers or endorsers may be held liable for physical harm based on a negligent undertaking or a negligent statement theory.[95] However, it appears that as a matter of policy those who examine or test samples of a product placed on the market, but do not qualify each and every item produced, do not face strict liability or liability in warranty. Negligence in the performance of an inspection and certification requires a showing of harm resulting from failure of the inspector or certifier to exercise reasonable care. A consumer injured by a product and alleging negligent certification of the product carries a heavy burden of proof. The product must be proven defective and not as advertised or represented. Furthermore, the consumer must show that the certifier did not exercise reasonable care in testing or inspecting the product. Finally, he must show that the defective product caused the injury.

Where a defendant such as a product certifier makes a statement or enters into an undertaking that is relied upon by a plaintiff, in the way intended by the defendant, there may be an assumption of responsibility sufficient to give rise to liability for harm flowing from the reliance. However, a plaintiff's reliance on a statement must be reasonable in order to give rise to a duty.[96] As late as 1951, in the case of *Candler v. Crane, Christmas & Co.*, the United Kingdom Court of Appeal held that there was no liability for negligent misstatement in the absence of a contractual or fiduciary relationship between the parties.[97] However, *Candler* was overruled by the House of Lords in *Hedley Byrne & Co., Ltd. v. Heller & Partners, Ltd*[98] in which it was held that a negligent misrepresentation

---

[93] Classification embodies the technical rules, regulations, standards, guidelines and associated surveys and inspections covering the design, construction and through-life compliance of a ship's structure and essential engineering and electrical systems. See website of International Association of Classification Societies at www.iacs.org.uk/brochure/classif.html.

[94] [1995] 3 All E.R. 307 at 320.

[95] *Halsbury's Laws of England* (4th ed. (reissue), Butterworths, London, 1997), Vol. 33, para. 614.

[96] *Hedley Byrne & Co., Ltd v. Heller & Partners, Ltd.* [1964] A.C. 465 at 486; [1963] 2 All E.R. 575 at 583, HL.

[97] [1951] 2 K.B. 164. Accounts of a company, that were requested by a potential investor for review, had been "carelessly prepared and gave a wholly misleading picture", *per* Lord Reid in *Hedley Byrne & Co., Ltd v. Heller & Partners, Ltd* (n. 96, above).

[98] *ibid.*

may create liability for damages for financial loss caused, apart from any contract or fiduciary relationship. The rationale for this position lies in the implied duty of care when information is sought from a person possessing a special skill and who knows, or should know, that reliance is being placed on his skill and judgment.[99]

Wrongful Denial of Approval

Can a product approver such as a trade organisation or test laboratory be held liable for wrongful withholding of approval of a product? Under a negligence theory a plaintiff manufacturer would have to establish a duty of care and prove a breach of that duty on a balance of probabilities. A term in the contract, implied or explicit, between the laboratory and the manufacturer, that the laboratory would exercise reasonable care in conducting the evaluation can establish the requisite duty of care. The potential harm caused to a company through negligent denial of certification of a product that is in fact worthy of certification is foreseeable. Therefore, a manufacturer who contracts with a testing laboratory for the technical evaluation of his product according to set standards and suffers actual loss through what proves to be negligent denial of approval presents a reasonable claim of negligence. For this reason, contracts with certification organisations often address liability issues, providing for a contractual disclaimer. **4–32**

Defamation

In order to avoid allegations of defamation, those testing and evaluating products must exercise due care as to the manner in which they communicate negative results of tests on products. Whereas in negligence the plaintiff must prove some actual loss recognised by law and that the loss was caused by the defendant, defamation protects the reputation of a person and is normally actionable *per se*.[1] In many cases the contract will specify that the testing and its results be carried out under conditions of non-disclosure to third parties. To be actionable as defamatory, words must impute to the plaintiff some quality which would be detrimental, or the lack of some attribute that is essential, to successful conduct of the business. **4–32A**

In the absence of any reflection on the plaintiff's business reputation, there can be no case for defamation. Thus, it is defamatory to publish of a trader that his goods are, among other things, unwholesome, adulterated, dangerous or unworkable,[2] but not that the goods fail to meet the standard for certification. A true statement will not incur liability for negligence or defamation.[3] Therefore, a product inspector or certifier making a true statement about a product that failed to meet the required standards for approval would not be liable for defamation. Neither is there liability because the truth is revealed in an unfair manner or the investigations on which it is based are not revealed in full[4] or are not complete.

---

[99] In *Hedley Byrne* (n. 96, above), there was a disclaimer of responsibility and so no such duty was implied.

[1] See *Gatley on Libel and Slander* (P. Milmo and W.V.H. Rogers eds, 9th ed., Sweet & Maxwell, London, 1998), Part One "The Defamatory Statement".

[2] *ibid.*, § 2.37.

[3] *Spring v. Guardian Assurance* [1995] 2 A.C. 296 at 335–336, 347.

[4] *Bell-Booth Group v. Attorney-General* [1989] 3 N.Z.L.R. 148, NZCA. See also *Lawton v. B.O.C. Transhield* [1987] 2 All E.R. 608; [1987] I.C.R. 7.

United States Perceptions of Tortious Negligence

4–33 The Restatement of Torts 2d, includes sections that are potentially applicable to certifiers.[5] These sections include provisions that define prerequisites for liability that appear relevant to, among other things, negligent certification of products. In this regard, key provisions of the Restatement, are those in section 311, which is concerned with the giving of false information (negligent misrepresentation) and sections 323 and 324A. Section 323 negligence could apply where certification services are necessary for the protection of the purchaser or user. By contrast, section 324A negligence arises in the rendering of services necessary for the protection of a third person.

The gist of each of the Restatement's negligence provisions is set forth in Table 4.1 (see paragraph 4–34, below) from which one discerns that *reliance* upon information given or on the undertaking itself can give rise to liability in all three modes of conduct. It is noteworthy that, under section 311, the harm must result from reasonable reliance upon the relevant information. By way of contrast, under sections 323 and 324A, liability for negligent undertakings requires that the harm result from the actor's failure to exercise reasonable care. Section 323 and 324A admit the possibility but not the necessity for the harm to have been suffered by virtue of reliance upon the undertaking.

4–34

Section	Actor's Mode of Conduct	Conditions for Liability	Comments
311	Negligent giving of false information to another	Physical harm caused by action taken by the other in reasonable reliance upon such information, where harm results to the other, or to third persons. Negligence may consist of failure to exercise reasonable care.	Particularly applicable where it is part of the actor's business or profession to give information upon which the safety of the recipient or a third person depends.
323	Negligent undertaking to render services to another which actor should recognize as necessary for the protection of the other's person or things.	Physical harm resulting from actor's failure to exercise reasonable care to perform his undertaking, if (a) his failure to exercise such care increases the risk of such harm, or (b) the harm is suffered because of the other's reliance upon the undertaking.	Applies whether the harm to the other or his things results from defendant's negligent conduct, or from failure to exercise reasonable care.

[5] Restatement of Torts 2d, c.12.

Section	Actor's Mode of Conduct	Conditions for Liability	Comments
324	Negligent undertaking to render services to another which actor should recognize as necessary for the protection of a third person.	Physical harm resulting from actor's failure to exercise reasonable care to protect his undertaking, if (a) his failure to exercise reasonable care increases the risk of such harm, or (b) he has undertaken to perform a duty owed by the other to the third person, or (c) the harm is suffered because of reliance of the other or the third person on the undertaking.	Applies whether the harm to a third person or his things results from the actor's negligent conduct in performing his undertaking, or his failure to exercise reasonable care to complete it, or to protect the third person when he discontinues it.

Table 4.1: Sections of the Restatement of Torts 2d Relevant to Liability of Certifiers

Approval of a product against a safety standard is a representation that the approved product is safe. When the product is found to be unsafe in practice and causes injury there may be negligence involved. Thus, there may be a cause of action of the kind set forth in section 311 of the Restatement. Since consumers or users are "third persons" having no relation to the actor (such as an inspection or testing laboratory) and section 324A deals specifically with liability to such third persons, section 324A provides a cause of action to consumers or users, provided the plaintiff can carry the burden of proof of negligence in the approval process. **4–35**

Two United States cases in particular were perceived, at the time, as breaking new ground in the establishment of potential tort liability of product approvers as against third parties. The first case was *Hempstead v. General Fire Extinguisher Corp. and Underwriters' Laboratories, Inc.,*[6] the second was *Hanberry v. Hearst.*[7]

In *Hempstead,* the plaintiff was seriously injured when an Underwriters-listed fire extinguisher exploded while in use. Underwriters neither manufactured nor sold the extinguisher. No privity of contract or any other legal relationship existed between Underwriters, the plaintiff, the plaintiff's employer, or the plaintiff's co-worker who was handling the extinguisher at the time it exploded. The plaintiff alleged that Underwriters was negligent in approving the design of the extinguisher and in allowing the manufacturer to affix Underwriters' label to the extinguisher. The court rejected Underwriters' assertion that it does not approve the "design" of products that it tests.[8] Holding that the fire extinguisher was "imminently dangerous" and therefore excepted from the privity doctrine, the court found Underwriters was negligent in approving the design of the fire extinguisher and liable to the plaintiff for injury.

---

[6] 269 F.Supp. 109 (D.Del. 1967).

[7] 81 Cal. Rptr. 519, Cal.Ct. App. (1969), 39 ALR3d 173.

[8] *ibid.* at p. 175. Underwriters' Laboratories (UL), established in 1894, is a non-profit Nationally Recognised Testing Laboratory, which lists in publications the products it approves and on which its certification marks may be used. Continued use of UL's certification marks is contingent upon satisfactory periodic inspections, by UL's representatives, of production at the manufacturer's premises.

Product Endorsers: Negligent Misrepresentation

4–36 As a matter of public policy, liability for negligent misrepresentation might exist where a purchaser relies on an endorsement seal and is injured because the product is defective and not as represented in the endorsement. The very purpose of such a seal of endorsement is to induce and encourage members of the public to buy the product. Therefore, as the court in *Hanberry v. Hearst* pointed out, endorsement cannot be denied to be the inducing factor in bringing about their sale. While wearing new shoes that were awarded the "Good Housekeeping Consumer's Guarantee" seal, the plaintiff-appellant slipped on a vinyl surface and was badly injured. The coefficient of friction between the material of the shoes and vinyl was dangerously low.

The Good Housekeeping magazine represented that "We satisfy ourselves that products advertised in Good Housekeeping are good ones and the advertising claims made for them in our magazine are truthful." The plaintiff had purchased the shoes believing them to have been "examined, tested and inspected" by the defendant and were good and safe for the use intended. The court concluded that liability may exist and that a cause of action for negligent misrepresentation had been pleaded. However, permission to proceed in warranty or in strict liability in tort[9] was denied. No authority was known for extending either theory to one not directly involved in manufacturing products for, or supplying products to, the consuming public. Furthermore, no representation had been made that the endorser had examined or tested each item marketed.

Trade Associations

4–37 Trade associations[10] that help their members with product design, development, standards, packaging, handling, furnishing educational material and public relations, may be liable in negligence for defective design of a product.[11] A trade association that comprises a large proportion of the traders in the goods may be assumed to speak with authority and be qualified to function as a certifier. Thus trade associations are often owners of one or more certification marks, which are used to indicate that certain attributes of a good or service, produced or sold by their members, are certified.

Through advertising and publicity, consumers are educated to the significance of an association's representations of adherence of its members' products to certain standards of safety or quality. Alternatively, such associations own collective marks used by their members to signify membership of the association and that by implication, their products meet the standards set for such membership. Authorised use of an association's certification mark or collective mark thus provides assurance to purchasers or potential purchasers that certain conditions or standards have been met in the product made and sold by the members.

4–38 In the United States, a consumer who understands and relies on the assurance conveyed by a trade association's mark and is injured because the product proves defective may have a cause of action under a theory of negligent misrepresentation as

---

[9] For the provision of special (strict) liability of a seller of a product for physical harm to user or consumer, see s.402A of the Restatement of Torts 2d.

[10] See generally, Sara, D. Schotland and Katherine L. Rhyne, "Product Liability Implications of Trade Association Activities", 7 Journal of Products Liability 215 (1984); and Theodore Voorhees, Jr., "Product Liability Faced by Trade Associations That Lobby the Government on Health and Safety Issues", 15 Journal of Products & Toxics Liability 55 (1993).

[11] *King v. National Spa & Pool Institute, Inc.*, 570 So.2d 612 (Ala1990)—the defendant promulgated safety standards for swimming pools. *FNS Mortgage Serv. Corp. v. Pacific General Group, Inc.*, 29 Cal.Rptr.2d 916 (Ct App1994)—responsibility assumed for approving plumbing products.

provided for in the Restatement of Torts 2d, s.311. However, an industry or trade association that does not itself make or sell products is not strictly liable for harm caused by an allegedly defective product if the member manufacturers do not delegate product safety and design functions to the association.[12] Nor may a trade association be held strictly liable or liable for breach of warranty or negligence for a member manufacturer's defective product, where the association has not been delegated functions such as formulating safety measures and does not mandate or monitor use of standards by members.[13]

Claims have been brought against United States trade associations in products liability cases spanning automobile and automobile parts accidents, swimming pool injuries, tobacco and alcohol litigation, toxic torts, asbestos-related illnesses, blood transfusions and medical treatment and other areas.[14] In these cases, the associations have faced allegations of conspiracy, concert of action, negligent giving of false information, failure to warn and instruct the public, attempts to misinform the public and other forms of tortious misconduct.[15]

Where voluntary standards are involved in products liability litigation, it is rare for claims to be directed at the standard developer, seeking damages for injuries alleged to be due to implementation of an unsafe or improperly drawn standard. The American National Standards Institute ascribes this rarity to "the basic integrity of the voluntary standards that result from a development process designed to achieve a consensus of materially interested parties.[16] However, where a trade or industry association formulates safety standards that members are required to meet, a cause of action for negligence may be recognised if a standard in fact fails to assure a safe product. A notable case is *King v. National Spa and Pool Institute*,[17] in which the intestate of the plaintiff sustained injuries, from which he later died, in a dive into a swimming pool manufactured by a member of the defendant trade association. Even though the pool met the association's minimum standards for allowing the type of diving board that had been installed, the pool was dangerous for diving from the board. The plaintiff's theory of liability against the trade association was that the standards that allowed placement of a diving board in a pool of the particular size created an unreasonable risk of harm.[18]

The Alabama Supreme Court, invoking section 324A of the Restatement 2d, reversed the lower court's decision in favour of the defendant. Although the deceased had not known of the trade association's standards and so clearly did not rely on them, the manufacturer had relied on the standards in constructing or installing the pool. Thus the association could be liable under the principles of section 324A (b) or (c), which stated the law of Alabama.

---

[12] *Swartzbauer v. Lead Indus. Assoc., Inc.*, 794 F. Supp. 142, (EDPa1992).

[13] *Beasock v. Dioguardi Enterprises, Inc.* 494 N.Y.S.2d 974, (Sup1985).

[14] For references to many such cases see, J.L. MacDonell and A. Burguieres, "Guilt by Association: Product Liability for Non-Manufacturers", Proceedings of the Product Liability Megaconference II, October 22–23, 1998.

[15] *ibid.*

[16] J.Q. Smith, J.P. Bolger and A. Marasco, Products Liability Claims Against Voluntary Standards Developers—An Update on Recent Developments, American National Standards Institute website www.web.ansi.org/public/library/guides/prod—liability.html.

[17] See n. 11 (2nd ser.), above.

[18] *ibid.*, at 613.

Ordinary Trade Mark Licensors

4–39 It is established law in the United Kingdom, United States and other jurisdictions that for the licensor of a trade mark to retain his rights in the mark and the use to inure to his benefit he must exercise quality control of the licensee's output.[19] Quality control, by definition, requires some licensor involvement in the licensee's production activities. What then is the minimum measure of such involvement for a licensor to incur liability for a dangerously defective product sold by the licensee under the licensor's mark?

Quality control in the licensing context is designed to assures a level of quality consistent with purchasers' expectations and previous purchasing experience. Through its trade mark, the licensor maintains a single source for uniform quality of the goods by controlling the quality to requirements put on the licensee. Failure to comply with the licensor's quality control requirements properly incurs suspension of the license pending remedial action on the part of the licensee.

In Table 4.1, (paragraph 4–34, above), three modes of negligent conduct that could conceivably be ascribed to third-party product approvers are set forth. However, these modes may also be considered applicable to the ordinary trade mark licensor as well; the licensor is an approver of the product, if not an independent third-party approver. His trade mark on the product is accepted by purchasers as an assurance of consistent product quality in accordance with their expectations.

The United States Apparent Manufacturer Doctrine

4–40 The apparent manufacturer doctrine is a feature of United States product liability litigation and in some states has been invoked since the early part of the twentieth century. Under the doctrine, a supplier unambiguously holding out the manufacturer's product as his own is held to the manufacturer's standard of care.[20] Section 400 of the Restatement (Second) of Torts, known as the apparent manufacturer doctrine, provides:

> One who puts out as his own product a chattel manufactured by another is subject to the same liability as though he were its manufacturer.

The same rule has been adopted under section 14 of the Restatement (Third) of Torts: Products Liability.[21] If a commercial seller sells a product manufactured by someone else under the seller's own trademark or logo, the seller is liable as though it were the manufacturer. This rule applies even if the seller discloses that the product was produced by an identified manufacturer specifically for the seller. This appears to represent a stronger position in favor of the consumer than in the United Kingdom

---

[19] Early in the twentieth century, quality control began to overcome judicial anathema to trade mark licensing. The anathema was founded on the belief that licensing would result in loss of identity of the trade marked goods with their "source", which would negate the accepted primary function of a trade mark. However, through the link imposed by quality control, a licensee's use of the mark could be imputed to the licensor, thereby preserving connectivity between the trade mark proprietor and the licensee's trade marked goods. In effect the mark could be construed as continuing to function as an indicator of source. See N.J. Wilkof, *Trade Mark Licensing* (Sweet & Maxwell, London, 1995), Chap. 12.

[20] For an early review of the apparent (or "ostensible") manufacturer doctrine and references to early cases see, "Recent Important Tort Cases", 28 *NACCA Law Journal*, 217–222 (1962).

[21] Section 14 of the Restatement (Third) of Torts: Products Liability, (St. Paul: American Law Institute 1998), states: "One engaged in the business of selling or otherwise distributing products who sells or distributes as its own a product manufactured by another is subject to the same liability as though the seller or distributor were the product manufacturer".

where an "own brander" can normally escape liability if he identifies the manufacturer on the product.[22] The rationale for the rule is that the seller's reputation is an implied assurance of the quality of the product and the seller should be estopped from denying that it stands behind that assurance.

The section 14 rule of the Restatement does not, by its terms, apply to a trade mark owner who licenses a manufacturer to place the trade mark on the manufacturer's product and distribute the product as though it were manufactured by the trade mark owner. Even though purchasers of the product might assume that the trade mark owner was the manufacturer, the trade mark owner does not sell or distribute the product. Trade mark owners are liable for harm caused by defective products distributed under the trade mark or logo when they participate substantially in the design, manufacture, or distribution of the products. In these circumstances they are treated as sellers of the products bearing their trade marks.

In the 1993 case of *Andujar v. Sears, Robuck & Co.*,[23] which involved a claim for injuries sustained while using a table saw, the New York Supreme Court affirmed judgment for the plaintiff because the seller had held itself out as the saw's manufacturer. The seller was held to the same duty as any other product manufacturer. In another case tried under New York law, the defendant true manufacturer (Atex) used defendant—appellee Kodak's logo on promotional material but not on the product. There was no suggestion that Kodak was the manufacturer in the promotional material and the plaintiff's apparent manufacturer theory, directed at Kodak, failed.[24] 4–41

In a 1994 Georgia case, where a ladder purchaser was injured when the ladder's bottom step collapsed, the trial court denied the defendant ladder wholesaler's motion for summary judgment. The Georgia Court of Appeals reversed, holding that the defendant was not liable as the manufacturer, because an entity that merely affixes its label to a product and sells it under its name is a product seller rather than a manufacturer under the Georgia Tort Reform Act. The court stated that the legislature had intended to eliminate the categories of "ostensible" or "apparent" manufacturer.[25]

Certain states, notably California, have held that all entities that significantly participate in the overall enterprise that places a product into the "stream of commerce" are "sellers" and have been held strictly liable for injuries caused by the product under the rule of section 402A of the Restatement of Torts 2d.[26] Regardless of the name given to such theories, the touchstone for liability is consistently one of significant participation in

---

[22] See paras 4–18 to 4–19, above.

[23] 193 A.D.2d 415, 597 N.Y.S.2d 78 (1993).

[24] *Fletcher v. Atex, Inc.*, 668 F.3d 1451 (1995).

[25] *Alltrade, Inc. v. McDonald*, 213 G.App. 758, 445 S.E.2d 856, 858 (1994).

[26] The Restatement of Torts 2d, section 402A, provides as follows:

(1) One who sells any product in a defective condition unreasonably dangerous to the user or consumer or to his property is subject to liability for physical harm thereby caused to the ultimate user or consumer, or to his property, if
  (a) the seller is engaged in the business of selling such a product, and
  (b) it is expected to and does reach the user or consumer without substantial change in the condition in which it is sold.

(2) The rule stated in Subsection (1) applies although
  (a) the seller has exercised all possible care in the preparation and sale of his product, and
  (c) the user or consumer has not bought the product from or entered into any contractual relation with the seller.

bringing the product to the consumer.[27] Therefore, an entity that stipulates and exercises a right to control the incidents of manufacture by another risks being deemed a seller and subject to strict liability under section 402A.[28]

Factors contributing to courts' findings of liability include the licensor's retention and exercise of the right to control the quality of the licensee's output, its provision and monitoring of compliance with product specifications, its advertising of the product and financial gain from sales. Additional trade mark-related factors include consumers' reliance on the licensor's trade mark, which conveys the message that the proprietor vouches for the licensed product.

Summary and Conclusion

4–42 This chapter has addressed the potential for liability of those who certify products that subsequently cause injury or damage. The reach of product liability rules is such that the third-party certifier cannot consider itself beyond the scope of claims for injury or damage. A third-party certification body that undertakes to certify a product may find itself subject to a claim if the body certifies as safe, or as conforming to a recognised safety standard, what is in fact a dangerously defective product. It therefore behoves certifiers to appreciate the measure of their liability exposure should certification of a product be shown to have been unjustified, causing injury or damage.

Later parts of the chapter have dealt especially with perceptions of products liability that impact certification mark and ordinary trade mark proprietors in the United States, where much of the more recent development of the conceptual framework in this particular field has taken place. The potential for tort liability of certifiers was tested in the United States in two important cases during the late 1960s.[29] These cases attributed liability to certifiers of defective goods under theories of negligent misrepresentation and negligent performance of an undertaking. While they attracted considerable attention at the time, the decisions have not brought certifiers within close and enduring reach of consumers in products liability actions. The various law and policy paradigms that have been adopted for manufacturers' and sellers' product liability do not extend easily to certifiers.

What are the reasons for the relatively small number of product liability cases against certifiers *qua* certifiers? Some factors endemic to the certification function may provide pointers to the answer. For example, the scope of the certifier's guarantee tends to stop short of being one of total quality or integrity of a product as a whole. This is well illustrated by the responsibility ascribed to classification societies, which set standards for the quality and integrity of vessels and survey vessels to determine whether they comply with the societies' standards. Without a classification certificate a vessel is in

---

[27] See *Kasel v. Remington Arms*, 101 Cal. Rptr. 314, 323 (Cal. Ct. App. 1972), "It is the defendant's participatory connection, for his personal profit or other benefit, with the injury-producing product and with the enterprise that created consumer demand for and reliance upon the product (and not the defendant's legal relationship (such as agency) with the manufacturer) which calls for imposition of strict liability." See generally, David J. Franklyn, "Towards a Coherent Theory of Strict Tort Liability for Trademark Licensors", 72 Southern Calif. Law Rev. 1 (1998).

[28] However, the Restatement (Third) of Torts: Products Liability, which issued in 1998, has been regarded as repealing s.402A of the Restatement (Second). Since its adoption in 1964, the Second Restatement had dominated the law of products liability in the United States. While retaining strict products liability for manufacturing defects, the Restatement (Third) adopts what is in effect a negligence approach to defective design claims and a reasonableness test for judging the adequacy of product instructions and warnings.

[29] See nn. 6 and 7 (2nd ser.), above.

effect unable to operate; it cannot obtain insurance. Nevertheless, as Clark has pointed out, the classification society's task is not necessarily interpreted as assuring the safety of worldwide shipping. Furnishing a seaworthy safe vessel is, under maritime law, the duty of the shipowner.[30]

The classification society/shipowner scenario is reminiscent of the product certifier/ manufacturer scenario. The product certifier tests to determine for compliance with certain specific standards, no more and no less. No guarantee of complete safety or satisfactory quality of the product as a whole is provided; neither should it be read into the certification. Third party certification is sometimes a legal requirement but the duty to provide a safe quality product resides with the manufacturer. The combination of narrow specificity in the certifier's remit and the manufacturer's responsibility for overall safety and quality in a product yields a low likelihood of the certifier being found blameworthy under a product liability theory. Claims against certifiers tend to fail because, among other things, of the inability to show causation. Consequently, a claimant is more likely to succeed in a strict liability action against the manufacturer than in a negligence action against a product certifier. **4–43**

As a matter of public policy, certifiers appear to enjoy a measure of immunity against product liability actions. As often as not they are accorded a status more reminiscent of arbiters, providing authoritative decisions about the conformity of a product, than links in the chain of supply. Potential product liability claims may not pose a daunting challenge to the stability and relative independence of certifiers in the delineation and regulation of their activities. However, the same cannot be said of liability attaching to their collateral activities within trade associations, professional institutions, membership corporations or other self-regulating undertakings. Trade associations are vulnerable to allegations of anticompetitive practices relating to a variety of association activities. Among such activities, the United Kingdom's Office of Fair Trading includes collective price agreements, certain cases of information exchange that could lead to price co-ordination, restrictions on advertising, joint buying and selling, and standard-setting that creates barriers to entry. Therefore, such undertakings must be especially diligent in the conduct of their affairs to avoid the antitrust "radar screens" of government agencies such as the Federal Trade Commission in the United States and the Office of Fair Trading in the United Kingdom. These issues are included in the subject matter of Chapter 6.[31]

---

[30] Peter D. Clark, *An American Admiralty Law Viewpoint on the Changing Role of Classification Societies*, www.navlaw.com/navlaw/menus/sealaw/class.htm.. See also the comments of Lord Lloyd (dissenting) in *Marc Rich & Co. v. Bishop Rock Marine* [1995] 3 All E.R. 307 at 318.

[31] See especially paras 6–36 to 6–39, below. See also the Office of Fair Trading guideline, *Trade Associations, Professions and Self-Regulating Bodies* (HMSO, London, 2000).

5

THE LEGAL AND COMMERCIAL SIGNIFICANCE OF CERTIFICATION MARKS

Introduction

This chapter examines the legal and commercial significance of certification marks in United Kingdom law. In Part 1 the legal status of the "guarantee" function of a certification mark is addressed first in light of consumer guarantees under the Unfair Contract Terms Act 1977 (UCTA 1977).[1] Then the possibility is considered of implication of a certification mark's guarantee in a breach of the implied terms of the Sale of Goods Act 1979 as amended by the Sale and Supply of Goods Act 1994 (together "SoGA"). The scope for such implication would appear to depend on the interpretation of the terms "description" and "quality" in the sale of goods setting, as well as the commercial circumstances of the particular transaction. **5–01**

Part 2 identifies features of United Kingdom trade mark and trade descriptions legislation, and related policies, that support purchasers' trust in certification- and certification-like marks. Suggestions are offered as to how such trust may be enhanced. At present, the TMA 1994 vindicates purchaser trust through, among other things, prohibitions on registration of misleading certification marks, provisions for infringement proceedings, and criminal sanctions against false trade marking and unauthorised use of a certification mark. The TMA 1994 in effect accords purchasers indirect protection only. The proprietor of the mark, in exercising his right to sue for trade mark infringement, may be protecting purchasers against deception, but such protection is largely outside the purchaser's sphere of influence.

Additional legal provisions that tacitly foster purchaser trust in certification marks are those of the Trade Descriptions Act 1968 (TDA 1968), which, *inter alia*, prohibits the application of a false trade description to any goods, which includes a false indication of compliance with a specified standard, such as might be used for certification.[2]

It is submitted that there is a case for a more directly consumer-oriented model of a certification mark. Such a model might emerge under the stimulation of relatively recent

---

[1] Certifers' liability in the context of product liability for defective goods that cause physical injury or property damage is the subject of Chap. 4, above.

[2] See paras 5–17 to 5–18, below. The TDA 1968 succeeded the Merchandise Marks Act, which had been in force from 1887.

E.U. regulations protecting geographical indications, and published United Kingdom government proposals requiring more informative product marking and greater accountability of certification service providers. Finally, the United Kingdom Competition Act 1998 and related government policy can be expected to affect certifying trade bodies' codes of practice in ways that could enhance consumer confidence in certification marks, as will the new provisions for certification of on-line and off-line commercial undertakings.

1 THE GUARANTEE IN A CERTIFICATION MARK

The "Guarantee" Function of Certification Marks

5–02 The meaning of the words "guarantee" or "warranty" as applied to certification marks must influence the view that traders and the public take of such marks. These words are often-used, nowadays interchangeably, in commerce generally. It is therefore in the interests of both buyers and sellers that there be a common understanding of the significance of the so-called guarantee function of a certification mark on goods or services.

The term guarantee is sometimes used in connection with legislation relating to trade marks, normally in the sense of safeguarding the individual source- or origin-identification function of a mark. Thus the TMA 1994 implements *inter alia* the E.U. Trade Mark Directive,[3] which states that the function of the registered trade mark is "in particular to guarantee the trade mark as an indication of origin". Furthermore, the E.U. regulation providing for use of a special logo for Protected Designations of Origin and Protected Geographical Indications on food products describes the logo as " [A] genuine guarantee for all European consumers, making it clear that the special nature of this product lies in its geographical origin. [4]

TMA 1994 offers no direct textual support for guarantee language in connection with certification marks. The Act recognises a "control and warranty" function for official signs and hallmarks,[5] but it does not accord a guarantee or warranty function to certification marks. However, the 1986 white paper which heralded the replacement of the Trade Marks Act 1938 by the TMA 1994, stated that examination of an applicant's regulations, submitted as part of his application for registration of a certification mark, was "to see that the mark does guarantee genuine qualities or characteristics."[6]

---

[3] Dir. 89/104 of December 21, 1988 to approximate the laws of the Member States relating to trade marks.

[4] Commission Reg. 1726/98 of July 22, 1998 amending Council Reg. 2037/93 laying down detailed rules for the application of Council Reg. 2081/92 on the protection of geographical indications and designations of origin for agricultural products and foodstuffs [1998] O.J. L224/1. Note that although PDOs and PGIs attest to product conformity to certain standards, they are not certification marks as such and do not constitute a registered property right as does a certification mark. In fact there is considerable tension between the certification mark paradigm and the E.U.'s protected geographical indication scheme. See para. 5–19 below, especially n. 92.

[5] TMA 1994, s.57(3) provides: A trade mark which consists of or contains an official sign or hallmark adopted by a Convention country and indicating control and warranty shall not, where the sign or hallmark is protected under the Paris Convention or the WTO agreement, be registered in relation to goods or services of the same, or a similar kind, as those in relation to which it indicates control and warranty, without the authorisation of the competent authorities of the country concerned.

[6] *Intellectual Property and Innovation*, Cm. 9712 (1986), at para. 5.01.

One finds a consensus in commentaries on the United Kingdom and other certification mark systems that guarantee usage is appropriate to certification marks. Thus Ladas observes that a certification mark "has principally a guarantee function. It certifies regional origin or material, mode of manufacture, quality or other characteristic of the goods. The guarantee is generally emphasized and the buyer relies on this."[7] Callman attributes a guarantee function to a certification mark, stating that "the guarantee function of a certification mark is much more evident than it is with respect to an ordinary trademark, service mark, or collective mark" and "a certification mark guarantees a specific standard of quality, place of origin, material, or mode of manufacture."[8] Rozas and Johnston invert this last proposition, saying that a mark that "guarantees the functional quality and safety of a product regarding the components of the product is certifying that the product has the standard level established by the rules of the certification."[9] **5–03**

Dawson asserts that "trade mark law permits an entire industry to protect itself by the registration of a *Certification Trade Mark* to act as a warranty that goods bearing the mark meet a certain standard or possess a particular characteristic."[original emphasis].[10] This last remark is important in the present context because it captures the mainstream United Kingdom perception that certification marks—like trade marks—exist primarily to protect traders or groups of traders from each other and have only an indirect bearing on consumer protection.[11]

Is a Certification Mark a Legally-Binding Guarantee?

Does a certification mark constitute a legally binding guarantee or other commitment to purchasers, on the part of the certifier, in respect of the certified characteristics? Such a commitment is tantamount to prescribing that, regardless of whether or not there be mutual assent, the certifier must stand surety to any and all remote purchasers.[12] The certifier would then have responsibility for reimbursement of the price paid or replacement, repair or other handling of the goods if they are found wanting with regard to the standard for certification. The position taken in the present work is that such a prescription would be unreasonable and unjust if only because a certification mark does not usually signify that each and every item manufactured has been inspected by the certifier (or his agents).[13] Unless the certifier contracts freely to stand surety and there is a contractually agreed examination of the goods, it does not seem equitable to make the certifier's position that of a legally bound guarantor. Furthermore imposing a legally binding guarantor function on the certifier would be a major disincentive to operators of certification mark schemes with little gain in economic utility. **5–04**

---

[7] Stephen P. Ladas, *Patents, Trademarks and Related Rights* (Harvard: Cambridge University Press, 1975), Vol. II, pp. 1290 *et seq.*

[8] Louis Altman, *Callman on Unfair Competition, Trademarks and Monopolies*(4th ed., St Paul: West Group, 1998), Vol. 3, § 17.18, p. 76.

[9] R. Rozas and H. Johnston, "Impact of Certification Marks on Innovation and the Global Market-Place" [1997] E.I.P.R. 598.

[10] N. Dawson, *Certification Trade Marks Law and Practice* (Intellectual Property Publishing, Ltd., London, 1988), p. 11.

[11] *ibid.*, at p. 100.

[12] By "remote purchaser" is meant one not contractually bound to the certifier.

[13] For this and other reasons, including economic efficiency, it is generally accepted as sensible policy that those certification mark proprietors or their agents who only examine or test samples of a product placed on the market should not face strict liability or liability in warranty for defective goods that cause harm. See Chap. 4, especially paras 4–12 to 4–14, above.

Guarantee of Consumer Goods

5–05 Though it may not be equitable, as a general proposition, to compel the certifier to be a legally bound guarantor there appear to be situations in which the certifier could be held liable to a non-contracting party. In particular, under the UCTA 1977 , a certifier could be liable if his mark is present on goods in consumer use that are defective and the mark comprises guarantee language. The UCTA 1977 treats goods as "in consumer use" when a person is using them, or has them in his possession for use, otherwise than exclusively for the purpose of a business.[14] Therefore, if goods in consumer use carry a written certifier's guarantee and they cause loss or damage (not limited to death or injury) the certifier, if shown to have negligently certified the product, faces liability under the UCTA 1977.[15] Anything in writing is treated as a guarantee under the UCTA 1977 if it:

> contains or purports to contain some promise or assurance (however worded or presented) that defects will be made good by complete or partial replacement, or by repair, monetary compensation or otherwise.[16]

"Writing" includes typing, printing, lithography, photography and other modes of representing or reproducing words in a visible form, and expressions referring to writing are construed accordingly.[17]

The UCTA 1977's provisions against a negligent person concerned in the manufacture or distribution of the goods do not apply as between the parties to a contract under or in pursuance of which possession or ownership of the goods has passed.[18] Thus UCTA reaches beyond the contractual relationship involving the buyer and implicates any negligent person or persons concerned in the manufacture or distribution of the goods, where such goods are defective and thereby cause loss or damage. If, as a matter of policy, the certifier were to be considered a party concerned in the manufacture or distribution of the goods,[19] a written expression of assurance or guarantee incorporated in a mark on goods that are found to be defective due to the certifier's negligence could result in liability of the certifier. The problem here is that it is notoriously difficult for a buyer to prove that a certifier was negligent. The difficulty lies in the burden that the plaintiff must carry of establishing a causal link between the certifier's act and the damage. Even if a chain of causation may have existed, it may have been broken by the intervention of the manufacturer or another party. The chain of causation is broken if an independent cause of damage, unrelated to the certifier's act, intervenes between his act and the damage.[20]

Certification Mark Implicated in Breach of Contractual Term

5–06 Now consider the contractual obligations of the seller towards the buyer of certification-marked goods. What is the status of the certification mark in relation to the obligations of the seller as reflected in the implied terms of the contract? More particularly, can the

---

[14] UCTA 1977, s.5(2)(a).
[15] UCTA 1977, s.5(1)(b).
[16] UCTA 1977, s.5(2)(b).
[17] Interpretation Act 1978, Sched. 1.
[18] UCTA 1977, s.5(3).
[19] As to product liability in United States law of entities that control the incidents of manufacture by another and so risk being deemed sellers under "apparent manufacturer" theories see Chap. 4, paras 4–39 to 4–41, above.
[20] See Chap. 4, para. 4–09, above.

implied terms be breached by the failure of the product to conform to what is claimed through the certification mark?

First, it is noted that in English law an implied term may be either a condition or a warranty. Whereas breach of a condition gives rise to a right to treat the contract as repudiated, breach of a warranty gives rise to a claim for damages but not to a right to reject the goods and treat the contract as repudiated.[21] Applicable to all transactions for the transfer of goods, whether by sale, hire-purchase, hire, barter, part-exchange or otherwise, section 12 to 14 of the Sale of Goods Act 1979 as amended by the Sale and Supply of Goods Act 1994 lay down implied terms.[22] The implied terms concern, among other things, correspondence of the goods with description[23] and satisfactory quality.[24] Furthermore, there is an implied term (classified as a condition) that the goods supplied under the contract are reasonably fit for any particular purpose made known to the seller, except where the buyer does not rely, or it is unreasonable for him to rely, on the skill and judgment of the seller.[25]

The significance of a certification mark in relation to the implied terms of the contract must depend fundamentally on the details and context of the transaction. Whether or not the buyer requires a certified product, relies on the certification in selecting the product, relies on the seller's judgment or recommendation to select a certification-marked product, was able to inspect the goods for defects, and so on, are key factors in a proceeding for breach of contract.

It is reasonable to expect the certification mark to vouch for characteristics that go to either the description of the goods and/or their quality. Therefore, to proceed in the present inquiry it is necessary next to consider the meanings of "description" and "quality" and their certification in the sale of goods setting.

Contractual Certification Can Impact Both Description and Quality

In the sale of goods setting certification of goods is normally regarded as relevant to quality only and not description, but it can also cover matters of quality which affect the description.[26] There is not always a clear distinction between quality and description. A characterisation of the quality may[27] or may not[28] form part of the description of the **5–07**

[21] Scots law does not make use of a distinction between a condition and a warranty. Law Commission Report, *Sale and Supply of Goods*, (Law Co. No.160, Scot Law Com. 104, 1987), para. 2.23 and para. 2.26(b).

[22] Implied terms may be read into contracts either because they are provided for under rules pertaining to a particular class of contract, such as for the sale of goods, or because they emerge necessarily out of the interpretation of the express terms of a particular contract. Such interpretation will depend on the subject matter and purpose of the agreement, as well as the circumstances in which the contract is made. See J. Salmond and J. Williams, *Principles of the Law of Contracts*, (Sweet & Maxwell, London, 1945), pp. 38–42. The implied terms of SoGA are an example of "default rules" in contract law. Defaults are terms which will be implied into contracts unless the parties positively exclude them. Economic efficiency considerations figure prominently in commentaries on justifications for implying default rules into private contracts. See C.A. Riley, "Designing Default Rules in Contract Law—Consent, Conventionalism, and Efficiency", 20 Oxford Journal of Legal Studies, 367 (2000).

[23] SoGA, s.13(1).

[24] See para. 5–10 below. For the purposes of SoGA, the quality of goods includes their state and condition and (where appropriate) certain aspects of quality, namely fitness for all the purposes for which goods of the kind in question are commonly supplied, appearance and finish, freedom from minor defects, safety and durability. SoGA, s.14(2)(b).

[25] SoGA, s.14(3).

[26] *Benjamin's Sale of Goods*, A. G. Guest, Gen. Ed. (5th ed., Sweet & Maxwell, London, 1997), §13–037.

[27] *Toepfer v. Continental Grain Co.* [1974] 1 Lloyd's Rep. 11, CA.

[28] *Ashington Piggeries Ltd. v. Christopher Hill, Ltd.* [1972] A.C. 441 at 470, 475.

goods. A defect in the composition or ingredients of the goods may be regarded as impacting the description, though the quality may meet the statutory standard of satisfactory quality. Alternatively, the quality may be so poor as to result in non-compliance with the contracted-for description. In *Gill & Duffus, S.A. v. Berger & Co., Inc.*,[29] Diplock, L.J., referring to *Toepfer v. Continental Grain Co.*,[30] which involved a sale by description,[31] stated that:

> One must look to the contract as a whole to identify the kind of goods that the seller was agreeing to sell and the buyer to buy. In *Toepfer's* case, it was not "No. 3 hard amber durum wheat" simpliciter but durum wheat of U.S. origin for which a certificate had been issued by a U.S. Government official stating that its quality was that which is described in the trade as "No. 3 hard amber."

Thus the description of the goods contracted for contained a quality requirement, a statement as to their quality, and provided that a certificate as to quality was to be final, the certificate was final as to the correspondence of the goods with that part of the description of them in the contract that referred to their quality (in this case "No. 3 hard amber") notwithstanding that the certificate was proved to have been inaccurate. Though this case concerned a sale by description in which the contract provided for delivery of quality-certified future goods, not only contracts for future or unascertained goods are sales by description. Sales of specific goods selected by the buyer and purchased over the counter, or in a self-service store (*i.e.* at the time of the contract) can meet the test for a sale by description if the seller's description is essential for identification of the goods.

Contractual Meaning of "Description"

5–08 A buyer who is able to show non-conformity of the goods with a contracted-for description, as expressed in a certification statement or the text of a certification mark, might prevail in an action against the seller for breach of contract.[32] The test for a contractually binding descriptive statement is whether the statement is essential to characterise the goods. The modern authority for this test, one which has been followed with approval by the House of Lords,[33] is *Couchman v. Hill*,[34] in which the court held that as a matter of law every item in a description which constitutes a substantial ingredient in the "identity" of the thing sold is a condition, although every such condition can be waived by the purchaser, who thereupon becomes entitled to treat it as a warranty and recover damages.[35]

A Certification Mark May Comprise Little or No Description

5–09 A purchaser who needs, at the time and point of sale, a description of the characteristics certified and the standard used for certification, may be left wondering. The statutorily defined purpose of a certification mark is to indicate that one or more characteristics of

---

[29] [1984] 1 A.C. 382 at 394.

[30] See n. 27, above.

[31] Where a seller provides a description of the goods, as a term of the contract, impliedly or expressly, in order to identify or define the goods, the sale is a sale by description.

[32] However, if the decision of the certifier is agreed by the parties as final, this may not be the case, even if the certifier is mistaken. See *Toepfer v. Continental Grain Co.*, n. 27, above.

[33] *Reardon Smith Line Ltd. v. Yngvar Hansen-Tangen*, [1976] 1 W.L.R. 989 at 998.

[34] [1947] K.B. 554 at 559.

[35] SoGA, s.11(3).

the goods are certified.[36] The fact of certification is normally apparent to the purchaser since it is usual for the Registrar to require that a certification mark include some indication that it is a certification trade mark.[37] If the applicant objects to putting the words into the mark, it is acceptable for the regulations to establish that the nature of the mark will always be made clear in advertising and on the goods. However, in some cases, the words appear in inconveniently small font.

Even if he is aware that the product is certified, the purchaser may not be able to identify the characteristics that are certified unless there is an informative statement on the goods, either apart from or within the words of the certification mark, or he happens to deal with a knowledgable and co-operative seller. It is noteworthy that, in principle, such positive attributes in a retailer may themselves be recognised as certifiable by certification mark in the United Kingdom. The Registry now recognises ordinary, collective and certification trade mark applications for aspects of a "retail service", as has been the case for some time in some other E.U. Member States.[38]

One could perhaps use the term "opaque" to characterise a certification mark that does not use words to identify basic features of the goods, their certified characteristic and the relevant standard. It is submitted that if consumer confidence in the certification of goods is to be encouraged, then increased transparency of certification marks, through addition of descriptive words, should be encouraged. Of course, product information may be obtained from inquiries to the manufacturer or vendor, together with the identity of the certifier, certified characteristics and standards. Such information may also be accessed from advertisements, the internet website of the certifier or manufacturer, and the like. This is frequently done before sophisticated technical products are purchased in the course of a business. Furthermore, a full description of the certified characteristics and the standard may be obtained from inspection of the certifier's regulations, which are open to public inspection in the same way as the register in the United Kingdom Trade Marks Registry.[39] However, such means are not necessarily appropriate or convenient for purchases of consumer products.

Contractual Meaning of Quality

The Sale and Supply of Goods Act 1994, introduced into the SoGA a satisfactory quality standard,[40] pinned to a reasonable person test. Thus: **5–10**

> [F]or the purposes of the Act, goods are of satisfactory quality if they meet the standard that a reasonable person would regard as satisfactory, taking account of any description of the goods, the price (if relevant) and all the other relevant circumstances.[41]

---

[36] TMA 1994, s.50.

[37] Pursuant to TMA 1994, Sched. 2, para. 5(2).

[38] See Practice Amendment Circular PAC 13/00, first published in Journal 6350, October 18, 2000. The Circular is reproduced in Appendix C, below. Retail services, are described in an explanatory note regarding Class 35 in the 7th edition of the International Classification of Goods and Services (Nice Classification) as "[T]he bringing together, for the benefit of others, of a variety of goods (excluding the transport thereof), enabling customers to conveniently view and purchase those goods."

[39] TMA 1994, Sched. 2, para. 10.

[40] Prior to enactment of the Sale and Supply of Goods Act 1994, which amended the Sale of Goods Act 1979, the standard for quality was *merchantable* quality, as it had been since enactment of the Sale of Goods Act 1893. The Law Commission regarded the term merchantable as a term that "refers to transactions between merchants and is not suitable for consumer transactions, even in its dictionary meaning." Law Commission Report, *Sale and Supply of Goods*, (Law Co. No.160, Scot Law Com. 104, 1987), para. 3.5(i).

[41] SoGA, s.14(2A).

However, tests of this type can be only of limited practical value in deciding if the implied condition of satisfactory quality is breached or not.[42] The contractual definition of satisfactory quality in the SoGA is not free of circularity or vagueness. As Atiyah has remarked, all such vague statements or definitions of the standard of quality required by the law are somewhat vacuous in practice. They appear to provide flexibility but they rest on circular logic, thereby providing fertile ground for the introduction of unsatisfactory criteria such as "reasonableness" and so are of little practical value in deciding if the implied condition of satisfactory quality is breached or not.[43]

Trade Marks: Meaning of Quality

5–11 Both certification and ordinary trade marks are bound up with quality perceptions, but in different ways. Where quality is concerned, a certification mark has a statutorily defined function—to indicate certification of goods to approved quality standards. A certification mark is protected without any of the judicial misgivings associated with upholding ordinary trade marks as quality "guarantees", with regard to which Isaac[44] explains:

> One of the functions of a trade mark is said to be that of guaranteeing the quality of the goods to the consumer. Although this guarantee is not legally binding it is in the trade mark owner's interest to maintain the quality of the goods to which the mark is applied, if not to improve them . . . Trade marks, unlike hallmarks, are not guarantees of quality in the strict sense although if a trade mark owner uses his mark in such a way that it becomes liable to mislead the public it is possible for a third party to apply to have the registration revoked.[45]

An ordinary trade mark may convey a message of consistent quality[46] to purchasers but the notion is still troublesome to the United Kingdom judiciary when tendered as justification for protecting an ordinary trade mark. The accepted, traditionally protected, notion of an ordinary trade mark is reflected in the statute, which requires that it must be "capable of distinguishing goods or services of one undertaking from those of other undertakings."[47]

However, an infringing trade mark on goods has been held to violate the contractual requirement for merchantable (now satisfactory) quality. Thus, in *Niblett, Limited v. Confectioners' Materials Company, Limited*,[48] two judges (Bankes and Atkin, L.J.) out of three, considered that the implied condition as to merchantable quality[49] had been

[42] Equally problematic is the "reasonableness" test as laid down under the UCTA 1977, s.11(1) of which states: "In relation to a contract term, the requirement of reasonableness for the purposes of this Part of this Act, section 3 of the Misrepresentation Act 1967 and section 3 of the Misrepresentation Act (Northern Ireland) 1967 is that the term shall have been a fair and reasonable one to be included having regard to the circumstances which were, or ought reasonably to have been, known to or in the contemplation of the parties when the contract was made." Factors influencing a decision as to whether a standard limitation clause is a fair and reasonable term include the strength of the parties' bargaining positions, the customer's knowledge of the clause and the reality of the customer's consent to that clause. See *Halsbury's Statutes*, (Butterworth, London, 2000), Vol. 11, *Contract*, p. 237. See also UCTA 1977, Sched. 2, "Guidelines for Application of Reasonableness Test".

[43] P.S. Atiyah, *The Sale of Goods* (8th ed., Pitman Publishing, London, 1990), p. 154.

[44] Belinda Isaac, *Brand Protection Matters* (Sweet & Maxwell, London, 2000), paras 2–107 and 2–108.

[45] TMA 1994, s.46.

[46] The pioneering proponent of this concept is widely held to be F.I. Schechter, who, in his article, "The Rational Basis of Trademark Protection", 40 Harv. L. Rev. 813 at 818 (1927), took it as axiomatic that the "true function" of a trade mark is the identification of a product as satisfactory.

[47] TMA 1994, s.1(1).

[48] *Niblett, Limited v. Confectioners' Materials Company, Limited* [1921] 3 K.B. 387.

[49] It was stated for the plaintiff-appellants that "[N]o reasonable man would in the circumstances of this case accept these goods in performance of an offer by him to buy sweetened condensed milk. That is the test of merchantable quality."

breached by the sale of goods (condensed milk) bearing the mark NISSLY BRAND, which infringed an ordinary trade mark (NESTLÉ).[50] The buyers were obliged to remove the infringing mark from the goods, before gaining possession from the Commissioners of Customs and Excise. Atkin L.J. considered that the goods were thus in such a state or condition that "no reasonable man would in the circumstances accept them in performance of an offer to buy." Despite this unusual case, the uncompromising recognition of the quality message in an ordinary trade mark as grounds for protection, a proposition that was beginning to be articulated widely in the United States at the time of *Niblett*, is still controversial in the United Kingdom.

In summary, it appears that the contract law notion of quality is not perhaps fully satisfied by the meaning of quality under conventional trade mark law. The owner of an ordinary trade mark may be expected to maintain a consistent level of quality in his product, but he is not normally subject to sanctions or loss of rights in his mark if he changes the ingredients or the nature of the product.[51] Where quality-related attributes are concerned certification marks appear to attest to attainment of a particular and absolute level of quality, and as such seem to come closer than ordinary trade marks to providing a meaning of quality that is more attuned to the notion of quality in a contractual setting.

2 NON-GUARANTEE SOURCES OF TRUST

Though a certification mark may not represent a legally binding guarantee of the certifier it is manifestly conducive to trust on the part of the buyer. Upon seeing a certification mark and recognising it as such the buyer is disposed to trust the mark as an attestation of product conformity to an objective requirement concerning its geographical origin, material or mode of manufacture, or some other characteristic. Furthermore, the buyer reasonably expects that legal measures are in place to deter use of the mark to falsely indicate conformity when there is none. Part 2 of this chapter addresses legal provisions and policies that serve to vindicate this trust and support an expectation of veracity in the certification mark's message. **5–12**

Proprietor's Right of Action Against Infringers

It would be an overstatement, in the context of United Kingdom law, to say, as has one commentator on United States trade mark law, that "protection of trademarks is merely a facet of consumer protection."[52] Nevertheless, the proprietor of a United Kingdom-registered trade mark or certification mark, through his right to sue for infringement, is cast by trade mark law in the putative role of guardian of the consumer's interests as well as his own. **5–13**

Under the TMA 1994 a person who uses in the course of trade a sign identical to a registered mark in relation to goods or services which are identical to those for which it

---

[50] Bankes, Scrutton and Atkin L.JJ. were unanimous in holding that the implied condition that the seller had the right to sell had been broken. In addition, Atkin L.J. held that the implied warranty that the buyers should have and enjoy quiet possession had also been broken.

[51] Nevertheless, in the United States at least, the owner may not be entitled to equitable relief for infringement or for unfair competition if he substantially altered the nature of the underlying product and did not make the fact known. See E.W. Hanak, "The Quality Assurance Function of Trademarks", 43 Fordham Law Review, 365 *et seq.* (1974).

[52] *McCarthy on Trademarks and Unfair Competition*, (St. Paul: West Group, 1998), Vol. 1 §2.33, pp. 2–58.

is registered infringes the mark.[53] Infringing use of a registered mark includes use in the course of trade, of a sign identical to the registered mark in relation to similar goods or services or a similar sign on identical goods or services, to cause a likelihood of confusion, which includes the likelihood of association with the mark.[54] For the purposes of the statutory provisions concerning infringement, "use" of a sign includes the affixing of the sign to the goods or their packaging, offering or exposing goods for sale, putting them on the market or stocking them under the sign, offering or supplying services under the sign, importing or exporting under the sign, or using the sign on business papers or in advertising.[55]

Exercise of the certification mark proprietor's right to act against infringers is intertwined with the prevention of confusion which can accompany deception or misrepresentation. The right to sue for infringement under the TMA 1994 is a potent means of fostering buyers' confidence that they will receive what they expect in a certification-marked good. However, the right is consequential in effect, rather than direct, as far as individual buyers are concerned.

Conditions for Registration of a Certification Mark

5–14 A basic vindication of purchasers' and traders' trust in certification marks stems from the stringency with which the United Kingdom registry applies the requirements for registration. The applicant must convince the registry of his ability, and intention, to control use of the mark. Additionally, the applicant must be well-known in the trade concerned and have the resources to ensure that its certification is authoritative.[56]

The TMA 1994 prohibits registration of a certification mark that is liable to mislead the public as to its character or significance, in particular if it is likely to be taken to be something other than a certification mark.[57] Furthermore, the registration of a certification mark may be declared invalid on the ground that the mark was registered in breach of this provision.[58] An application for revocation may be made by any person.[59] Another perceived source of trust may be the prohibition on registration of a certification mark if the proprietor carries on a business involving the supply of goods or services of the kind certified.[60] This long-applied prohibition appears to be considered necessary to the public interest in avoiding the compromise of certifier impartiality or openness of access for all qualified products.[61]

Criminal Offences Under the Trade Marks Act 1994

5–15 Trust in certification marks is enhanced by the criminal sanction provisions of the TMA 1994, which can be invoked against false trade marking of goods and unauthorised use of a trade mark.[62] These provisions apply not only to ordinary trade marks but to

---

[53] TMA 1994, s.10(1). For further discussion of infringement of a certification mark, see Chap. 3, para. 3–24, above.
[54] TMA 1994, s.10(2)(a). As to the significance of "likelihood of association" see Chap. 3, n. 94, above.
[55] TMA 1994, s.10(4).
[56] *Trade Marks Registry Work Manual*, Chap. 12, *Certification Marks*, p. 5, June 1996.
[57] TMA 1994, Sched. 2, para. 5(1).
[58] TMA 1994, Sched. 2, para. 16.
[59] TMA 1994, s.46(4).
[60] TMA 1994, Sched. 2, para. 4
[61] See Chap. 3, paras 3–21 and 3–22, above.
[62] TMA 1994, ss.92–96.

certification marks and collective marks as well (by virtue of section 1(2) of the TMA 1994). In particular, section 92 of the TMA 1994 makes it an offence for a person to apply to goods or their packaging without the proprietor's consent, a sign identical to, or likely to be mistaken for, a registered trade mark.[63] Furthermore, a person who, without the proprietor's consent sells or lets for hire, offers or exposes for sale or hire or distributes goods which bear, or the packaging of which bears, such a sign, commits an offence.[64] Additionally, it is an offence to apply without the proprietor's consent a sign identical to, or likely to be mistaken for a registered trade mark to material intended to be used for labelling or packaging goods, business papers in relation to goods, or for advertising of goods.[65]

Enforcement of the provisions of section 92 of the TMA 1994 is the duty of local weights and measures authorities.[66] For purposes of information disclosure facilitating enforcement of the TDA 1968,[67] section 92 of the TMA 1994 is to be applied as if it were contained in the TDA 1968.[68] Also noteworthy are the provisions of section 95, which make it an offence to falsely represent a trade mark as registered[69] or to make a false representation as to the goods or services for which a trade mark is registered.[70]

False Indication of Conformity to Certification Standards

Where a trader uses a certification mark which indicates that goods are certified as complying with a particular standard and the goods do not in fact comply, the trader commits an offence under the TDA 1968.[71] A false indication includes anything likely to be taken as an indication that goods comply with a standard specified or recognised by any person or implied by the approval of any person if there is no such person or no standard so specified, recognised or implied.[72] In *Downland Bedding Co. v. Retail Trading Standards Association*[73] a label was attached to each article (pillows) bearing the words "This article conforms with Kite Mark Standards". In fact, three pillows were found to contain extracted matter in a concentration of 1.7 per cent above the amount prescribed by the standard. The defendant was convicted under the Merchandise Marks Act 1887. Dismissing an appeal, the Divisional Court rejected the argument that although some of the pillows might not have conformed with the prescribed standard, taken in bulk they did conform. Each pillow was required to conform with the prescribed standards. **5–16**

The Trade Descriptions Act 1968

The TDA 1968 is a primary statute for the protection of purchasers against deception. **5–17**
The TDA 1968 prohibits the application of false descriptions to goods offered in trade or

63 TMA 1994, s.92(1)(a).
64 TMA 1994, s.92(1)(b).
65 TMA 1994, s.92(2)(a).
66 TMA 1994, s.93(1). However, s.93(5) states that nothing in s.93 shall be construed as authorising a local weights and measures authority to bring proceedings in Scotland for an offence.
67 See paras 5–17 to 5–18, below.
68 TMA 1994, s.93(4).
69 TMA 1994, s.95(1)(a).
70 TMA 1994, s.95(1)(b).
71 See para. 5–17, below. TDA 1968 succeeded the Merchandise Marks Act, which had been in force from 1887.
72 TDA 1968, s.3(4).
73 [1959] Crim. L.R. 217. The case was brought under the Merchandise Marks Act, which preceded the TDA 1968.

business. A "false trade description" includes a false indication that certain characteristics of the goods comply with a certain standard.[74] These characteristics include origin,[75] material-related characteristics,[76] method of manufacture of goods,[77] quality-related characteristics[78] and accuracy-related characteristics.[79] It is noteworthy that characteristics of this type are recited as certifiable in the definition of a certification mark in the TMA 1994.[80] The TDA 1968 prohibits, among other things, false or misleading descriptions of goods, services,[81] accommodation, and facilities provided in the course of trade. Under the TDA 1968, it is a criminal offence for a person, in the course of a trade or business to apply to goods a false trade description to any goods,[82] or to supply or offer to supply any goods to which a false trade description is applied.[83] Thus a trade description is defined as an indication, direct or indirect, and by whatever means given, with respect to goods, of matters covering a wide range. Furthermore, the TDA 1968 confers powers to make mandatory the marking of information or instructions relating to goods on or to accompany the goods[84] or to be included in advertisements.[85]

Indications of Origin

5–18 There is no general requirement under the law of the United Kingdom or E.U. for goods to carry an indication or certification of origin.[86] However, where a mark is used to indicate certification of origin it must not fall foul of the requirements of the TDA 1968, which make it a criminal offence for a person, in the course of business, to apply false or misleading trade descriptions to goods. Included in the term "trade description" are the place or date of manufacture, production, processing or reconditioning of the goods.[87] Furthermore, the TDA 1968 provides that where a false indication is applied to any goods outside the United Kingdom and the false indication is an indication of the place of manufacture, production, processing or reconditioning of the goods or any part thereof, there is a prohibition of importation of the goods into the United Kingdom.[88]

---

[74] See para. 5–16, above.
[75] TDA 1968, s.2(1)(h)—"place or date of manufacture, production, processing or reconditioning".
[76] TDA 1968, s.2(1)(c)—"composition".
[77] TDA 1968, s.2(1)(b)—"method of manufacture, production, processing or reconditioning;".
[78] TDA 1968 s.2(1)(d)—"fitness for purpose, strength, performance, behaviour or accuracy." *cf.* SoGA, s.14(3), which, in the quality of goods, includes, where appropriate, fitness for all the purposes for which goods of the kind in question are commonly supplied, SoGA, s.14(3).
[79] *ibid.*
[80] TMA 1994, s.50(1).
[81] TDA 1968 treats misdescription of goods and services differently. Whereas a trader who misdescribes goods commits an offence, a trader who misdescribes services will have committed an offence only if it is proved that he did so knowingly or recklessly. In its White Paper "Modern Markets: Confident Customers" (Cm. 4410, July 1999) the U.K. government proposes, subject to consultation, to amend TDA 1968 to align the provisions relating to services with those relating to goods. As to certifiers' liability for erroneous or inaccurate opinions on the safety of goods already in a consumer's possession and amendments to TDA 1968 that have been proposed in this connection see paras 5–21 to 5–22, below.
[82] TDA 1968, s.1(1)(a).
[83] TDA 1968, s.1(1)(b).
[84] TDA 1968, s.8.
[85] TDA 1968, s.9.
[86] See also Chap. 3, especially paras 3–07 to 3–08, and 3–10, above.
[87] TDA 1968, s.2(1)(h).
[88] TDA 1968, s.16.

Protection of Geographical Indications

As part of its agricultural policy, the E.U. protects, by Regulation, geographical indications and designations of origin for agricultural products and foodstuffs.[89] Two classes of protected geographical denominations exist for agricultural products and foodstuffs, namely, Protected Designations of Origin (PDOs) and Protected Geographical Indications (PGIs). A PDO product must originate from a particular area, be fully produced, processed and prepared in that area and have quality or characteristics which are essentially or exclusively due to a particular geographical environment with its inherent natural and human factors.[90] The qualifications for PGI status appear to be less demanding and closer to the TRIPS definition.[91] While the good must still originate in a particular area, the production and/or processing and/or preparation must take place in that area, with the goods possessing a specific quality ("given quality" in TRIPS), reputation or other characteristics ("characteristic" in TRIPS) attributable to that geographical origin.[92] **5–19**

Only a group of producers or processors, regardless of its legal form, may apply for registration of a PDO or PGI. The application, which must comprise a product specification, is filed in the Member State in which the geographical area is located. Following formal examination by the Commission and verification that the designation is not generic, the main elements of the application are published. If no statement of objection is filed within six months of publication the application proceeds to registration. Among the first United Kingdom registrations were White Stilton and Blue Stilton cheeses, both of which are PDOs and coexist with the United Kingdom registered certification marks STILTON and STILTON CHEESE. Other registrations include Orkney beef and Orkney lamb (PDOs), Scottish beef and Scottish lamb (PGIs), Jersey Royal potatoes (PDO) and Newcastle brown ale (PGI).[93]

---

[89] Council Reg. 2081/92 of July 14, 1992. Art.2(2)(b) of the Reg. defines a "geographical indication" as the name of a region, a specific place or, in exceptional cases, a country, used to describe an agricultural product or a foodstuff originating in that region, specific place or country, and which possesses a specific quality, reputation or other characteristics attributable to that geographical region and the production and/or processing and/or preparation of which take place in the defined geographical area. The Reg. does not apply to wines and spirits, which are subject to specific rules. For a detailed discussion of the subject of geographical indications and appellations of origin see *Kerly's Law of Trade Marks and Trade Names* (D. Kitchin, D. Llewelyn, J. Mellor, R. Meade, and T. Moody-Stuart eds, 13th ed., Sweet & Maxwell, London, 2001). See also B. Schwab, "The Protection of Geographical Indications in the European Economic Community", [1995] E.I.P.R. 242, and N. Dawson, "Locating Geographical Indications—Perspectives From English Law", 90 T.M.R. 590 (2000).

[90] Council Reg. 2081/92 of July 14, 1992, Art.2(2)(a). The Reg. entered into force on July 25, 1993.

[91] *ibid.*, Art.2(2)(b). See Chap. 3, paras 3–07 and 3–09, above.

[92] The PDO/PGI scheme is the subject of a U.S. complaint, filed against the E.U. in the WTO. The U.S. contends that Reg. 2081/92, as amended, is inconsistent with the E.U.'s obligations under TRIPS, because it denies national treatment with respect to geographical indications and fails to adequately protect pre-existing trade marks that are similar or identical to a geographical indication registered under this Reg. According to Art.14 of Reg. 2081/92, once a PDO or PGI is registered, the application for registration of a trade mark corresponding to such indication or designation shall be refused, if submitted after its date of publication in the Official Journal of the European Communities. The U.S. contends that Reg. 2081/92, violates, among other things, TRIPS, Art. 3 (national treatment), Art. 16 (trade mark rights conferred—exclusive right to prevent unauthorised use), and Art. 63 (transparency of dispute prevention and settlement). See American Bar Association (ABA), Section of Intellectual Property Law, Committee 202, International Trademark Practice, Treaties and Laws, Report for 1999–2000, *WTO Disputes: Pending Consultation Between the U.S. and the E.C. Affecting Geographical Indications,* at ABA website www.abanet.org/intelprop/99–00/ipl4.html. The United States Trade Representative regards the E.U.'s treatment of geographical indications for foodstuffs under Reg. 2081/92 as a basis for the E.U.'s inclusion on the Special 301 Priority Watch List.

[93] The first accepted applications under the Reg. 2081/92 of July 14, 1992, were granted under Commission Reg. 1107/96 of June 12, 1996 on the registration of geographical indications and designations of origin under the procedure laid down in Art.17 of Council Reg. 2081/92 [1996] O.J. L148/01.

Informative Logos for E.U. Geographical Indications

5–20 An E.U. Regulation, promulgated in 1998, allows producers to use a special logo for PDO and PGI food products.[94] The presence of this logo is described in the Regulation as:

> [A] genuine guarantee for all European consumers, making it clear that the special nature of this product lies in its geographical origin. Because of this, products will inspire more confidence.

Use of the logo is intended to ensure a minimum level of standardised information when a producer and/or processor wishes to use the PDO/PGI system of geographical indications and designations of origin established by the original Regulation. The logo Regulation states that:

> [T]o strengthen the credibility of the symbol characterising the agricultural products or foodstuffs qualifying for a PGI or PDO, the name of the inspection service or body should be indicated on the label used to market the product.

An E.U. Member State may stipulate that the name of the inspection authority or body referred to in Article 10 of the original Regulation falling-within its own inspection structure must appear on the label of the agricultural product or foodstuff. The logo graphics are based on the logo for Guaranteed Traditional Speciality but differ from it in colour. A graphical representation of furrows in a ploughed field has been incorporated as a reference to the origin and geographical provenance of the products.

Certification of Goods in Buyer's Possession: Statements by Experts

5–21 To what extent should the consumer be protected against a certifier who provides an erroneous or inaccurate opinion on the safety of goods already in the consumer's possession? Section 1 of the TDA 1968 is intended to prohibit the provision of goods with false descriptions applied in the course of trade. But what if there is no provision of goods? In *Wycombe Marsh Garages Ltd. v. Fowler*,[95] the appellants' garage served as a Ministry of Transport test station for the issue of test certificates. The appellants' foreman mechanic had failed a car for having defective tyres. Subsequent examination of the tyres by experts revealed that the mechanic's diagnosis was wrong and that the tyres were not unsafe. The appellants were charged and convicted of applying a false trade description by means of a notification of refusal of a test certificate to certain goods (the car's nearside tyres). The appeal court quashed the conviction suggesting that it was not Parliament's intention that one who, in the course of rendering a service is required to give an opinion as to the condition of goods, gives a false opinion, however honestly, is liable to a penalty under section 1 of the TDA 1968. Furthermore the court pointed out that the TDA 1968 was enacted to prohibit misdescriptions of goods, services, etc., provided in the course of trade. In this case there was no provision of goods in the course of trade at all.

Statements by Certifiers: Proposed Amendments to the Trade Description Act 1968

5–22 Amendments to the TDA 1968, proposed by the previous Labour Government, were intended to protect the interests of consumers possessing goods that require certification, such as cars. Such amendments would likely make inroads into the quasi-immunity

---

[94] See n. 4, above.
[95] [1972] 3 All E.R. 248.

traditionally enjoyed by professional certifiers. With situations of the type that arose in *Wycombe Marsh Garages Ltd. v. Fowler*[96] in mind, the Government had proposed to amend the TDA 1968[97] to introduce liability for statements made by service providers or suppliers of goods such as professional testers and certifiers,[98] which relate to the condition of goods in the possession of the customer.[99] These amendments would have made public bodies and persons acting as nominees or sub-contractors for a Minister of the Crown, performing a statutory function, fully accountable.[1] However, in bringing such statements within the scope of the TDA 1968, it would be necessary for the enforcement authority to establish that a person knew the statement was false when it was made. Nevertheless, professional experts and their associations, who certify the condition of goods including cars and real property and services applied to them, could be expected to oppose such proposals on the grounds that they encroach on the special position enjoyed by certifiers status.[2]

United Kingdom Policy on Trade Association Codes of Practice

Trade Associations figure prominently as owners of certification marks and as standard-setting institutions. It is therefore important that trade bodies who set standards and certify goods and services act and are seen to act in ways that do not violate the laws against anticompetitive practices, such as Articles 81 and 82 (ex 85 and 86 respectively) of the Treaty of Rome and of their counterparts in the United Kingdom Competition Act 1998. The conduct of trade bodies in the United Kingdom is subject to the Competition Act 1998, which brought into United Kingdom domestic legislation the E.U. prohibitions of anticompetitive behaviour on the part of undertakings and associations of undertakings.[3] **5–23**

The United Kingdom Government has stated that it considers self-regulation through codes of practice run by trade associations to be an effective way of strengthening protection for consumers.[4] The monitoring of the effects of trade association codes on

---

96 *ibid.*

97 See n. 99, below.

98 While not becoming subject to criminal liability, the Crown would be subject to enforcement authorities' applications to the High Court for a declaration that an act or omission of the Crown, which would otherwise amount to an offence, is unlawful.

99 See paras 19–22 of the policy document *Amendments to the Trade Descriptions Act 1968*, at the Department of Trade and Industry website, http://dtiinfo1.dti.gov.uk/consumer/law/4.htm (visited November 14, 2000). Shortly before this Special Report went to press the policy document was no longer available on the DTI website. However, copies can be obtained from the DTI Consumer Affairs Directorate. Part of the concern about such statements is that they may be used in order to induce the customer to buy additional goods or services, such as the fitting of spare parts by garages, that may not be needed. A new provision was proposed, which related to statements made by experts about goods or property which they are not selling. Under the proposed amendments it would have been an offence to make false or misleading statements that are made as an inducement for a person to enter into a transaction or with a view to influencing the terms of any transaction, about *inter alia* the condition of goods, physical state of real property, and services applied in the past to goods or real property. Recent inquiries to DTI indicate that these proposals are unlikely to reach the legislative agenda during the present Government's term.

1 As an example of a Ministry test station held liable for negligent issue of a test certificate, see *Rutherford v. Attorney-General* [1976] 1 N.Z.L.R. 401, (Claim was allowed for economic loss).

2 See Chap. 4, above.

3 Any body formed to represent the interests of its members in commercial matters may be an association of undertakings. See *Trade Associations, Professions and Self-Regulating Bodies*, OFT Guideline, para. 1.2. Trade bodies are encouraged by government to issue voluntary codes of practice to ensure that their members' activities remain within the law. See *Voluntary Codes of Practice*, OFT Trading Consultation paper, OFT Report OFT 183, December 1996.

4 According to Mr Richard Caborn, Minister for Trade, the DTI "has no plans to regulate trade associations", House of Commons Hansard Debates for November 30, 2000 (Pt 3), col.1129.

competition policy in the United Kingdom is part of the brief of the Office of Fair Trading (OFT). The OFT treats "any code of practice which binds or recommends anyone to restrict their freedom to make decisions as a restrictive trade agreement", which is "thus registrable under the Restrictive Trade Practices Act, whether or not it is supported by OFT."[5] However, where the OFT supports a code of practice it has determined that any restrictions on competition are "not significant".[6] The OFT aims to extend its reach to traders who are not members of trade associations and appears to believe its task would be simplified if all traders were members of associations. However, the OFT could not support a rule requiring compulsory association membership.[7]

The Office of Fair Trading Proposal to Certify Codes of Practice

5–24 The OFT has published a plan to provide and market a seal of approval for approved codes so that consumers would be able to see whether trader members of trade associations are committed to a code. United Kingdom policy on trade association codes of practice focuses sharply on safeguarding and promoting the interests of United Kingdom consumers. Sections 124(3) and (4) of the Fair Trading Act 1973, put a duty on the OFT to promote trade associations' codes of practice for guidance in safeguarding and promoting the interests of consumers.[8] Supported by the OFT in some cases, trade associations promulgate codes of practice specifying minimum standards of behaviour for their members. While accepting that codes play a useful role, the OFT position is that even where a code of practice is in place a statutory basis for intervention is required if the code is not effective. The Government has accepted that the OFT be accorded new powers to approve, monitor and assure compliance with trade association codes of practice, based on core principles set forth in a White Paper.[9]

Summary and Conclusion

5–25 Part 2 of this chapter focused on the guarantee function and contractual significance of certification marks. It is concluded that the epithets "guarantee" and "warranty", commonly applied to certification marks, appear to be largely the result of semantic

---

[5] See *Voluntary Codes of Practice, OFT Consultation Paper*, OFT report, OFT 183, December 1996. Summary available at www.oft.gov.uk/html/rsearch/oft183.htm

[6] *ibid.*

[7] In this connection, the ongoing struggle in the U.S. courts against compulsory association in the agricultural sector and mandatory contributions to the development of certification marks, a vestigial policy of the New Deal, may be of interest. See for example, *Gallo Cattle v. California Milk*, Opinion of the U.S. Court of Appeals for the Ninth Circuit, Case No. 97–17182, filed July 14, 1999. Gallo argued, unsuccessfully, that the compulsory assessments payable to the California Milk Advisory Board to support, among other things, the REAL CALIFORNIA CHEESE certification mark, violated Gallo's rights under the First Amendment of the United States Constitution. Gallo also claimed that the mark implied a message that Gallo's cheese was not better than any other California produced cheese. See also *Dan Glickman, Secretary of Agriculture, Petitioner v. Wileman Brothers & Elliot, Inc.*, U.S. Supreme Court Opinion No. 95–1184, June 25, 1997 (Imposed assessments on respondents to cover costs of generic advertising of California treefruit not abridgement of freedom of speech within the meaning of the First Amendment. No First Amendment right against coerced subsidisation of commercial speech). Followed in *Gerawan Farming, Inc. v. Ann M. Veneman, as Secretary etc., et al.*, California Appeal Court, Fifth Appellate District, (Super. Ct. No. 94–167877), Opinion filed June 8, 1999.

[8] s.124(3) provides: "[I]t shall be the duty of the Director to encourage relevant associations to prepare, and to disseminate to their members, codes of practice for guidance in safeguarding and promoting the interests of consumers in the United Kingdom". And s.124(4): "In this section relevant association means any association (whether incorporated or not) whose membership consists wholly or mainly of persons engaged in the production or supply of goods or in the supply of services or of persons employed by or representing persons so engaged and whose objects or activities include the promotion of the interests of persons so engaged."

[9] White Paper "Modern Markets: Confident Customers" (Cm. 4410, (July 1999)).

infiltration. A certification mark neither imposes a legal requirement on the certification mark proprietor to act as a surety towards a buyer nor creates any particular obligations with respect to contractual or tort obligations. In Part 2 attention has been drawn to United Kingdom and E.U. laws and policies that are commensurate with purchaser trust in certification and certification-like marks. At present, purchasers' trust in certification marks is vindicated by the policy of the United Kingdom trade marks registry in requiring convincing evidence of well-known status in the trade and resources to ensure certification is authoritative. Trust in a certification mark also flows from the proprietor's statutory right to initiate infringement proceedings and additional provisions of the TMA 1994, which prohibit registration of certification marks that are liable to mislead the public and make false certification marking and unauthorised use of a certification mark a criminal offence.

Finally, it is observed that in the absence of clear wording in a certification mark or on the product, the certifying body, the product attributes that are certified, and the standard to which they are certified are not always readily apparent from the mark. Put differently, there is a lack of transparency in many certification marks. Transparency could be increased by proprietors' requiring, in the regulations for use of their marks, that a minimum standard textual content be contained in a label comprising the mark.

Certification marks can and should be a means of offering more direct assurance to buyers, especially first-time buyers who are not familiar with the mark or what it stands for. It is submitted that the stage is set for a more directly consumer-oriented model of a certification mark. New forms of registration of protected geographical indications, regulations for more informative product marking, possible amendments to trade descriptions law with respect to certification service providers, recent changes in competition law and policy affecting trade bodies' codes of practice, and certification of e-commerce undertakings all appear to be compatible with a more consumer-oriented certification trade mark.

6

REGULATIONS AND STANDARDS

Introduction

A certification mark is underpinned by the proprietor's regulations or standards, conformity to which is a *sine qua non* for legitimate use and legal protection of the mark. Therefore, the development and implementation of regulations and standards is of major consequence for certification marks, particularly when they are used for regulatory purposes. This chapter identifies the frameworks for development and implementation of technical regulations and standards. Included is an outline of the principles behind international mutual recognition agreements for recognition of product conformity assessment procedures, of which certification is but a part. In addition, the mechanisms promoting common or "harmonised" standards for products are described in light of their declared purpose of eliminating unnecessary technical barriers to trade. 6–01

Presentation of the content is based on the world economic groupings, in "top down" order. Thus regulation and standard-setting frameworks and processes are described firstly in the context of the world trade system. Then, institutions responsible for regulation and standardisation within the E.U., which is a single trading block or customs territory within the world trade system, are described. Finally, some examples are given of ways in which the rules, guidelines and practices set forth by these supranational regulation and standardisation institutions are being interpreted and applied within the United Kingdom.

Technical Regulations, Standards and Indicia of Conformity

Promulgated by governmental[1] or non-governmental bodies in all areas of national and international trade, technical regulations and standards are directed to the construction, performance, safety, quality, environmental acceptability, material, mode of manufacture, and many other characteristics of products. In many instances, conformity to technical regulations or standards is necessary before products can be legally placed into the stream of commerce. The use of certification and certification-like marks on goods 6–02

[1] In their regulatory capacity governments may generate technical regulations themselves, in collaboration with trade and industry bodies, or incorporate by reference regulations and standards developed by such bodies. For the difference in definitions between standards and regulations see para. 6–04, below.

that conform to technical regulations and standards provides a convenient visual attestation to such conformity, which benefits the trading community and regulators alike. For example, the E.U. requires that many categories of products, from machinery, construction products, weighing instruments, and medical devices, to pressure vessels, gas appliances, and telecommunications terminal equipment, display a specific, visible attestation, the "CE" mark, of conformity to statutorily prescribed minimum health and safety requirements.

Another type of standard, certification of conformity to which is demanded increasingly, concerns the interoperability or "compatibility" of a product with other products or systems. Interoperability standards are specially important to the development of telecommunications and information technology because evolution and growth of these sectors is synonymous with ever more extensive networking.[2] A familiar example of standardisation for interoperability in computer systems is the Intel-Windows PC architecture, in which computers produced by many different manufacturers conform to a single set of standards and can work with the same operating system.

The subject of interoperability standards is highly controversial, if only because governments tend to equate their intervention or non-intervention in the development of such standards with promotion of social and economic welfare.[3] An obvious manifestation of intervention is the enactment of legislation designed to promote competition among rival developers of the technologies that enable interoperability. However, in the information technology field at least, interoperability now appears to be driven primarily by the market rather than government.

Regulations and Standards as Technical Barriers to Trade

6–03 The nexus between unilateralism and protectionism in the application of technical regulations and standards in international trade is notorious. Protectionist measures include the one-sided imposition of excessively strict testing and conformity requirements, insistence that conformity assessment be done by a body in the importing country, unreasonably high costs for such conformity assessment, and confusingly voluminous technical regulations. Furthermore, non-transparency in the form of secrecy and delays in de-restricting documents relating to regulations and standards, and

---

[2] The interoperability of the components and sub-systems of global telecommunications is fundamental for international e-commerce. For example, data from a purchaser's local system must be able to reach a buyer's local system that may be located on the other side of the world, and vice versa. Interoperability of hardware and software is achieved through standards, thereby facilitating the various transactions of e-commerce, such as electronic payment, encrypted communication, electronic contracting, identity authentication, and non-repudiation.

[3] Regarding the role of government in the development of standards for networking, particularly for e-commerce, see report, *A Framework for Global Electronic Commerce*, The White House, July 1, 1997, at www.ecommerce.gov. The report stated that "The United States believes that the marketplace, not governments, should determine technical standards and other mechanisms for interoperability. Technology is moving rapidly and government attempts to establish technical standards to govern the Internet would only risk inhibiting technological innovation. The United States considers it unwise and unnecessary for governments to mandate standards for electronic commerce. Rather, we urge industry driven multilateral fora to consider technical standards in this area." Nevertheless, the report favoured strong government intervention in the sensitive area of encryption standards. See Mark A. Lemley, "Standardizing Government Standard-Setting Policy for Electronic Commerce", 14 Berkeley Technology Law Journal 745 (1999).

policies for their enactment and enforcement, are additional protectionist measures.[4] All measures of this type can amount to technical barriers to trade.

While there may be a consensus as to the advantages of standardisation, efforts to "level the playing field" through uniform technical regulation and harmonisation of standards continue to be dogged by difficulties at the regional and global trading levels. Why, within a purportedly liberalised multilateral trading system does adoption of uniform regulations and standards remain problematic? Evidently, there is a blurring of the distinction between the ideal and the reality. The notion that the establishment of the World Trade Organisation (WTO),[5] in 1995, would be the dawn of true multilateralism, with traders taking unilateral action only to the extent permitted by the system itself, has yet to be realised. Nevertheless, the WTO has made impressive headway in instituting and operating mechanisms for dealing with regulations and standards, and trade disputes concerning them, even if it is a less than ideal system.

1 THE WTO/GATT FRAMEWORK

Difference Between Regulations and Standards

The definitions of "technical regulations" and "standards" used here are those adopted by the Contracting Parties to the Uruguay Round of multilateral trade negotiations, which resulted in the 1994 General Agreement on Tariffs and Trade (GATT). The successor to GATT 1994 is the WTO, which was inaugurated on January 1, 1995.[6] The WTO is the internationally accepted legal and institutional basis for world trade. Its key objectives have been described as "to provide a forum to negotiate and monitor the liberalization of trade, to improve policy transparency and resolve trade disputes."[7] The **6–04**

---

[4] "An opaque legal or regulatory regime is one which imposes significant information-acquisition costs or barriers upon a party subject to the law or regulation. . .It is highly unlikely that these information-gathering costs in opaque legal regimes will be borne by anyone other than the regulated party. In a few countries and a few settings, information costs are shared by governments [*e.g.* the United States' Freedom of Information Act, 5. U.S.C.A. §552, Pub. L. 89–487, 80 Stat. 250 (1966)], but this is not common . . . By contrast, a transparent legal regime imposes none of these costs. Although there will naturally be costs associated with ascertaining and evaluating business risks, there will be no or minimal costs associated with locating, acquiring, and confirming the regulatory requirements and consequences associated with investment." William B. T. Mock, "An Interdisciplinary Introduction to Legal Transparency: A Tool for Rational Development", 18 Dickinson Journal of International Law 293 at 302–303 (2000).

[5] See nn. 6 and 7, below.

[6] The Marrakesh Agreement Establishing the World Trade Organisation states that the General Agreement on Tariffs and Trade 1994 (GATT 1994) is an instrument legally distinct from the General Agreement on Tariffs and Trade dated October 30, 1947, annexed to the Final Act of the United Nations Conference on Trade and Employment (Havana Conference), and referred to as GATT 1947.

[7] Kym Anderson, "The Future Agenda of the WTO" in *From GATT to the WTO: The Multilateral Trading System in the New Millenium*, (Kluwer, Dordrecht, 2000), Chap. 3, p. 8. However, the view that these declared objectives manifest a genuine desire among nations for a liberalised world trading order, premised on free trade and the elimination of protectionism, is not accepted by all commentators. Some argue that such a view is naive and that the WTO/GATT is primarily an expedient bargain struck between the political leaders of the WTO. See for example, A.O. Sykes, "Protectionism as a "Safeguard": A Positive Analysis of the GATT "Escape Clause" with Normative Speculations", 58 Univ. of Chicago Law. Rev. 255 (1991). Sykes saw the safeguard measures clause of Art. XIX of the GATT (now embodied in Annex 1A of the Marrakesh Agreement as part of the Agreement on Safeguards), which allows import restrictions when a Member's domestic industry is caused or threatened with serious injury, as allowing signatories "to renege upon their commitments to reduce trade barriers." Note, by way of comparison, that there is no such escape clause in the treaty establishing the European Community (the Treaty of Rome). Arts 28 and 29 (ex Arts 30 and 34) of the Treaty absolutely prohibit quantitative restrictions on imports and exports between Member States.

WTO/GATT Agreement places legally binding basic obligations on WTO Members, obligations that determine how governments draft and enforce domestic trade legislation and regulations.[8] All Agreements negotiated in the Uruguay Round are contained in Annexes to the Agreement establishing the WTO. The Agreement on Technical Barriers to Trade (TBT) is one such Agreement and Annex 1 of TBT sets forth terms and definitions, which among other things distinguish between "technical regulations" and "standards". A technical regulation is defined as a

> Document which lays down product characteristics or their related processes and production methods, including the applicable administrative provisions, with which compliance is mandatory. It may also include or deal exclusively with terminology, symbols, packaging, marking or labelling requirements as they apply to a product, process or production method.

In contrast to a regulation, a standard is defined as a

> Document approved by a recognised body, that provides, for common and repeated use, rules, guidelines or characteristics for products or related processes and production methods, with which *compliance is not mandatory*.[9] It may also include or deal exclusively with terminology, symbols, packaging, marking or labelling requirements as they apply to a product, process or production method. [Emphasis added]

The TBT requires that, wherever appropriate, Members shall specify technical regulations based on product requirements in terms of performance rather than design or descriptive characteristics.[10], although both approaches are permitted

Because the mode of manufacture of a product can affect its characteristics, in certain cases it may be considered more appropriate to draft technical regulations or standards in term of the production process rather than the final product's characteristics. However, regulatory measures based on the process or production method, instead of the physical characteristics of the product, where applied to restrict imports, are normally perceived as violating Article XI of the WTO/GATT Agreement, which prohibits such restrictions. There is controversy among commentators on this point. Howse and Reagan[11] question whether there is textual support in the Agreement for the perceived violation and argue that Members should be free to impose unilateral import prohibitions where, for example, protection of the global environment is concerned. An example of a recent WTO case concerning such a prohibition is *United States—Import Prohibition of Certain Shrimp and Shrimp Products*,[12] in which imports of shrimp were banned from countries that did not require shrimping technology that avoided the incidental killing of sea turtles. Jackson[13] defends the more widely accepted position that such restrictions are not permitted.

---

[8] Within the current rules, access to WTO dispute settlement is reserved to Member governments, *i.e.* the system of protection is diplomatic, with *locus standi* granted only to governments. Individual companies or trade associations must therefore persuade their governments to take up their case if it is to reach the WTO. This aspect of the system is currently the subject of considerable scrutiny and commentary, see for example, Petros. C. Mavroidis et al., "Is the WTO Dispute Settlement Mechanism Responsive to the Needs of the Traders? Would a System of Direct Action by Private Parties Yield Better Results?" Panel Discussion, 6th Geneva Global Arbitration Forum, 32 J.W.T. 147 (1998). See also Jean Charles Van Eeckhaute, "Private Complaints against Foreign Unfair Trade Practices, The EC's Trade Barriers Regulation", 33 J.W.T. 199 (1999).

[9] However, it should be noted that certain governmental agencies, such as the U.S. Department of Labor's Occupational Safety and Health Administration, continue to apply "standards" usage to mandatory technical regulations.

[10] TBT, Art. 2.8.

[11] R. Howse and D. Regan, "The Product/Process Distinction—An Illusory Basis for Disciplining 'Unilateralism' in Trade Policy", 11 E.I.J.L. 249 (2000).

[12] Report of the Appellate Body, October 1998, WT/DS 58/AB/R,

[13] H. Jackson, "Comments on Shrimp/Turtle and the Product/Process Distinction", 11 E.I.J.L. 303 (2000).

Principle of Mutual Recognition

The TBT requires that WTO Members give positive consideration to accepting as equivalent technical regulations of other Members, even if these regulations differ from their own, provided they are satisfied that these regulations adequately fulfil the objectives of their own regulations.[14] Perhaps even more important for practical purposes is the requirement that Members shall ensure, "whenever possible", that results of conformity assessment procedures of central government bodies in other Members are accepted, even when those procedures differ from their own. However, Members are entitled to satisfy themselves that other Members' procedures offer an assurance of conformity equivalent to their own procedures.[15] TBT recognises the possible need for prior consultations among Members regarding the technical competence of the relevant conformity assessment bodies in the exporting Member. Therefore, accreditation by international standardising bodies is to be taken into account as an indication of technical competence.[16] There is also recognition that some Members may limit the acceptance of conformity assessment results to those produced by designated bodies in the exporting Member.[17] **6–05**

Mutual Recognition Agreements

Mutual recognition agreements (MRAs) are designed to institute formally mutual recognition of the parties' conformity assessment procedures and results, reports, certificates and other evidence of conformity, normally in relation to particular categories of products. MRAs provide for recognition by one party of certificates issued by designated conformity assessment bodies in the country of the other party, and vice versa. Such steps are intended to eliminate duplicative product assessments. A major MRA was signed on June 18, 1998 between the world's two major economies, the United States and the E.U. The MRA is composed of a "framework agreement" and six subsections containing specific provisions indicating the products and activities covered. The E.U.-U.S. MRA initially covered the mutual recognition of the testing of electrical equipment, machinery, medical devices, medicinal products, personnel protection equipment and toys. During a three year transition period, the E.U. and United States were to have conducted joint inspections, train auditors, and set up a market surveillance system.[18] **6–06**

MRAs allow exported products to be placed on the market and taken into service in the importing country without conformity assessment in the importing country or

---

[14] TBT Art. 2.7. For a useful review and discussion of the mutual recognition principle and its application to world trade post GATT see, Sherry M. Stephenson, "Mutual Recognition and its Role in Trade Facilitation" 33 Journal of World Trade 141, (1999).

[15] TBT, Art. 6.1.

[16] TBT, Art. 6.1.1.

[17] TBT, Art. 6.1.2.

[18] Within the framework of the U.S.-E.U. MRA, on January 17, 2001, implementation of an agreement was announced in respect of the reduction of barriers to transatlantic trade of telecommunications and electronic products. Under the Agreement, 33 U.S. and 32 E.U. conformity assessment bodies are recognised to be competent by U.S. and E.U. regulatory authorities to test and certify equipment under two annexes to the U.S.-E.U. MRA, which entered into force in December 1998, covering telecommunications, terminal equipment, including radio transmitters, and information technology equipment. When fully implemented, the MRA will also eliminate duplicative conformity assessment of network and electromagnetic compatibility for electrical products; electrical safety for electrical and electronic products; good manufacturing practices for pharmaceuticals; product evaluation for certain medical devices; and safety of recreational craft. For further details of the U.S.-E.U. MRA see website of the United States Trade Representative, www.ustr.gov.

territory. This is because MRAs provide for mutual recognition of conformity procedures carried out, and certificates issued, in the territory of the exporter. An MRA is not premised on one country's acceptance of another's technical regulations or standards. Rather, it is an undertaking to accept the other party's test data and indicia of conformity. Recognition is essentially limited to recognition of the other party's competence to satisfactorily evaluate and certify products to a level acceptable to the other party. Activities with respect to mutual recognition take place at (a) the technical level, which is the level of the testing laboratories and the bodies responsible for administering accreditation of testing laboratories; and (b) the "acceptance level" which is the level comprising the regulators such as customs, health and safety authorities, environmental or other government agencies, and purchasers.

Commercial Treaties in Historical Context

6–07 Agreements governing trade have been made between nations since ancient times and instances are referred to by the Roman and Greek writers.[19] The common form of trade agreement was bilateral rather than multilateral. England's first commercial treaty is said to be the England-Norway Treaty of 1217, designed to protect merchants of each signatory country when visiting the territory of the other.[20] England later signed bilateral treaties with other European states, including Flanders, Portugal, the Baltic cities,[21] France and Florence. England's 1654 Treaty of Peace with Sweden is an early example of mutual most-favoured-nation assurance, under which treatment had to be no less favourable than that accorded by any third state. The treaty provided that for the parties:

> [T]rade shall be absolutely free and unconfined in their respective dominions, and the subjects have all the privileges, exemptions, and immunities, which any foreigners have in either.[22]

Illustrative of treaties designed to remove prohibitions on imports is the 1703 Treaty of Commerce between Great Britain and Portugal, signed at Lisbon, December 27, 1703, under Article I of which Portugal agreed to

> [A]dmit, for ever hereafter, into Portugal, the woollen cloths, and the rest of the woollen manufactures of the Britons, as was accustomed, till they were prohibited by the laws[23]

in exchange for which Great Britain agreed, under Article II, to

---

[19] "Commercial Treaties", Encyclopaedia Britannica, (Encyclopædia Britannica, Inc., Chicago, 1971), Vol. 6, pp. 152–156.

[20] *ibid*.

[21] *ibid*. In this connection, the Hanseatic League (from the Old High German word hansa, meaning "league"), was a federation of cities in northern Germany, and of communities of German merchants in the Low Countries, England, and the Baltic region, organised for the protection and enhancement of mutual commercial interests. The League was established in the early 13th century, when German merchants who had settled on the Baltic island of Gotland established a mercantile association, consisting of Cologne and 29 other towns. The Gotland association negotiated important trading privileges abroad, notably with England, Flanders, and Russia. See http://hjem.wanadoo.dk/~wan04430/Denmark/Hanseatic_League/body_hanseatic_league.html.

[22] Treaty between England and Sweden, signed at Uppsala, April 11, 1654, Art.IV. *The Consolidated Treaty Series*, Clive Parry, Ed., (Dobbs Ferry, Oceana Publications, Inc., New York, 1969), (Years 1653–1655), Vol. 3, pp. 257 and 268.

[23] *The Consolidated Treaty Series* (Clive Parry ed., Dobbs Ferry, Oceana Publications, Inc., New York, 1969), Vol. 25, (Years 1703–1706), pp. 37 and 42.

> [A]dmit the wines of the growth of Portugal into Britain; so that at no time, whether there shall be peace or war between the kingdoms of Britain and France, anything more shall be demanded for these wines by the name of custom or duty, or by whatsoever other title,. . .than what shall be demanded from the like quantity or measure of French wine, deducting or abating a third part of the custom or duty.[24]

Establishment of the Standards Code

By the 1930s, bilateral trade agreements between many countries, or co-operation arrangements in international trade, were in place. Many of these agreements were destabilised or suspended as a result of World War II. The first post-war multilateral trade agreement to be established was the GATT 1947. However, the subject of technical regulations and standards as barriers to trade was not addressed in depth in GATT 1947.[25] While it was acknowledged that technical regulations formed a major class of barrier to entry into international markets, it was to take another thirty years before the Standards Code, a major landmark on the road to removal of discriminatory practices among trading nations, was reached.[26] **6–08**

The Standards Code (the Code) was an agreement which 32 Contracting Parties signed and which became effective on January 1, 1980, following the Tokyo Round negotiations of the GATT. Principal aims of the Code were to encourage national treatment and non-discrimination for product testing and certification programmes. Adoption of standards or technical regulations by governments or other bodies for reasons of health, safety, environmental protection, or other purposes, was to be permitted, but without creation of unnecessary obstacles to trade.[27]

By addressing, among other things, the preparation, adoption and application of technical regulations and standards, by central government, local government and non-governmental bodies, the Code provided a framework, albeit a voluntary one, for reducing or removing technical barriers to trade. Also included in the Code were procedures for determination of conformity, systems of certification of conformity and dispute settlement procedures. Free flow of information among signatories about their technical regulations, standards and certification systems was stipulated as well. However, the Code did not provide solutions to some major issues, including, reciprocal testing and certification arrangements and access to certification systems. These and other issues comprised the subsequent agenda of the Committee on Technical Barriers to Trade, constituted under Article 13 of the Code.

The GATT Uruguay Round: Agreement on Technical Barriers to Trade

In the most recent round of multilateral negotiations, the Uruguay Round, the substantive provisions of the Standards Code were incorporated into a binding Agreement, namely the Agreement on Technical Barriers to Trade, as Annex III of the GATT. The **6–09**

---

[24] *ibid.*, at p. 43.

[25] Nevertheless GATT 1947 did relate to standards and regulations, to some extent, in Arts. III, XI and XX. Thus Art. III required national treatment so that, *inter alia*, "internal quantitative regulations requiring the mixture, processing or use of products in specified amounts or proportions should not be applied to imported or domestic products so as to afford protection to domestic production". Art. XI was directed towards general elimination of quantitative restrictions on importation and exportation. But prohibitions or restrictions were allowed where necessary for the application of standards or regulations for the "classification, grading or marketing of commodities in international trade". Furthermore, Art. XX allowed for national treatment to be waived if necessary to protect life or health, patents, trade marks and copyrights, or deceptive practices. For the text of these articles of GATT 1947, see P. Raworth and L.C. Reif, *The Law of the WTO*, (Oceana Publications, Inc., New York, 1995), pp. 836 *et seq*.

[26] The Code applied to agricultural and industrial products.

[27] For a detailed history of the Standards Code see, *The GATT Uruguay Round: A Negotiating History*, (Terence P. Stewart ed., Kluwer Law & Taxation, Deventer, 1993), pp. 1067 *et seq*.

format of TBT is similar to the Standards Code and comprises fifteen articles covering, for industrial and agricultural products, the preparation adoption and application of technical regulations by central and local government bodies and non-governmental bodies.[28] An important change from the Standards Code is the use in TBT of the term "conformity assessment" instead of "certification", which is but one aspect of conformity assessment. Conformity assessment covers a manufacturer's self-declaration of conformity with prescribed standards or regulations, third-party verification, inspection or testing and certification, and quality system registration (which requires the manufacturer's facility to be registered and audited periodically).

Procedures for assessment of conformity by central government bodies[29] are required to assure access to suppliers of like products from other Members' territories.[30] This means *inter alia* that they shall not be more strict or be applied more strictly than is necessary, taking account of the risks that non-conformity would create.[31] Members are also obligated to ensure that conformity assessment procedures are undertaken and completed as expeditiously as possible and in a no less favourable order than for suppliers of like products from other Members' territories.[32]

WTO/GATT-Designated Standard-Setting Bodies

6–10 Two international standard-setting bodies were expressly nominated in the GATT to co-ordinate the implementation of technical agreements which give expression to political decisions embodied in the Agreement on Technical Barriers to Trade. These bodies are the International Organisation for Standardisation (ISO) and the International Electrotechnical Commission (IEC), which date from 1947 and 1904 respectively.

ISO is a federation of national standards bodies with representation from virtually every country. The most widely known function of ISO is the publication of International Standards, which ISO regards as "international agreements" containing "technical specifications or other precise criteria to be used consistently as rules, guidelines, or definitions of characteristics, to ensure that materials, products, processes and services are fit for their purpose."[33] Eighty per cent of ISO's work is paid for by the member organisations, and 20 per cent from sales, mainly of standards.

6–11 Co-ordinated from its Geneva headquarters, ISO's standard-setting activity is devolved to about 3,000 committees throughout the world. Its programs reflect the drive to liberalise international trade, accommodate new technologies, recognise the interpenetration of industry sectors, create a uniform worldwide communications system and

[28] TBT, Art. 1 contains general provisions; Arts 2 and 3—Preparation, Adoption and Application of Technical Regulations by Central Government, and Local and Non-Governmental Bodies, respectively; Art. 4—Preparation, Adoption and Application of Standards; Art. 5—Procedures for Assessment of Conformity by Central Government Bodies; Art. 6—Recognition of Conformity Assessment by Central Government Bodies; Arts 7 and 8—Procedures for Assessment of Conformity by Local Government and Non-Governmental Bodies, respectively; Art. 9—International and Regional Systems (for positive assurance of conformity); Art. 10—Information About Technical Regulations, Standards and Conformity Assessment Procedures; Art. 11—Technical Assistance to Other Members; Art. 12—Special and Differential Treatment of Developing Country Members; Art. 13—The Committee on Technical Barriers to Trade; Art. 14—Consultation and Dispute Settlement; Art. 15—Final Provisions. Annex 1 to TBT contains Terms and their Definitions for the Purpose of this Agreement; Annex 2—Technical Expert Groups established under Art. 14; Annex 3—Code of Good practice for the Preparation, Adoption and Application of Standards.

[29] TBT, Art. 5.

[30] TBT, Art. 5.1.1.

[31] TBT, Art. 5.1.2.

[32] TBT, Art. 5.2.1.

[33] See ISO website at www.iso.org.

aid the productivity, competitiveness and export capabilities of the developing countries. Probably the best-known series of ISO standardisation and compliance auditing programmes are for the overall management of organisations and establishment of quality assurance management programmes[34], and for management of the environmental effects of an organisation's activities.[35] However, ISO also develops and publishes standards in many different areas, including the oil and gas industries, steam turbines, cryogenic vessels, multimedia applications (MPEG standards), and end-to-end digital television systems (ISO/IEC 16500:1999).[36]

The IEC is the other international standards body nominated in the TBT Agreement. Most countries of the world are members of IEC. Their national committees contribute two-thirds of the budget for IEC. They represent the electrotechnical interests of their countries' industry, commerce, government, scientific and professional bodies. IEC was founded in 1904 at the International Electrical Congress in St Louis, USA. Its original brief was to encourage international standardisation of "nomenclature and ratings of electrical apparatus". By the late 1930s the Commission had published international standards for many kinds of electrical equipment and components, their safety, ratings and symbols. Today IEC standards extend to information technology and business equipment and robotics. IEC and ISO work in collaboration, so that, jointly, under the brief accorded them by the GATT Agreement,[37] they oversee and co-ordinate the standardisation of the entire range of products, technologies and processes in the developed and developing worlds.

Central Government Standard-Setting: Code of Practice

In the WTO/GATT system all central government bodies are obligated to accept and 6–12
comply with a code of good practice concerning standardisation.[38] The Code of Good Practice for the Preparation, Adoption and Application of Standards provides for notification of a standardising body's acceptance of, or withdrawal from, the Code via ISO/IEC in Geneva. The Code requires treatment of products of any WTO Member to be no less favourable than products of national origin, there must be no unnecessary obstacles to international trade, use of international standards where possible, involvement in international standardising bodies, standards based on performance rather than design characteristics, and periodic publication of standards preparation programmes.

Local Government and Non-Governmental Bodies' Codes of Practice

With regard to local government and non-governmental standardising bodies, the GATT 6–13
Agreement on Technical Barriers to Trade provides that Members "[S]hall take such reasonable measures as may be available to them to ensure that local government and non-governmental standardising bodies. . .accept and comply with this Code of Good

34 ISO 9000 series.

35 ISO 14000 series.

36 ISO Annual Report, 1999.

37 TBT, Annex 1, "Terms and their Definitions for the Purpose of this Agreement"; Annex 3, "Code of Good Practice for the Preparation, Adoption and Application of Standards"; "Decision on Proposed Understanding on WTO-ISO Standards Information System"; and "Decision on Review of the ISO/IEC Information Centre Publication." See *The Results of the Uruguay Round of Multilateral Trade Negotiations—The Legal Texts* (GATT Secretariat, Geneva, 1994), pp. 138 *et seq.*

38 TBT, Annex 3.

Practice."[39] In the years following the Tokyo Round, strenuous but unsuccessful efforts were made, by the European Community in particular, to have a Code formally incorporated for non-governmental bodies (NGOs).[40] But conformity to the Code, for non-central government standardising bodies, remains beyond the direct reach of the GATT provisions. Applicability of Codes of Practice to such bodies is on a "best-effort" basis. This situation has been criticised because both local government and non-governmental standard-setting institutions wield substantial economic influence, which is felt in most areas of commercial activity.

Non-Governmental Standard-Setting Bodies

6–14 Under the GATT/TBT Agreement, Members are to "take such reasonable measures as may be available to them" to ensure that non-governmental bodies within their territories which operate conformity assessment procedures comply with the provisions of Articles 5 and 6.[41] This language stops short of an outright requirement and may be construed as acknowledging a measure of self-regulation, or regulation by the local Member, of its domestic non-government standard-setting bodies. Operation by non-governmental bodies' of conformity assessment procedures may be relied upon by Members only if such bodies comply with the provisions of Article 5 and 6. However, provided central government bodies do not rely on conformity assessment procedures operated by such non-governmental bodies, the obligation to notify proposed conformity assessment procedures does not apply to them.[42]

WTO Relations with Non-Governmental Organisations

6–15 Under Article V(2) of the Marrakesh Agreement, which established the WTO "the General Council may make appropriate arrangements for consultation and co-operation with non-governmental organisations concerned with matters related to those of the WTO". In its General Council Decision of July 18, 1996, the WTO recognised the role NGOs can play in increasing the awareness of the public in respect of WTO activities and decided on guidelines for its relations with NGOs.[43] Members resolved to improve transparency[44] and develop communication with NGOs by ensuring more information and documents about WTO activities would be made available by derestricting and

[39] TBT, Art. 4.

[40] See Stewart, *op. cit.*, pp. 1076–1078.

[41] TBT, Art. 8.1. Arts 5 and 6 lay down procedures for conformity assessment and its recognition by central government bodies.

[42] *ibid.*

[43] WT/L/162. Between October 2, 2000 and January 26, 2001, NGO Position Papers received by the Secretariat of WTO, circulated for the information of Members, included, among others, *Statement on Electronic Commerce* (Confederation of Asia and Pacific Chambers of Commerce and Industries), *Developing Countries and the Multilateral Trade System* (European Chemical Industry Council); *Priorities for WTO Agriculture* (Food and Drink Federation); and *WTO Negotiations for Liberalizing Trade in Services* (Keidanren/Japan Services Network). Between January 26, 2001, and April 26, 2001, NGO Position Papers received included *Paper on the proposed Regulation laying down the General Principles and Requirements of Food Law, establishing the European Food Authority and laying down procedures in matters of Food Safety* (E.U. Committee of the American Chamber of Commerce in Belgium); *Paper regarding the draft Directive on invoicing* (European e-business Tax Group); *World Trade Organization (WTO) Negotiations on agriculture* (European Union of Alcohol Producers—UEPA); and *Position préliminaire de l'UNICE sur l'Antidumping en vue d'un nouveau cycle de négociations commerciales multilatérales à l'OMC* (Union of Industrial and Employers' Confederation of Europe -UNICE). These and other NGO position papers are at www.wto.org.

[44] See para. 6–03, above.

publishing more promptly than in the past. To enhance this process the WTO Secretariat makes available an online computer network the material on which is accessible to the public, including derestricted documents.

Nevertheless, since the WTO is both a legally binding intergovernmental treaty of rights and obligations among its Members and a forum for negotiations, NGOs cannot be directly involved in the work of the WTO or its meetings. Furthermore, chairpersons of WTO councils and committees who participate in discussions or meetings with NGOs do so in their personal capacity unless that particular council or committee decides otherwise.

2 THE E.U. FRAMEWORK

The E.U.: Product Conformity Assessment Standards and Mandatory Marking

Operation of the single market of the E.U. is predicated on the fundamental principle of free movement of goods across national boundaries as required under Articles 28–30 (ex 30–36) of the Treaty of Rome. Implementation of the principle requires that goods be subject to a mutually acceptable and recognised conformity assessment approach in all Member States. To achieve this goal of mutual recognition the E.U. supports a program of harmonisation of technical regulations and standards applicable to a number of industrial product categories. The legislative mechanism used to drive harmonisation of standards is the promulgation of Directives. Unlike an E.U. Regulation, a Directive is not self-executing and its provisions must be implemented in the domestic legislation of each Member State.[45] The so-called New Approach Directives stipulate essential requirements that products must meet, creating, as declared by the Commission: **6–16**

> [c]onditions which will enable the principle of mutual recognition of proofs of conformity to operate in both the regulatory and the non-regulatory sphere.[46]

It is this mutual recognition of acceptability among all Member States that provides the overarching rationale for mandatory use of a single conformity mark, the "CE" mark, on many categories of goods.

European Harmonised Standards

Under mandates originating in the European Commission, recommended harmonised technical standards (EN standards) are either drawn up or adopted from pre-existing national standards (frequently British Standards Institution standards) for use in conjunction with the New Approach Directives. Products manufactured to the recommended technical standards automatically conform to the essential requirements. If **6–17**

---

[45] Alternatives to the traditional ways of implementing E.U. legislation are included in the Commission's White Paper on European Governance COM(2001) 428 final, July 25, 2001. Among other approaches, the White Paper contains proposals for defining criteria for creation of new autonomous E.U. regulatory agencies and initiatives for "co-regulation", which provides for a more cooperative approach between regulators and industry, and enforcement of a fair trading Directive by use of standardisation. See also B. Sheridan, "Understanding Alternative Regulation", Global Counsel, February 2001. p. 21 *et seq.*

[46] Council Resolution of December 21, 1989 on a global approach to conformity assessment [1990] O.J. C10/1.

products do not conform to the recommended technical standards, the manufacturer carries the burden of showing conformity to the essential requirements of the relevant Directive. While the New Approach focuses on the voluntary nature of compliance with European harmonised standards compliance with the essential health and safety requirements set forth in a given directive is always mandatory. Furthermore, where a directive does directly refer to an EN standard it is *de facto* mandatory.[47]

Mandatory Marking in the E.U. Single Market

6–18 As indicated in the foregoing, conformity with the essential requirements of the applicable New Approach Directives is compulsory. The manufacturer, or his representative in the E.U., must issue an E.C. Declaration of Conformity and affix a prescribed mark, the CE mark, to the product to signify conformity with, at least, the essential requirements of the applicable directives.[48] The mark *may* additionally signify third party certified conformity with the recommended standards, where the third party is a competent or notified body, depending on the type of product.

The New Approach was born out of the lack of progress that had become self-evident by the late 1970s towards creation of what could truly be called a single European market. In some spheres, such as cosmetics, absolute harmonisation requiring mandatory compliance to Community-wide regulations had been introduced. However, in other sectors, a two-tier system operated under which a manufacturer could elect to conform to Community-wide regulations, in which case his products could be admitted into all Member States, or he could conform to the regulations of individual Member States' regulations, and so settle for access to correspondingly fewer Member States. Thus, for example, manufacturers of industrial machinery were faced with the choice of forgoing access to some Member States or carrying out modifications to meet the technical standards of those States. This led to the promulgation of the "Machinery Directive", Article 8(1) of which requires that

> the manufacturer or his authorized representative established in the Community must, in order to certify that machinery and safety components are in conformity with this Directive, draw up for all machinery or safety components manufactured an EC declaration of conformity based on the model given in Annex II(A) or (C) as appropriate.
>
> In addition, for machinery alone, the manufacturer or his authorized representative established in the Community must affix to the machine the CE marking referred to in Article 10.[49]

All Member States effect legislation implementing Directives in national law, thereby making obligatory the affixing of the CE mark on all products covered by the Directive

[47] Such a reference to a specified standard may be justified by the Commission on grounds of necessity to assure public health and safety, or protection of the environment.

[48] The CE Marking Directives, their reference numbers and dates of commencement of mandatory marking are: Simple Pressure Vessels 87/404, July 1, 1992; Safety of Toys 88/378, January 1, 1990; Construction Products 89/106, June 27, 1991; Electromagnetic Compatibility 89/336, January 1, 1996; Safety of Machinery 89/392, January 1, 1995 (now 98/37); Personal Protection Equipment 89/686, July 1, 1992; Lifts 95/16, June 30, 1999; Non-automatic Weighing Instruments 90/384, January 1, 2003; Medical Devices 93/42, June 14, 1998; Active Implantable Medical Devices 90/385, January 1, 1995; Low Voltage 73/23, January 1, 1997; Gas Appliances 90/396, January 1, 1996; Telecommunications Terminal Equipment 91/263, November 6, 1992; New Hot Water Boilers Fired with Liquid & Gaseous Fluids 92/42, January 1, 1998; Equipment and Protective Systems for Use in Explosive Atmospheres 94/9, July 1, 2003; Pressure Equipment 97/23, May 29, 2002; Explosives for Civil Use 93/15, December 31, 2002; and Recreational Craft 94/25, June 30, 1998.

[49] Dir. 89/392 of June 14, 1989 [1989] O.J. L183/9 as last amended by Dirs 91/368 [1991] O.J. L198/16, 93/44 [1993] O.J. L175/12 and 93/68 [1993] O.J. L220/1. The original Directive and all the amending Directives have now been combined into a single Directive, namely, Dir 98/37 of June 22, 1998 on the approximation of the laws of the Member States relating to machinery [1998] O.J. L207/1. This is merely a consolidation and does not change the law in any way.

that are placed on the market or taken into service within the E.U. Harmonisation provided by the Directive is only to the degree necessary for meeting *essential* requirements for safety of machinery, in accordance with the minimum standards principle.

The Information Directive

6–19 Among the problems that prevented progress towards harmonisation were the lack of a legal requirement for mutual notification of regulations to be promulgated by Member States. In addition, there were difficulties in conformity assessment in the face of non-harmonised technical regulations throughout the E.U. The problem of mutual notification was addressed in the so-called "Information Directive" of 1983, which required Member States' new regulations to be notified to the E.C. and so to all Member States.[50] Notified regulations are examined by a committee consisting of Member States and the Commission. Where there are potential conflicts between a proposed national regulation and E.C. regulations, Member States' relevant ministries and standards bodies, the Commission and the European standards bodies are all invited to comment. The Commission is empowered to propose measures to deal with possible violations of Community law arising from conflicting national and Community regulations.

Scope of "technical specification" and "technical regulation" under the Information Directive

6–20 Questions of interpretation of the scope of the terms "technical specification" and "technical regulation" under the Information Directive[51] have been referred to the ECJ. In *Bic Beneleux SA v. Belgian State*[52] the ECJ had to decide if the Belgian Government's mandatory requirement to affix a distinctive sign on disposable razors subject to an environmental damage tax constituted technical specifications or technical regulations within the meaning of Articles 1(1) and 1(5) of the Directive. The Belgian Government's position was that the duty to notify applies only to marking requirements implementing a technical standard which is capable of constituting an obstacle to free movement of goods (across national boundaries). However, the court held that according to Article

[50] The "Information Directive" (83/189 of March 28, 1983) lays down a procedure for the provision of information in the field of technical standards and regulations ([1983] O.J. L109/8 as amended by Council Directive 88/182 of March 22, 1988 [1988] O.J. L81/75 and European Parliament and Council Directive 94/10 of March 23, 1994 [1994] O.J. L100/3). Thus, for example, when the U.K. Motor Cycles (Protective Helmets) Regulations 1998, which came into force on August 21, 1998, required helmets "to bear an approved certification mark of an approved body attesting to compliance with British Standard 6658/1985 as amended or to any other standard accepted by an EEA state which offers in use equivalent safety, suitability and fitness of purpose", the requirement was duly notified to the European Commission. It should also be noted that under the WTO/GATT TBT Agreement, Art. 2.11, WTO Members must ensure that all technical regulations issued which have been adopted by central government bodies are published promptly or otherwise made available in such a manner as to enable interested parties in other Members to become acquainted with them.

[51] Art. 1(1) of the directive defines "technical specification" as "a specification contained in a document which lays down the characteristics of a product such as levels of quality, performance, safety or dimensions, including the requirements applicable to the product as regards terminology, symbols, testing and test methods, packaging, marking or labelling and the production methods and procedures for agricultural products as defined in Article 38(1) of the Treaty. . ." Art. 1(5) of the directive defines "technical regulation" as "technical specifications, including the relevant administrative provisions, the observance of which is compulsory, *de jure* or *de facto*, in the case of marketing or use in a Member State or a major part thereof, except those laid down by local authorities."

[52] Case C–13/96 [1997] E.C.R. 1753.

1(5) the marking requirement constituted "a *de jure* technical regulation in that 'its observance. . .is compulsory. . .in the case of marketing' of the product concerned and in that it is, according to the definition given in Article 1(1), a technical specification, since the enactment defines 'the characteristics required of a product such as . . .the requirements applicable to the product as regards. . .marking or labelling'."

In *Criminal Proceedings against Roelf Donkersteeg*, the alleged failure by the Netherlands Government to notify technical specifications or regulations pursuant to the Information Directive was used as a defence against conviction for failing to provide footware disinfecting facilities and have pigs on the defendant's agricultural holding vaccinated, as required by Netherlands legislation.[53] Finding for the Netherlands Government, the ECJ held that no production methods or procedures for agricultural products were laid down within the meaning of the Directive. The requirements of the Netherlands law at issue were held not to be a technical specification for the purposes of the Directive.

Minimum Requirements and Mutual Recognition Within the E.U. Single Market

6–21 The New Approach provided the means for remedying the problem of non-harmonised technical regulations, which amounted to a lack of mutual recognition of conformity assessment among the Member States. The New Approach is founded on the twin principles of minimum essential requirements for product conformity and E.U. Member States' obligatory mutual recognition of conformity assessment.[54] Regarding the first principle, the minimum essential requirements are those necessary to protect consumers and are the only requirements justifying restriction of access of goods to a Member State market. It is not the E.U. legislators' function to prescribe details not deemed essential to protect consumer health and safety. More detailed, harmonised standards are developed by a specially created standardisation body. Compliance with such standards is prima facie compliance with the essential requirements.

As to the second principle, mutual recognition implies that where there is no harmonised European standard, conformity to the standard of any one Member State's standard is acceptable for the product to gain admission to one or all other Member States. Prior to the New Approach, differing mandatory requirements and technical standards among Member States had constituted barriers to trade. However, with the establishment of the principle of mutual recognition came the intriguing possibility of regulatory competition among Member States. This perception is predicated on the reasonable notion that business and industry are attracted to the more favourable regulatory regimes. Realisation of the single European market thus entails striking a balance between harmonisation and regulatory competition among Member States. The correct balance can only be struck if there is mutual trust among the regulators of

---

[53] ECJ Case C–37/99, Opinion of Advocate General Fennelly, 6 April 2000; Judgment of the Court (Sixth Chamber), November 16, 2000.

[54] These principles emerged out of the 1979 ECJ judgement in the celebrated *Cassis de Dijon* case (Judgment of February 20, 1979, Case 120/78 [1979] E.C.R. 649). In this case, the ECJ ruled against a German government prohibition on importation of alcoholic beverages containing less than the 25% minimum alcohol content required by the German standard. Conformity to French standards, meant, in the ECJ's view, there could be no valid reason to exclude the low alcohol cassis beverage from any other Member State. The court also held that trade barriers were allowed only to satisfy mandatory requirements relating to, amongst other things, public health. Since *Cassis de Dijon*, when public health is an issue and import prohibitions are justified, the Commission provides *minimum standards* in the form of a Directive.

Member States to assure adherence to minimum E.U. requirements in matters under their national jurisdiction.

E.U. Conformity Assessment Procedures

Some of the marking directives distinguish between different categories of products in relation to their conformity assessment procedures. For some categories, the "self-certification" procedure is sufficient to allow the obligatory CE mark to be affixed. However, there may be other categories or product types which are subject to special rules. Such products are commonly considered to involve a higher health and safety risk, and therefore require some level of third-party involvement in their health and safety clearance for the market. **6–22**

A manufacturer wishing to affix the CE mark to a product that is subject to these special rules, when it does not fully comply with European harmonised standards covering the essential safety requirements, must submit the product for so-called "type examination" by a notified body, which examines the product in the light of an expert's report.[55] A "notified body" is a third party accredited as competent to perform conformity assessment specific to a given Directive or Directives and which has been designated by a Member State as a body meeting the criteria for competence and notified to the European Commission.

Principle of Notification

Notified bodies carry out tasks pertaining to certain conformity assessment procedures under the applicable New Approach Directives where a third party assessment is required.[56] Responsibility for notification rests with the Member States, who may choose from the bodies under their jurisdiction. A body seeking notification must be assessed and accredited for technical competence and capability of carrying out the conformity assessment procedures in question. Competence and capability are deemed reflected in, among other things, availability of technically competent personnel and suitable equipment, independence, impartiality, integrity and civil liability insurance coverage.[57] Notified bodies are free to offer any type of certification and markings where the products are intended for the markets of third countries, for example in the context of mutual recognition agreements. **6–23**

Where notified bodies are concerned, the Commission views conformity with a particular series of European harmonised standards, the EN 45000 series, and accreditation, as important instruments to help in establishing conformity of a body with the requirements of the applicable directive. The EN 45000 standards comprise parts dealing with organisation and management of the body and parts concerning technical requirements. Standard EN 45004 specifies general criteria for the competence of bodies

---

[55] See para. 6–23, below. This procedure applies for products cited in Annex IV of the Safety of Machinery Directive (see n. 48, above).

[56] Under certain New Approach directives the body may be called by another name, for example inspection body (Directives relating to simple pressure vessels and construction products), a testing laboratory and a certification body (Directives relating to construction products). It is irrelevant whether the body calls itself a laboratory, a certification body or an inspection body as long as it carries out the tasks in the conformity assessment procedure and has technical ability to do so in an independent and impartial way. See n. 57, below.

[57] See Guide to the implementation of directives based on the New Approach and the Global Approach", edited by the European Commission, Chap. 6, at www.europa.eu.int/comm/enterprise/newapproach/newapproach.htm.

performing inspection. In the term "inspection" are included examination of a product design, product, service, process or plant and determination of its conformity with specific requirements or, on the basis of professional judgment, general requirements. Under EN 45011, product certification by a notified body "entails assurance that a product conforms to specific requirements such as standards, regulations, specifications or other normative documents."

Accreditation of United Kingdom Notified Bodies

6–24 In the United Kingdom, the United Kingdom Accreditation Service (UKAS), under a memorandum of understanding with the Standards and Technical Regulations Directorate of the Department of Trade and Industry (DTI), is recognised as the sole body for the accreditation of certification, testing and inspection bodies to the EN45000 standards. Incorporated in 1995, UKAS is a not-for-profit company, limited by guarantee, which accredits bodies that certify, test and inspect companies' systems and products.[58] UKAS is licensed by DTI to use and confer the national accreditation marks which symbolise Government recognition of conformity assessment services.[59] UKAS-accredited certification bodies and companies registered by UKAS-accredited certification bodies are listed in the United Kingdom Register of Quality Assessed Companies, published by the Stationery Office. Accreditation is not normally offered to organisations outside the United Kingdom. Maintenance of accreditation is confirmed on an annual basis by surveillance visits, with a full re-assessment every fourth year.

6–25 UKAS-accredited bodies are entitled to use accreditation marks in connection with their accredited activities, provided they adhere to the regulations governing use of the marks, which comprise the Royal Crown. The Crown signifies government backing, through the DTI, for UKAS in its role as the sole national accreditation body. The Department of Trade and Industry has licensed UKAS to use the marks and to sub-license their use to UKAS-accredited bodies. It is UKAS's responsibility to ensure compliance to the rules for the use of marks, rules which are laid down by the Lord Chamberlain.[60]

The Same Mark is Applied to Many Classes of Product

6–26 Within the E.U., a single mark, the CE mark, is applied to, and suffices for, many classes of products placed on the market or taken into service within the E.U. This one mark thus has a far wider reach than each of the mandatory marks required, for example, by

---

[58] See www.dti.gov.uk/strd/certify.htm.

[59] Information on UKAS and accredited organisations is available from the UKAS website at www.ukas.org.uk.

[60] The Secretary of State for Trade and Industry is the registrant for, and licenses use of, UKAS design and word service marks comprising the Royal Crown, in international classes 35, 41 and 42, including UKAS, UKAS TESTING, UKAS ENVIRONMENTAL MANAGEMENT, UKAS INFORMATION SECURITY MANAGEMENT, UKAS INSPECTION, UKAS TESTING, UKAS UNITED KINGDOM ACCREDITATION SERVICE, UKAS PERSONNEL CERTIFICATION, UKAS PRODUCT CERTIFICATION and UKAS QUALITY MANAGEMENT. The registrations in class 35 are for: Business consultancy and business advisory services in connection with the accreditation of the competence of organisations in the fields of certification of systems, products and personnel. Registrations in class 41 cover: Training and education services in connection with the accreditation of the competence of organisations in the fields of certification of systems, products and personnel. Registrations in class 42 are for: Accreditation of the competence of organisations in the fields of certification of systems, products and personnel. www.ukas.com/new_docs/accredit-marks.htm.

government agencies in the U.S. For it to be acceptable, the CE mark must be distinct from other inscriptions on the machinery and large enough to be clearly visible (5mm minimum height).[61] Affixing of other marks, such as the manufacturer's logo or an optional quality mark is not prohibited. However, marks having shapes or meanings which could be confused with the CE mark are prohibited.

Is the CE Mark a Certification Mark?

One question that arises from the foregoing is whether or not the CE mark is a certification mark. It appears that sometimes the mark is, and sometimes it is not, in effect a certification mark, depending upon the circumstances under which it is used. Certainly, access to the mark is open to all qualified products as must be a certification mark; indeed there are penalties for the failure to affix the CE mark when its use is mandated. Where, as for most classes of products, there is no legal requirement for third-party examination of the product or its technical file, and self-declaration of conformity is all that is required, the mark may be considered not to rise to the status of a certification mark. However, where, before affixing the CE mark, a manufacturer either elects or is required to submit his product for an expert's report, and the technical file is submitted to an accredited body for evaluation against the requirements of applicable directives, the CE mark appears to have attributes of a certification mark, albeit without any identifiable owner. **6–27**

European Standards Bodies

The European Commission or EFTA Secretariat can initiate promulgation of a European technical standard where required to accompany the enactment of a new directive. Responsibility for developing European standards is vested by the Commission in three nominally independent bodies, which are CEN (Comité Européen de Normalisation), CENELEC (Comité Européen de Normalisation Electrotechnique) and ETSI (European Telecommunications Standards Institute). The first two of these bodies existed before the New Approach was adopted by the Council of the E.C. in 1985. ETSI was created in 1987. These three bodies interact closely with ISO,[62] IEC and ITU-T (the International Telecommunication Union Telecommunications Sector).[63] Such interaction is directed in large part to ensuring that the Commission is fully cognisant of standards developed outside its own territory in order to ensure compatibility between such standards and the E.U.'s own standards. **6–28**

In the CEN/CENELEC process of producing standards, drafts are prepared by a technical committee and submitted to the national committees for comment. The technical committees then take account of the comments they receive to produce a final draft, which is then distributed for voting. Members' votes are weighted according to the size of the countries they represent. Larger countries, such as Germany, France, Italy and the United Kingdom each have ten votes, whereas smaller countries have one or two votes. A majority of national committees must be in favour of the standard.

CEN is an international association, incorporated under Belgian law. The National Members of CEN are standards bodies of the E.U., EFTA and the Czech Republic.[64] In

[61] See Amendment to Dir. 89/336 [1993] O.J. L220/7.
[62] See para. 6–29, below.
[63] See generally Brian Rothery, *Standards and Certification in Europe* (Gower, Aldershot, 1996).
[64] BSI (the British Standards Institution) is the designated body for the U.K.

addition there are several European consumer, trade and industry associations that have Associate Member status.[65] One of CEN's declared strategic objectives is to achieve a "coherent approach to conformity assessment and to certification marks at European level).[66] CENELEC, also incorporated under Belgian law as a non-profit organisation, was instituted in 1973. Its responsibilities are similar to those of CEN, but for standards in the fields of electrotechnology.[67] CEN is officially recognised as the European Standards Organisation in its field by the European Commission.[68] ETSI is an independent organisation comprising more than 200 telecommunications equipment manufacturers (the largest single membership category), about 70 public network operators, national standards bodies, users, service providers and research bodies. The ETSI voting structure is somewhat different from CEN/CENELEC. Elaboration, approval and implementation of European standards and structural changes to ETSI itself require a 71 per cent majority weighted vote by national delegations. Other decisions are based on weighted voting by all full members.[69]

Technical Co-operation Between GATT/TBT-Nominated Standardisation Bodies and their E.U. Counterparts

6–29 Two important agreements on technical co-operation, the Vienna Agreement and the Dresden Agreement, were concluded in the 1990s between the GATT/TBT-nominated standardisation bodies, namely ISO and IEC, and their respective E.U. counterparts, CEN and CENELEC. These agreements are important not only because they expedite the establishment of a common standards base and production of harmonised standards within Europe, but also because they provide a formal mechanism for drawing on European standards work and promoting its acceptance worldwide. Through the agreements the acknowledged world standards bodies can draw on standards developed in Europe and promote them for adoption throughout the world, and vice versa. Co-operation between ISO and CEN is the subject of the Vienna Agreement, concluded in 1991.[70] The corresponding IEC-CENELEC agreement is the Dresden Agreement, which came into effect in September 1996.[71] The objectives of such agreements are to make the standards development process more efficient, quicker and more international through sharing plans for the development of new standards and the institution of parallel voting on proposed standards at international and European levels.

---

[65] Examples are ANEC (European Association for the Co-operation of Consumer Representation in Standardization), CEFIC (European Chemical Industry Council) and other organisations specific to the machine tool, medical device, and construction industries. The 1999 annual budget for the CEN Management Centre was 10.64 M EUR, of which 46% was provided by membership fees and 41% from the European Commission. For further details see the CEN website at www.cen.be.

[66] *ibid.*

[67] CENELEC website at www.server.cenelec.be.

[68] Dir. 83/189.

[69] R. Bekkers and I. Liotard, "European Standards for Mobile Communications: The Tense Relationship between Standards and Intellectual Property Rights" [1999] E.I.P.R. 110 at 113.

[70] Formally known as the Agreement on Technical Co-operation between the International Organisation for Standardisation (ISO) and CEN, the Agreement was approved on June 27, 1991 in Vienna by the CEN Administrative Board following its approval by the ISO Executive Board at its meeting on May 16 and 17, 1991 in Geneva. For the text of the Agreement see the ISO website at www.iso.org.

[71] The Dresden Agreement is the successor to the Lugano Agreement of 1991.

The Vienna Agreement

6–30

The Vienna Agreement provides for substantive exchanges and sharing of information, including work programmes, proposed standards and texts of draft standards, between ISO and CEN technical committees and subcommittees and joint participation at committee meetings. The Agreement provides a mechanism whereby CEN, as a body whose members (with the exception of Luxembourg) are also members of ISO, can opt to transfer the development of a given standard to ISO. The Agreement is reciprocal in nature and is based on equal rights. Therefore, CEN is not compelled to use ISO work products for its own standard-setting activities, such as those mandated by the European Commission.

Co-operation between ISO and CEN can extend from planning and sharing of plans for new standards to the outright deferral of one body to the other in the substantive committee work of development of a new standard. Where there is a common ISO-CEN interest in seeing a particular standard developed, either ISO or CEN is free to lead the work, although in practice CEN would defer to ISO. As an example, the CEN Technical Committee on Lasers and Laser-related Equipment, CEN/TC 123, has recently decided to disband the working groups in its organisation because the work was being done by the ISO Technical Committee for Electro-optical Systems, ISO/TC 172/SC.[72]

The Dresden Agreement

In addition to its co-operation provisions, the Dresden Agreement between IEC and CENELEC requires IEC to have the right of first refusal for standards development work proposed in CENELEC. Thus CENELEC will initiate standards development only in exceptional cases, where, for example, work by IEC would entail too long a timeframe for a standard to issue, or would not be likely to succeed because of inherent technical, legislative, or commercial differences between regions. Where IEC exercises its right to undertake the work of development of a CENELEC-proposed standard, CENELEC must cease its work on the project. If IEC decides not to take up the project, CENELEC will proceed while keeping IEC, and through IEC, the IEC's non-European members, informed monthly of progress. The final draft of a CENELEC-developed standard (*i.e.* an EN, or "European Norm") must be offered to the IEC as a Committee Draft for Vote but the final decision as to the content of the EN rests with CENELEC. 6–31

Illustrative of the results of deferral of the standardisation process pursuant to the Dresden Agreement is the situation in the field of laser safety, where, nearly all the working groups at the European level, under the CENELEC Technical Committee for Optical Radiation Safety and Laser Equipment, CENELEC/TC 76, continue to exist but are no longer active, having deferred to the international level through the counterpart IEC Committee IEC/TC 76. However, CENELEC reserves the right to take over an IEC project if agreed desirable, for example, in the face of unsatisfactory progress. A case in point is the development of a standard for laser safety training, which was handed over to working group WG4 of CENELEC/TC 76, following a decision by IEC/TC 76 not to pursue the work.[73]

---

[72] See "International vs. European Standards" at website of Technical University of Vienna, www.tuwien.ac.at/islt/tmp/section 6/6_1_5.htm.

[73] *ibid*. The text of the Dresden Agreement is at the IEC website www.iec.ch/cenelec.htm.

Standard-Setting by Individual Companies and Consortia

6–32 Official standards promulgated by government or government-nominated and accredited bodies in a consensus-building process, must be distinguished from standards that emerge from the activities of individual companies or groups of companies in the course of their technology development programmes. Thus many important standards are generated not as formal standards directly sponsored by government but as the result of collaboration between companies in a particular industry sector without involvement of central or local government bodies.

In some cases, companies organise as a trade or industry association that, among other things, may set industry standards. Membership of such an association must be open to all parties meeting the requirements for membership, which must be reasonable and non-discriminatory. However, in other cases, standards, particularly interoperability standards for computers, electronic appliances and communications products, may emerge from the technical development initiatives of a single company or a small group of companies. The membership of an industry standard-setting group, often constituted out of business considerations accompanied by a need to access important technology through intellectual property pooling, may form only a small percentage of companies in the sector. Where the emerging standards achieve significant market penetration and are adopted by the sector as a whole they are known as *de facto* or "proprietary" standards. The emergence may be preceded by several years of competition between rival standards, during which time market growth is delayed as purchases are deferred pending resolution of the contest. Examples of *de facto* standards are the Intel-owned standard for microprocessor technology, which is backed by its patent estate, and the VHS videocassette standard.

6–33 Major market advantages can inure to the firm or consortium that generates a standard which embodies intellectual property rights and acquires the status of a *de facto* standard. Once such a standard emerges, manufacturers' products must conform or be denied a realistic competing role in the marketplace. If their products are not interoperable with those of the standard-setting company or companies, they are effectively ousted from the market. The problem has received relentless government, public and judicial attention in recent years, especially in relation to the telecommunications[74] and computer industries.

Ownership of the *de facto* standard PC operating system has been said to be largely responsible for Microsoft's market power. This market power has been maintained through copyright in software and contractual arrangements including tying arrangements, free product offerings, and exclusionary licensing and marketing practices,[75] determined by the United States courts to be restrictive of trade.[76] In what was probably

[74] For a comprehensive review of the tensions between standards and intellectual property rights in the European communications sector see R. Bekkers and I. Liotard, "European Standards for Mobile Communications: The Tense Relationship between Standards and Intellectual Property Rights" [1999] E.I.P.R. 110.

[75] See nn. 76 and 78, below. See also M.A. O'Rourke, "Striking a Delicate Balance: Intellectual Property, Antitrust, Contract, and Standardization in the Computer Industry", 12 Harvard Journal of Law & Technology, 2 (1998). Microsoft was found to have offered uniform license agreements to the 20 largest original equipment manufacturers (OEMs), allowed OEMs to modify its operating system, disclosed application programming interfaces, communications interfaces and technical information to OEMs, independent software vendors, and independent hardware vendors, in violation of the U.S. Sherman Act, ss.1 and 2.

[76] *United States v. Microsoft Corporation*, 84 F.Supp.2d, 9 (findings of fact); 87 F.Supp. 2d, 30 (conclusions of law); and 97 F.Supp.2d, 59 (2000), (entry of appropriate relief for violations of Sherman Act, §§ 1 and 2, as amended, 15 U.S.C.A. and various state laws).

the most important antitrust case since *United States v. American Telephone & Telegraph Co.*,[77] Microsoft Corporation, as manufacturer of a PC operating system, internet web browser and applications, was held to have maintained its monopoly power in the operating system market by anti-competitive means, attempted to monopolise the web browser market and tied illegally its operating system to its web browser. As a result, the appropriate remedy was deemed to be conduct modification and structural reorganisation, under which there would be separation of Microsoft's operating systems and applications businesses.[78] Microsoft was banned *inter alia* from taking adverse actions against original equipment manufacturers who supported similar products made by Microsoft's competitors.

E.U. Policy on Intellectual Property Rights in Standards

The owner of an intellectual property right vested in a standard may license third parties in respect of the right, thereby permitting manufacture and access to the standard in question. However, what happens if the rightholder is informed of a formal standard-setting body's wish to base a standard on the rightholder's technology? The *de facto* standard, which is likely to be a commercially successful standard, is thus a candidate for conversion into a formal standard. Clearly the agreement of the rightholder to license the technology must be sought if the process of promulgating the formal standard is to continue, but under what terms? The European Commission's policy on this issue is less than clear cut. On one hand the Commission acknowledges the freedom of the rightholder to refuse to license and regards such freedom as absolute, since his exclusive intellectual property rights cannot be subject to expropriation or compulsory licensing except in exceptional circumstances.[79] Furthermore the Commission recognises that **6–34**

> [I]f the rightholder is to be satisfied that his investment in research and development can be adequately recovered, he would expect the royalty rate to relate in some way to the normal freely-negotiated

[77] 552 F.Supp. 131 (1982), affirmed as *Maryland v. United States*, 460 U.S. 1001 (1983).

[78] Much of the United States Government's case against Microsoft was premised tacitly on consumer reliance on interconnection within a network. The economic implications of anticompetitive conduct in cultivating, sustaining and developing a networked clientele are of major importance in cases such as *Microsoft*. So-called "network externalities", benefits that accrue increasingly to users and stakeholders as the size of the network increases, play a key role in the anticompetitive analysis. The archetypal case is that of the average telephone user's demand for access, which grows with the network. Where there is no interoperability or compatibility standard operative for "seamless" communication between networks, consumers tend to opt for linkage within the network having the greatest number of subscribers. As a result, subscribers can find themselves "locked-in" to one particular network. Lock-in also creates a technical barrier to entry of rival network operators into the market, since they are disadvantaged when trying to accumulate sufficient subscribers to assure growth of the rival network. For a discussion of network externalities and the appropriateness of antitrust divestiture as a remedy for anticompetitive conduct in networked industries. See G.J. Werden, "Network Effects and Conditions of Entry: Lessons from the Microsoft Case," 69 Antitrust Law Journal 87 (2001), and H.A. Shelanski and J.G. Sidak, "Antitrust Divestiture in Network Industries", 68 The University of Chicago Law Review, 1 (2001). For arguments that a positive effect on consumer welfare can arise from lock-in and single firm dominance of a product which serves as a platform, see Orin G. Hatch, "Antitrust in the Digital Age," in *Competition, Innovation and the Microsoft Monopoly: Antitrust in the Digital Marketplace*, J.A. Eisenach and T.M. Lenard eds., (Kluwer, Norwell, 1999), p. 23. Hatch says that where there is domination of the market for a platform product "—one to which other software developers will write their programs—that firm creates a *de facto* standard, a uniform platform. Software developers thus are not faced with the cost, in terms of time and resources, to develop applications that run across a variety of platforms." This, according to Hatch, can significantly boost "productivity and innovation."

[79] Intellectual Property Rights and Standardization, COM (92) 445 at para. 4.3.5. Examples of exceptional circumstances are "reasons of national security or over-riding public interest."

> commercial rate, allowing for the greatly increased market for his technology which standardisation will bring.[80]

On the other hand, where compliance with a standard is elevated to a mandatory requirement in E.U. legislation the Community requires that the contents of the standard be made available to all interested parties, albeit on a "fair, reasonable and non-discriminatory basis." [81] Ultimately, the burden for assuring proper negotiated access to standards in such cases falls on the relevant European standardisation bodies. While accepting that the end effect of refusal to provide access on reasonable terms would be an inability to implement the standard under Community law, requiring steps for withdrawal of the standard,[82] the Commission's position is that

> [I]f a European standardisation body consistently failed to ensure non-discriminatory access to its standards, the status of the standardisation body itself under Community law would have to be reviewed. [83]

Conversion of *de facto* Standards into Official Standards

6–35 How may a *de facto* standard be converted into an official standard, assuming that there is scope for negotiating an agreement between the proprietor of the intellectual property vested in the standard and an official standard-setting body? From a public policy point of view, the adoption of official standards based on *de facto* standards has the advantage of exploiting well-tried, tested and normally well-documented solutions that have gained market acceptance. However, where a *de facto* standard concerns a technology embodying IP rights, the rightholder must be put on notice that a standard is to be promulgated using the technology in question. The owner of a proprietary standard might be prepared to see his standard converted to an official industry standard by a recognised standard-setting body, perhaps forgoing exclusive control and royalty rates that he would negotiate in bilateral agreements in favour of potentially large growth in market share and interoperability-induced increases in the value of his own products.

The approach to IP rights used by ISO/IEC , CEN/CENELEC and ETSI, do not make it easy for a reluctant rightholder to say "no" to negotiating a license. True, holders of patents and "like rights" must be canvassed to provide a statement as to whether they would be willing to negotiate a license.[84] Furthermore, absent a statement from the rightholder, the relevant Technical Committee may not proceed with inclusion of a patented item—unless the respective Council gives its permission. If such permission is forthcoming the work on development of the standard continues and the standard is published. Only if it emerges after publication of an International Standard that a license cannot be obtained under reasonable terms and conditions is the International Standard referred back to the Technical Committee for further consideration.

ETSI's Intellectual Property Rights Policy[85] sets out detailed procedural rules for dealing with an essential intellectual property right relating to a particular standard or

---

[80] *ibid.*, at para. 4.3.3.
[81] *ibid.*, at paras 6.3.1—6.3.3.
[82] *ibid.*
[83] *ibid.*
[84] ISO provides a basic text for return by a patent holder willing to negotiate a license relating to use of patented items envisaged for reference in an ISO proposed standard. The patent holder is required to state that it is willing to negotiate licenses with an unlimited number of applicants throughout the world "under reasonable and non-discriminatory terms and conditions that are demonstrably free of any unfair competition." See ISO website at www.iso.org.
[85] ETSI Rules of Procedure, November 22, 2000, Annex 6, at www.etsi.org.

technical specification. Where such a right is brought to the attention of ETSI, the owner is requested to give a written undertaking that it is prepared to grant irrevocable licenses on fair reasonable and non-discriminatory terms to manufacture, sell, lease, repair, use, or operate equipment and use methods.[86] Faced with a Member's refusal to license an intellectual property right in respect of a standard or technical specification, the ETSI General Assembly reviews the requirement for the standard or technical specification to identify an alternative technology. If no viable alternative exists, work on the standard or technical specification ceases while the Member is requested to reconsider its position, and if it does not withdraw its refusal to license the right in question it must provide a written explanation to ETSI's Director General.[87]

E.U. Competition Law: Trade Associations' Conformity Assessment and Standard-Setting Activities

Certification marks and seals of approval awarded by trade associations must be **6–36**
accessible to non-members as well as members of the association. The Treaty of Rome prohibits in absolute terms agreements that have as an object or effect prevention, restriction or distortion of trade within the common market.[88] Trade associations must therefore act, and be seen to act, in ways that do not violate competition principles, which prohibit collusion and monopolistic interference with the natural flow of commerce. In the E.U., associations for the joint use of a quality label are deemed not to restrict competition if other competitors, whose products objectively meet the stipulated quality requirements, can use the label on the same conditions as the members.[89] Nor do the obligations to accept quality control of the products provided with the label, to issue uniform instructions for use, or to use the label for the products meeting the quality standards constitute restraints of competition.[90] But, there may be restraint of competition if the right to use the label is linked to obligations regarding production, marketing, price formation or obligations of any other type, as is for instance the case when the participating enterprises are obliged to manufacture or sell only products of guaranteed quality. Furthermore, the standards underpinning the mark must be reasonable and objective, and the producer's right to sell and advertise products other than those certified must not be restricted.[91]

The E.U. regards associations for the joint use of a quality label as not restrictive of competition if qualifying products of other competitors can use the label on the same conditions as the members. A case in point is NAVEWA/ANSEAU,[92] in which a non-profit association of water supply companies in Belgium required washing machines and dishwashers intended for use in Belgium to carry a safety conformity label. The labels were available only from manufacturers or sole importers who received them from CEG, a non-profit association comprising electric utilities, manufacturers and importers of electric appliances and professional and technical bodies. The Commission held that the programme of conformity assessment discriminated against importers other than sole importers.

---

[86] *ibid.*, at para. 6.1.
[87] *ibid.*, at paras 8.1.1 and 8.1.2.
[88] Arts 81 and 82 (ex 85 and 86) of the Treaty of Rome.
[89] Notice on Co-operative Agreements [1968] O.J. C75/3, para. 8.
[90] *ibid.*
[91] *ibid.*
[92] *NAVEWA/ANSEAU* [1982] O.J. L167/39; corrigendum [1982] O.J. L325/20. On appeal, *NV IAZ International Belgium v. E.C. Commission* [1983] E.C.R. 3369.

Where members of an association are free to use an association's seal purely as an advertising symbol, it would not normally be regarded as a restriction of competition. Joint advertising agreements designed solely to draw buyers' attention to the products of an industry are viewed as not restrictive of competition between the participating enterprises. However, if the participating enterprises are partly or wholly prevented, by agreements or concerted practices, from themselves advertising or if they are subjected to other restrictions, there may be a restraint of competition.[93] Where joint advertising services are rendered to members by the association by staff financed by membership fees, it is regarded as reasonable for such services to be generally reserved for members.[94]

Consumer Protection—The Move to Increase Office of Fair Trading Powers

6–37 The government elected in 1997 accepted that OFT be accorded new powers to approve, monitor and assure compliance with trade association codes of practice, based on core principles set forth in a White Paper.[95] The OFT would provide and market a seal of approval for approved codes so that consumers would be able to see whether trader members of trade associations are committed to a code. These proposals are in line with proposals for co-regulation and increased accountability under self-regulation that were announced by the E.U. Commission in its White Paper on Governance in July 2001.[96]

Trade Association Standards: United Kingdom Competition Law

6–38 The Competition Act 1998 transposes into United Kingdom legislation the prohibitions embodied in the Treaty of Rome, which aim to ensure free competition within the European Union. Thus two fundamental prohibitions were introduced explicitly into United Kingdom law, namely (1) the prohibition of anti-competitive agreements and practices[97] and (2) abuse of a dominant market position.[98] Changes in enforcement of international anti-cartel laws in the United Kingdom, discernable in the last two years can be attributed in part to the Competition Act.[99]

Chapter 1 of the Act, adopts the language of Article 81 (ex 85) of the E.C. Treaty in prohibiting agreements between undertakings, decisions by associations of undertakings or concerted practices which may affect trade within the United Kingdom and have as their object or effect the prevention, restriction or distortion of competition within the United Kingdom. Chapter II follows Article 82 (ex 86) of the Treaty in prohibiting any conduct by one or more undertakings which amounts to the abuse of a dominant position in a market if it may affect trade within the United Kingdom. Where an

---

93 Notice on Co-operative Agreements [1968] O.J. C75/3, para. 7.

94 See Commission Decision of October 16, 1980 relating to a proceeding under Art. 81 (ex 85) of the EEC Treaty (IV/97—*Industrieverband Solnhofener Natursteinplatten eV*) [1980] O.J. L138/32.

95 See Chap. 5, para. 5–24, above.

96 See n. 45, above.

97 Competition Act 1998, s.2.

98 Competition Act 1998, s.18.

99 "If you want to see a country that has completely changed its attitude towards cartel enforcement in terms of the law, as well as in terms of enforcement personnel and enforcement priorities, take a look at the U.K. That is a night and day situation, compared to a couple years [*sic*] ago." Interview with Gary Spratling (ex U.S. Department of Justice Prosecutor), 14 Antitrust 6,11 (2000).

agreement has intentionally or negligently infringed the Chapter I or Chapter II prohibition, the Director General of Fair Trading may require a party to the agreement to pay him a penalty.

Codes of Practice in E-commerce

The E.U. Directive on electronic commerce, which Member States are required to transpose into domestic law before January 17, 2002, requires the encouragement of the creation of codes of conduct by trade, professional and consumer associations or organisations, to govern the provision of information society services and promote safe use of the internet for electronic commerce ("e-commerce").[1] In order to ensure that such codes of conduct comply with Community law, subparagraph (b) of Article 16(1) encourages interested parties to inform the Commission of any draft codes. Article 8 of the Directive sets out the general principle that commercial communication is permitted for regulated professions to enable them to provide an Information Society service while meeting the applicable professional rules of conduct. Given the differences in approach and the fact that bodies in the regulated professions have a tradition of self-regulation, the Directive aims to encourage such bodies at the European level to identify necessary adjustments and common solutions, in compliance with Community law, in the interest of the professions themselves, consumers, and the competent national authorities. Information on regulated professional bodies' specialties and their fees is considered vital to economic activity and to consumer protection. Other indications that might also be important include photographs, logos, customer information and customer testimonials. 6–39

In the United Kingdom, there is some concern, shared by traders and Members of Parliament that security and confidence in online shopping and business generally have yet to develop fully. One Government-backed policy that has been considered to enhance public confidence is to certify the codes of conduct of e-commerce traders. An example of a Government-backed scheme is TrustUK, which, at its website,[2] declares itself to be "a non-profit Organisation endorsed by the United Kingdom Government to enable consumers to buy online with confidence." The website explains that "Most reputable companies are members of trade associations or subscriber bodies which operate codes of practice to which their members are required to adhere—for the purposes of TrustUK, they are known as code owners. When you visit a web site bearing the TrustUK e-hallmark you'll know that this company subscribes to a strict code of practice approved by TrustUK." However, the proliferation of certification schemes, some either created by, or under the auspices of the Government and some not, has been said to carry a danger of confusing the public.[3]

[1] Dir. 2000/31 of the European Parliament and of the Council of June 8, 2000 on certain legal aspects of information society services, in particular electronic commerce, in the internal market ("Directive on electronic commerce") [2000] O.J. L178/1, Art. 16(1).

[2] See TrustUK website, www.trustuk.co.uk.

[3] "Many people in the internet industry have come to view trust marks and certification schemes as an excellent opportunity to further the e-commerce market. Trust marks will help to provide confidence and a system of recourse in buying and selling online and in business-to-business transactions. However, there are many certification schemes and trademarks, and the number of them is rapidly increasing. I am worried that, instead of building public confidence, it might cause confusion . . . I emphasize that my concerns about TrustUK are based on a belief that it is a good idea. The Government are to be commended for creating it . . . I have looked at TrustUK's website to see what it is trying to achieve. I am worried about self-declaration. TrustUK seems to be setting itself up as a body that recognises codes of practice instead of providing a mechanism so that buyers can have confidence in individual merchants." Mr. Brian White, M.P. for Milton Keynes North-East, in House of Commons Hansard Debates for November 30, 2000 (Pt 3), col. 1129.

Another example of an e-commerce "hallmark" is that of the Net Retailers Federation[4] which, according to its website was formed "to offer legitimate on-line Retailers a visible, instantly recognisable Hallmark of service reliability in the eyes of the Consumer".

Conclusion

6–40 The WTO/GATT TBT provides a worldwide framework of basic rules, guidelines and procedural principles for promulgation of technical regulations, standards, and conformity assessment procedures. The TBT urges the multilateral trading system away from the notion of product certification towards the wider, more holistic, concept of conformity assessment, which entails not only certification of a product *qua* product, but also the environment and management system within which it is produced. Certification marks appear to be as applicable to conformity assessment as they are to product certification. Therefore, increased utilisation of certification marks seems likely as conformity assessment increasingly replaces product certification in the multilateral trading system.

Much of the WTO approach to technical regulation and standardisation, particularly its focus on mutual recognition of technical requirements, mutual acceptance of competence to assess conformity, and the harmonisation of standards, is reminiscent of E.U. principles established under the "New Approach", which commenced in the mid-1980s, a decade before the WTO was established. Ironically, as the E.U. plans for enlargement of the single market and the integration of e-commerce into its legislative and judicial institutions, the E.U. now sees a need to modify its regulatory strategy. There is likely to be increased emphasis on a mixed regime combining autonomous regulatory agencies at E.U. level with co-regulation based on enforceable formalised co-operation between the interested parties.[5] It remains to be seen if and how the new proposed modalities of E.U. regulation will influence WTO regulatory principles on one hand and the United Kingdom regulatory regime on the other.

---

[4] See Net Retailers Federation website at www.netretailfederation.com.

[5] Commission of the European Communities, Communication COM(2001) 130 final, Brussels, March 3, 2001, and White paper on European Governance COM(2001) 428 final, Brussels, July 25, 2001.

7

AUTHENTICATION OF DIGITAL PRODUCTS

Introduction

This chapter puts forward the proposition that a legally protectible "authentication mark" is associable with digital products.[1] The proposition builds on the notion that an authentic digital product is one reproduced or distributed with legitimate authority or approval. The digital watermarks and digital signatures currently used in digital products are, it is suggested, forms of authentication mark. They are means of authenticating digital content through embedded ownership and other data, which can be used to detect and prevent unauthorised reproduction and distribution. 7–01

A review of judicial constructions and definitions indicates that something is authentic if it is established or verified as genuine or that it is what it purports to be.[2] A person who controls a machine by which an infringement of copyright might be committed, makes the means available to other persons knowing that it could be put to infringing use, and omits to take reasonable steps to limit its use to legitimate purposes, "authorises" any infringement that results from its use.[3] Thus the term "authentic" is reserved here for legitimate copies, by which is meant copies made by the right holder or with his authorisation or approval. Such copies may be said to result from the exercise of an *authentication right*, cognate to copyright, as signified by an authentication mark which is embedded in or attached to the digital content of the product.

The initial sections of the chapter reflect upon the differences between the proposed authentication mark and a conventional certification mark. Then, the technical measures that are synergistic with protection of an authentication mark are described in more detail. Later sections review recent legislation that comports with the idea of a digital authentication right. Of particular relevance is recent legislation granting full legal recognition to digital signatures and treaty-based E.U. and United States laws that interdict unauthorised circumvention of access control and copyright protection devices, trafficking in devices that facilitate circumvention, and interference with rights management information.

---

1 Examples of digital products in the present context are digital books, videos, music, films and software, all of which may be delivered on tangible carriers such as CDs or DVDs, or via electronic communications channels such as the internet, satellite or cable.

2 See "Words and Phrases" and cumulative supplements, (St. Paul: West Publishing, 1966–2000).

3 *Moorhouse and Angus and Robertson v. University of N.S.W.* [1976] R.P.C. 151.

Towards a Digital Authentication Mark: The Nexus between Authenticity and Authorisation or Approval

7–02 Why is the concept of a legally protectible authentication mark necessary for digital products? It is submitted that certification marks, as currently conceived under the law, do not seem to be suitable for certifying the authenticity of digital content. The function of a certification mark is to indicate certification to objective standards of particular characteristics such as geographical origin, material, mode of manufacture, quality or accuracy. However, an attempt to determine the authenticity of a digital product by reference to an objective technical standard may well yield an inconclusive result. State-of-the-art copying is such that, for many digital products, there is no discernible difference between unauthentic and authentic copies as far as an observer is concerned. Instead, the essential difference between the unauthentic and the authentic resides in the legal status of the copy.

The key question for both the right holder and the consumer is whether the information content that is vested in the product and accessed by the customer is authentic in the sense that it is produced by or with the legitimate authority or approval of the right holder. Consequently, unless the concept of a certification mark can be expanded to include the very legitimacy of the product as the standard or requirement to be complied with, the certification mark paradigm does not appear to be appropriate.

7–03 Another important reason why a certification mark is not adapted for authentication of digital products has to do with the right of user. Under United Kingdom law, and in similar jurisdictions in this regard, the proprietor of a registered certification mark authorises others to apply the mark to their own products. The proprietor is excluded from using the mark himself on goods of the kind certified. By way of contrast, the proposed authentication right provides expressly for the use of a proprietor's own (digital) mark on his products and copies legitimately made by others, in order to designate such products and copies of them as authentic. Unless United Kingdom and United States law were to reconceive of a certification mark so as to extend the right of user to the proprietor of the mark, as is the case for example under Australian law,[4] the proposed digital authentication mark could not be viewed as a certification mark.

Furthermore, authentication of digital products is different from certification of products as discussed in previous chapters because the notion of "product" is different. Music, books, films, software and other digital products comprise digital representations of information, which are protected by copyright. Indeed, it has been noted that there must be uncertainty as to whether information can in fact be sold at all, since a sale under the United Kingdom law of sale and supply of goods predicates transfer of ownership rights. Instead, the nature of the transaction is in the nature of a license, so as to control use and further copying.[5]

---

[4] Australian Trade Marks Act 1995, s.169. The owner may use the certification trade mark on goods or services which it deals with or provides, or allow other persons to become *approved users* of the certification trade mark. In either case, the use must be in accordance with rules governing use of the mark, rules which must be approved by the Australian Competition and Consumer Commission.

[5] See Reid (n. 31, below), at p. 97.

Digital Watermarks

Digital watermarks are widely applied to the products released by the copyright industries[6] as a useful contribution to the prevention, among other things, of illegal copying. They are just one legally supported technological tool for limiting revenue loss[7] due to "piracy". Digital watermarking serves to evince the authenticity of digital products on tangible and electronic communication carriers[8] alike; it can also identify illegal copies and track their propagation and distribution across networks. **7–04**

Comprising a concealed series of data bits embedded within the digital representation of the work, a watermark is intended to be an immutable identifying connection between the work and the right holder.[9] Although not perceptible to human observers, the bits can be read by a detection device to determine the origin of the product and whether it is authentic.

Although watermarks are vulnerable to technological attack[10] they are finding widespread use, particularly in connection with internet delivery of music and video online. For such applications a personalised bitstream watermark is embedded into the work during delivery to the customer. The bitstream can be used to identify and track unauthorised copying from and to various media. For example, methods exist for revealing unauthorised copies on the internet by using computer programs known variously as "worms", "web-spiders" or "web-crawlers", that work their way through web pages, checking for and signalling the detection of unauthorised copies.

Advanced digital watermarks can also be used to actively control access, reproduction and subsequent distribution or communication of the product to others. However, access control requires that computers, receivers, playback, record and other devices incorporate means for detecting and reading the watermark information. There is here a problem

[6] The term "copyright industries" is applied broadly to include the creators, owners and producers of text, software, music, video, film and multimedia products.

[7] The Recording Industry Association of America (RIAA) reports that during the year 2000 some 2560 DMCA notices were sent to link sites that facilitated the downloading of unauthorised files. Counterfeit and pirate CD-Rs seized in 2000 increased by 79% over 1999, resulting in 1,669,394 counterfeit/pirate CD-Rs seized. Between April and December 2000, there were 1035 arrests in New York City alone for distribution of unauthorised recordings, compared to 316 for all of 1999. The 1,035 arrests resulted in the confiscation of approximately 600,000 unauthorised CD-Rs. Confronted with advances in internet technology such as MP3, which compresses large audio files into small files for computer storage and uploading and downloading over the internet, RIAA initiated suits for various types of illegal conduct, including creation of commercial music databases (MP3.com) and the deliberate aggregation of links to illegal music downloads (MP3Board.com). A summary judgment against MP3.com was entered in favour of the plaintiffs on April 28, 2000. In *RIAA v. Napster*, the Ninth Circuit Court of Appeals upheld a federal district court ruling that Napster was liable for contributory and vicarious infringement of copyrighted material. On March 6, 2001, Federal District Court Judge Marilyn H. Patel issued a modified preliminary injunction in the case requiring Napster to remove Plaintiff's works from its system. See Recording Industry Association of America website www.riaa.com.

[8] Typical physical carriers include DCC (Digital Compact Cassette), MD (Mini Disc), CD-R (Compact Disc-Recordable) and CD-RW (Compact Disk-Rewritable), DVD-RW (Digital Versatile Disc-Rewritable) and DVD-RAM (Digital Versatile Disc Random Access Memory). Electronic communication carriers include on-demand cable, satellite and internet.

[9] Historical Note: Watermarking of papers was first practiced in Europe in Fabriano, Italy, in the late 13th century, when paper makers began to incorporate designs such as crosses and circles into the moulds in which the paper was cast. The dried paper was thinner in the area contacted by the device, resulting in a permanent impression or "watermark" that was visible when held up to light and that was impossible to copy exactly. Later marks included the initials or names of the paper makers. The original reason for their use is not clear. See *Encyclopaedia Britannica*, "Paper Manufacture" (Encyclopaedia Britannica, Inc. 1971), Vol. 17, p. 280.

[10] Studies of attacks on commercially available image watermarking schemes, carried out at the University of Cambridge Computer Laboratory by Petitcolas *et al.* show that the use of web crawlers to download images from the internet and check them for the presence of a watermark, creation of supposedly inalterable watermarks, use of Java applets to encase images on a web site and other techniques can all be successfully attacked. See www.cl.cam.ac.uk/~fapp2/watermarking.htm.

arising from the resistance of manufacturers of computers and consumer electronics to design their products with built-in capabilities for detecting and reading the bit sets associated with copyright protection measures.[11] Requirements for such capabilities if imposed by either the law or stipulated by the copyright industries might have far-reaching consequences for the manufacturers, encompassing technological, economic and liability considerations. Nevertheless, there are precedents for statutorily required technical protection measures in equipment. For example, in enacting the United States Audio Home Recording Act of 1992, Congress required manufacturers of digital audio tape recorders to fit their products with detectors to disable further copying of copyright digital music if attempts are made to copy from a copy that is itself second- or higher-generation.[12]

Watermark Robustness versus Perceptibility

7–05 In robust watermark technology, the mark must remain invariant not only under attempts to tamper with the mark but also under normal operations such as intentional size, shape or orientation changes of a digital image and legitimate extraction and security checks.[13] Furthermore, the probabilities of failing watermark detection (false-negative error) and detecting a watermark when one is not in fact present (false-positive error) must be very low if watermarking is to be treated as unambiguous evidence of authenticity. Other factors affecting usefulness of the watermarking approach are the cost and time penalties associated with embedding, extracting, reading and operating on the data bit sets. Additionally, while a large number of bits make for a robust watermark they also render the mark more perceptible (as an audio or visual distortion).[14]

Digital Watermarking Technology Evaluation

7–06 The interplay between the various technological and economic factors in watermarking and their optimisation for commercial exploitation is illustrated by reference to the recent evaluations conducted by JASRAC, the Japanese Society for Rights of Authors, Composers and Publishers. JASRAC coordinated an international test, named "STEP 2000", with various other copyright management bodies around the world to evaluate audio digital watermarking technologies.[15] Particular attention was given to the robustness-audibility tradeoff. The evaluation also took into consideration the time elapsed in embedding and extracting the watermarked information. The watermarked music that was submitted for evaluation included requirements for copy control bits[16]

---

[11] See D.S. Marks and B.H. Turnbull, "Technical Protection Measures: The Intersection of Technology, Law and Commercial Licenses" [2000] E.I.P.R. 198 at 202.

[12] See *Nimmer on Copyright* (Mathew Bender, New York, 1999), Chap. 12A, p. 90.

[13] The robustness of data embedded for state of the art electronic copyright management systems (ECMs) for videos is such that, for example, the data stay with the video even when it is converted to analogue form and retain their ability to control the behavior of video devices and software. See for example Digimarc ECMs for video products at www.digimarc.com. On the other hand, if *fragile* watermarking technology is used, the watermark is designed to be destroyed by illegal activities.

[14] In the music recording industry one test for determining how many bits can be used with a particular watermarking technology is whether professionally trained listeners can detect the watermark.

[15] Besides Japan, collection societies from the following jurisdictions supported the STEP 2000 evaluation project: Australia, United States, The Netherlands, Hong Kong, Germany, Great Britain, France, Spain, Italy and Finland. See JASRAC website at www.jasrac.or.jp/ejhp/.

[16] Copy control bits serve as flags to indicate whether copying is permitted when the work is inserted in the receiver or playback device. Such flags may be of questionable value since they are easily identified and circumvented by "content pirates". See D.S. Marks and B.H. Turnbull, "Technical Protection Measures: The Intersection of Technology, Law and Commercial Licenses" [2000] E.I.P.R. 198 at 212.

and separate copyright management bits. As a result of the programme, JASRAC has concluded that watermarking technology has "moved beyond the research and experiment stage" and has "reached a level of practical utilization".[17]

Authentication and Encryption

Although digital watermarking makes a useful contribution to protecting the proposed authentication right in digital products, it frequently is incapable, by itself, of withstanding piratical attack. Stronger forms of protection are available by resorting to advanced encryption techniques. Complete transactions in digital products, from initial inquiry through to ordering, delivery and download are now commonplace on the internet. In such transactions, encryption of the digital content can assure that it is decrypted, accessed and used solely by the authorised recipient under the agreed terms and conditions.[18] Encryption technology for secure distribution, downloading and use that complies with the contractual terms and conditions of supply and that controls further copying and dissemination, is of great importance for authentication of digital products over the internet.[19] 7–07

Public Key Infrastructure Cryptography

Securing of the proposed authentication right through encryption and decryption is premised on the use of special "keys", which are mathematical algorithms that operate on the digital content. Symmetric or private key encryption systems use the same key for encryption and decryption. The same key is thus known to both the sender and the recipient. Asymmetric, or public key encryption, provides a more secure form of encryption in which each network subscriber is assigned a key pair comprising a public key and a private key. The public key is published; the private key is in the sole possession of the subscriber. One key of the pair is used for encryption and the other for decryption. Thus if X wishes to encrypt digital content for receipt by Y, X can use Y's public key to encrypt and Y uses Y's private key to decrypt. 7–08

Digital Signatures as Evidence of Authenticity

Besides encryption and decryption of transacted-for digital content, Public Key Infrastructure (PKI) cryptography is also used to evidence the authenticity of the transacting parties' identities by associating with each a unique "digital signature". A digital signature comprises an additional block of encrypted data that is attached to the encrypted digital content. If X wishes to impress his digital signature on to the particular copy of the product that he sends to Y, X signs using his private key. The digital signature can be decrypted by anyone who has access to X's public key, thereby authenticating X as the sender of the digital content, which may take the form of 7–09

---

[17] The enterprises whose technologies were certified under STEP 2000 were IBM, MarkAny (Korea), Victor Company of Japan, Signum (England) and BlueSpike (USA).

[18] Such terms and conditions may include, for example, the number of times that the recipient is permitted to access and use the work.

[19] See, for example, Competitive Technologies, Inc., January 19, 2000, news release announcing incorporation of its licensed encryption technology for use in digital music security and media distribution security, at www.competitivetech.net/pr_000119c.htm.

documents, communications or data, and which may or may not contain sound, images or both.

One example of the joint use of digital content encryption and digital signatures is the SafeDisc® system for CDs.[20] During premastering, the content is encrypted and carries with it authentication instructions. A unique SafeDisc digital signature is subsequently added to the title during mastering. When a user plays an original disc, the authentication software reads the digital signature, thus allowing the program to be decrypted and to play normally. The signature cannot be copied by CD-Rs or by professional mastering equipment. The original CD must be present in the CD-ROM drive to allow the authentication process, which is transparent to the user, to occur. When an unauthorised copy is played back, the absence of the signature will prevent decryption of the program and the copy will not play.[21]

Thus technologically advanced electronic signatures serve to both verify the identity of the sender and detect any loss of integrity of the information in the product.[22] This dual function is recognised in the E.U.'s Electronic Signatures Directive,[23] which distinguishes between an "electronic signature" *simpliciter*[24] and an "advanced electronic signature", which is not only capable of identifying the signatory[25] but also is linked to the data to which it relates in such a manner that any subsequent change of the data is detectable.[26] Thus Y can be confident that what he receives was sent by X and furthermore that the content has not been changed in any way since it was signed.

Digital Signatures as Authenticators in United Kingdom Law

7–10 The primary purpose of a signature in English law is to authenticate the document to which it is affixed. In conventional terms, a signature is the writing, or otherwise affixing, of a person's name or a mark to represent his name with the intention of authenticating a document as being that of, or as binding on, the person whose name or mark is so written or affixed.[27] In his study of English statutory definitions and usage of the word "signature" and the pertinent case law Reid considered that

> The most important conclusion which can be drawn from the analysis . . . is that the primary reason for requiring a signature is to authenticate a document. If, therefore, some technological method of authentication can be adopted which additionally evidences the primary characteristic of a signature, namely that it is an act whose performance evidences that the "signatory" intended to authenticate or adopt the contents of the document as his own,[28] that method of authentication is arguably a digital signature which will satisfy any legislative requirement for other than a personal signature.[29]

---

[20] See www.macrovision.com/scp.html.

[21] SafeDisc includes anti-hacking technology that is intended to prevent the compromise of its security features. The anti-hacking technology is designed to not only deter casual copying, but also to stop destructive hackers and commercial pirates. Nevertheless, "cracking" and "hacking" information is posted on the internet by individuals and groups that promote and assist circumvention of protection measures. SafeDisc, which is used to protect a long list of computer games, has not escaped their attention.

[22] The term "integrity" comprises the correctness of the information, its origin and the functioning of the system which processes it.

[23] Dir. 99/93 on a Community Framework for Electronic Signatures (commonly known as the Electronic Signatures Directive), Art.2(2). The Directive was published at [2000] O.J. L13/12. See also n. 35, below.

[24] *ibid.*, Art. 2(1).

[25] *ibid.*, Art. 2(2)(b).

[26] *ibid.*, Art. 2(2)(d).

[27] *Stroud's Judicial Dictionary of Words and Phrases* (D. Greenberg and A. Millbrook eds., 6th ed., Sweet and Maxwell, London, 2000), Vol. 3, p. 2449.

[28] *Goodman v. J. Elban, Ltd* [1954] 1 Q.B. 550; [1954] 1 All E.R. 763; [1954] 2 W.L.R. 581, CA.

[29] C. Reid, *Digital Information Law: Electronic Documents and Requirements of Form* (Centre for Commercial Law Studies, London, 1996), p. 248.

Thus a physical signature evidences (1) the identity of the signatory,[30] (2) that the signature is intended to be that of the signatory and (3) that the signatory approves of and adopts the document.[31] A mapping of these evidential elements to the digital environment is effected in the Electronic Communications Act 2000 (ECA 2000).[32]

The Role of Certification Authorities

It should be borne in mind, in connection with item (1) in the foregoing, that there is no innate one-to-one correspondence between a digital signature and the identity of the signatory.[33] Instead there must be intervention of a third party, a "Certification Authority" (CA) or "Trusted Third Party" (TTP) which, after verifying a person's identity using real world identification documents, issues the person with a registered encryption key, backed by a certificate of identity. A subscriber's registration record at the CA links his public key to his identity. The CA issues a certificate digitally signed by the CA, containing the registrant's name and other information. The certificate guarantees that the public key belongs to the registrant (network subscriber), who can be a real person or a corporate entity. 7–11

CAs are service providers who must have the confidence of the public. In order for such confidence to accrue, their services must be secure and not open to fraud. A necessary minimum level of such confidence is provided by approvals schemes for businesses and other organisations providing the required services. Annex 1 of the E.U.'s Electronic Signatures Directive requires "qualified" certificates to contain, among other things, the identity of the certification-service-provider and the State in which it is established, the name of the signatory, signature-verification data which correspond to signature-creation data under the control of the signatory, the period of validity of the certificate, the "advanced electronic signature" of the issuing certification-service-provider and, if applicable, limitations on the scope of use of the certificate, including limits on the value of transactions for which the certificate can be used.

The Electronic Communications Act 2000

The ECA 2000, Part II of which is relevant to the present discussion, came into force on May 25, 2000.[34] The ECA 2000 makes provision for the legal recognition of electronic signatures and aims to facilitate the use of electronic communications or electronic storage of information as an alternative to traditional means of communication or 7–12

---

[30] "The virtue of a signature lies in the fact that no two persons write exactly alike, and so it carries on the face of it a guarantee that the person who signs has given his personal attention to the document." Denning L.J., dissenting in *Goodman v. J. Elban, Ltd*, see n. 28, above.

[31] C. Reid, "Legally Binding Electronic Documents: Digital Signatures and Authentication", 35 The International Lawyer, 89, 93 (2001).

[32] See para. 7–12, below.

[33] See Denning L.J.'s comment in *Goodman v. J. Elban, Ltd*, n. 25, above.

[34] Pt I of the Act, addresses the provision of cryptography services, which is at present regulated by a "statutory voluntary approvals programme" established by the Government, which took appropriate powers under Pt I. Pt III of the original Bill, "Investigation of Protected Electronic Data", was removed, but has re-emerged as the Regulation of Investigatory Powers Act 2000.

storage. The Act implements the E.U. Directive on Electronic Signatures[35] and is intended to encourage confidence in electronic commerce and the technology on which it is based. Section 7 of the ECA 2000 provides for admission of electronic signatures in evidence in relation to any question as to the authenticity of an electronic communication or data or as to the integrity of the communication or data. In any legal proceedings an electronic signature incorporated or logically associated with a particular electronic communication or particular electronic data *together with* the certification by any person of such a signature shall be admissible in evidence in relation to any question as to the authenticity of the communication or data or as to the integrity of the communication or data.[36]

Under the ECA 2000, the term "communication" includes a communication comprising sounds or images or both and a communication effecting a payment; "electronic communication" means a communication transmitted (whether from one person to another, from one device to another or from a person to a device or vice versa)—(a) by means of a telecommunication system (within the meaning of the Telecommunications Act 1984); or (b) by other means but while in an electronic form.[37] The key notion of authenticity is defined by (i) whether the communication or data comes from a particular person or other source; (ii) whether it is accurately timed and dated; and (iii) whether it is intended to have legal effect.[38] References to the integrity of any communication or data are references to whether there has been any tampering with or other modification of the communication or data.[39]

Standards for Electronic Signatures

7–13 The development of authentication products is in its infancy and there is as yet no internationally accepted comprehensive suite of industry standards. Wherever electronic signatures are used at the national and international levels standards are needed to provide a uniform minimum level of security. In the European context, the European Electronic Signature Standardization Initiative (EESSI)[40] foresees standardisation requirements in the areas of qualitative and procedural standards for information security and

---

[35] See n. 23, above. The due date for implementation of the Directive was July 19, 2001. The Directive requires each Member State to establish a system to supervise certification-service-providers which are established on its territory and issue qualified certificates to the public. In March 2001, the Government issued a consultation paper, seeking views by June 19, 2001, on the implementation of obligations of Member States and areas where Member States have discretion whether to act on issues, including supervision, accreditation and liability of cryptography service providers, standards for electronic signature products and requirements for use of electronic signatures in the public sector. Section 1 in Part I of ECA requires the Secretary of State to establish and maintain a register, open to the public, of approved providers of "cryptography support services" and specifies information to be contained in the register. However, implementation of Pt I of the Act has not been commenced because the Government preferred to see an industry-led approval process instead of the statutory scheme envisaged in Part I. The Alliance for Electronic Business have drawn up an industry led scheme (known as the "tscheme"), which, if it continues to satisfy the Government's requirements will replace the scheme of Pt I of the Act. Details of the scheme are available at www.tscheme.org.

[36] ECA 2000, s.7(1).

[37] ECA 2000, s.15(1).

[38] ECA 2000, s.15(2)(a).

[39] ECA 2000, s.15(2)(b).

[40] The European Electronic Signature Standardization Initiative (EESSI website at www.ict.etsi.org/eessi/EESSI-homepage.htm) was launched by European industry and standardisation bodies to analyse the standardisation activities needed to support the E.U. Directive on electronic signatures (see nn. 23 and 35, above). Acting on a mandate from the European Commission, EESSI operates under the auspices of the Information and Communications Technologies Standards Board (ICTSB website at www.ict.etsi.org/main.htm), which was set up by the three European standards bodies CEN, CENELEC and ETSI. For more about these three bodies, see, Chap. 6, above.

technical standards for interoperability of authentication. EESSI considers the following standardisation activities to be of high priority.

Security requirements for signature products; certification/registration of conformance of electronic signature products; security management and certificate policies of certification service providers that issue qualified certificates; signature creation and verification; electronic signature syntax and encoding formats, and technical aspects of signature policies; the standard to be used for qualified certificates based on X.509 public key certificates[41]; and the protocol to interoperate with a time stamping authority.[42]

Standardisation programmes are being conducted concurrently by various groups.[43] In Europe, the E.U. Directive for a Community framework for electronic signatures[44] aims to harmonise the legal acceptance of certain electronic signatures throughout the E.U. The Directive identifies requirements for qualified certificates,[45] certification service providers[46] (CSPs), secure signature-creation[47] devices, and recommendations for secure verification[48] devices. Member States' laws, regulations and administrative provisions necessary to comply with the Directive were required to be in force before July 19, 2001.[49] Under the Directive,[50] the European Commission is to establish criteria for the appointment of notified bodies[51] charged with responsibility for assessing the conformity of secure signature creation devices with the requirements of Annex III. Furthermore, the Commission may publish reference numbers of standards, compliance with which shall create a presumption of compliance with the requirements for CSP use of trustworthy systems and products and the technical and cryptographic security of the process supported by them.[52]

World Intellectual Property Organization Copyright Treaty

Besides making certified digital signatures admissible in evidence when attached to communications and data, as described in the foregoing, how else can the law protect the proposed authentication right when exercised through the use of technological measures? The answer would appear to depend on the nature of any given technological measure and the treatment it is accorded in Contracting Parties' laws implementing a 7–14

---

[41] X.509 is a widely accepted standard based on the use of public-key cryptography and digital signatures, which defines a framework for the provision of authentication services. The X.509 standard is premised on the public-key certificate concept, in which each user, or subscriber, is allocated a certificate by a CA, as explained above. The certificate contains basic information, including a certificate serial number, the identity of the issuing CA, the period of validity, the subscriber to whom the certificate refers, the subscriber's public key and the CA's signature. The CA or the subscriber enters the certificate into a directory. The directory server provides the location at which users can obtain certificates.

[42] See European Electronic Signature Standardization Initiative (EESSI), Final Report of the EESSI Expert Team, July 20, 1999.

[43] Examples of bodies that are active in the field of electronic signature standardisation are the Internet Law Policy Forum, the Internet Engineering Task Force, the World Wide Web Consortium and the American Bar Association.

[44] Dir. 99/93 of December 13, 1999 [2000] O.J. L13/12.

[45] *ibid.*, Annex I.

[46] *ibid.*, Annex II.

[47] *ibid.*, Annex III.

[48] *ibid.*, Annex IV.

[49] *ibid.*, Art. 13.

[50] *ibid.*, Art. 3(4).

[51] A notified body in the present context is a national public or private body, designated by a Member State as responsible for accreditation and supervision, and notified to the European Commission and the other Member States as such. See Art. 11.

[52] See n. 44, above, Art. 3(5).

key treaty in this regard—the World Intellectual Property Organization (WIPO) Copyright Treaty (WCT), which was concluded in Geneva, on December 20, 1996.[53]

The WCT recognises that viable protection against unauthorised access and use of digital representations of creative works requires both technological and legal measures, and sets norms for legal protection. The impact of WCT on protection of technical protection measures such as watermarking and digital signatures may be gauged by reference to Articles 11 and 12. These two articles obligate Contracting Parties to provide legal protection and remedies against the circumvention of effective technological measures (Article 11), and the removal or alteration of rights management information in works, and distribution or communication to the public of works which have been subjected to removal or alteration (Article 12).

WCT, Article 11 Protects Against Circumvention

7–15 The intention of Article 11 is to protect rightholders by prohibiting unauthorised circumvention of right holders' *effective* technologies for purposes of copyright infringement. Thus:

> Contracting Parties shall provide adequate legal protection and effective legal remedies against the circumvention of effective technological measures that are used by authors in connection with the exercise of their rights under this Treaty or the Berne Convention and that restrict acts, in respect of their works, which are not authorized by the authors concerned or permitted by law.[54]

Much therefore depends on the interpretation of the term "effective technological measures", which the WCT does not define. Furthermore, the WCT does not recite any specific form of technological measure; neither does it characterise directly what functions the measures are to perform other than to be used in connection with the authors' exercise of their rights under the treaty or the Berne Convention. As will be discussed in paragraphs 7–16 to 7–19, below, the conduct and devices that the technological measures are supposed to be effective in defending against are to be viewed as acts of circumvention of devices that control access, devices that circumvent access control, and devices that circumvent copyright protection.[55]

E.U. Implementation of WCT, Article 11

7–16 On April 9, 2001 the E.U. agreed to a new copyright Directive,[56] which concerns the legal protection of copyright and related rights in the framework of the Internal Market, with particular emphasis on the "Information Society" (by which is meant the internet).

---

[53] As of October 15, 2001, there were 51 Signatories to WCT, including Argentina, Austria, Belgium, Canada, Chile, Denmark, Finland, France, Germany, Greece, Hungary, Indonesia, Ireland, Israel, Italy, Luxembourg, Mexico, Monaco, Netherlands, Nigeria, Portugal, South Africa, Spain, Sweden, Switzerland, United Kingdom, United States of America, Uruguay, Venezuela, and the European Communities. As of October 15, 2001, the only leading industrialised countries on the list of 28 Ratifications and Accessions were Japan and the USA. The Treaty will come into force when the number of ratifications reaches 30. See WIPO website at www.wipo.int/treaties/docs/english/u-page31.doc.

[54] WCT, Art. 11.

[55] See commentary of E. Elizafon Katz, in "RealNetworks, Inc. v. Streambox, Inc. and Universal City Studios, Inc. v. Reimer" 16 Berkeley Technology Law Journal, 53 at 54 (2001).

[56] For the initial proposal for a European Parliament and Council Directive on the harmonisation of certain aspects of copyright and related rights in the information society, see COM (97) 628 [1998] O.J. C108/6. For the Amended Proposal, see COM (1999) 250 final [1999] O.J. C180/6. For the Commission Opinion on the European Parliament's amendments to the Council's common position regarding the proposal, see COM (2001) 170 final March 29, 2001.

Using the same terminology as the WCT, Art. 11, the Directive requires Member States to protect against activities of

> [C]ircumvention without authority of any effective technological measures designed to protect any copyright or any rights related to copyright.[57]

and activities including the manufacture or distribution of devices, products or components or the provision of services, carried out without authority, which:

> (a) [a]re promoted, advertised or marketed for the purpose of circumvention[58] of, or
> (b) have only a limited commercially significant purpose or use other than to circumvent,[59] or
> (c) are primarily designed, produced, adapted or performed for the purpose of enabling or facilitating the circumvention of,
>
> any effective technological measures designed to protect any copyright or any right related to copyright.[60]

The Directive deems a technological measure "effective" where the access to or use of a protected work or other subject matter is controlled through application of an access code or any other type of protection process.[61] Such measures may include decryption, descrambling or other transformation of the work. Thus the E.U. approach to implementation of the WCT, Art. 11 is based on protection against acts of circumvention of access controlling devices and acts, including provision of devices or services, that facilitate circumvention. Therefore a watermark or digital signature that does not control access or use is not likely to be protected under Article 6 of the E.U. Directive.

The Directive accords right holders total control over the manufacture, distribution, etc., of devices designed to circumvent anti-copying devices. This has led to considerable criticism, much of which centres on whether legally enforceable access control by the right holder, through technological means, is compatible with "fair use" or "fair dealing" for education, research, private study and other non-commercial use.[62] Indeed, it is submitted that fair use or fair dealing in copyright should not involve the right holder at all. Such use should be totally decoupled from, and outside, the right holder's domain. The same comments apply in relation to the United States approach to implementation of the WCT, Art. 11.[63]

United States Implementation of WCT, Article 11

Title I of the Digital Millennium Copyright Act[64] (DMCA) amends the United States Copyright Act to implement the WIPO Internet Treaties. Sections 1201 and 1202, address the circumvention of copyright protection systems and the integrity of copyright management information (CMI), respectively. Considering firstly section 1201, there is a broad statement of prohibition on circumvention devices that control access to a copyrighted work. Thus: 7–17

> No person shall circumvent a technological measure that effectively controls access to a work protected under this title.[65]

---

57 See n. 56, above, Amended Proposal, COM(1999) 250 final [1999] O.J. C180/6, Art. 6.1.
58 *ibid.*, Art. 6.2.
59 *ibid.*
60 *ibid.*
61 *ibid.*, Art. 6.3.
62 M. Dohert and I. Griffiths, "The Harmonisation of European Copyright Law for the Digital Age" [2000] E.I.P.R. 17 at 18.
63 See para. 7–17, below.
64 Public Law 105–304 [H.R. 2281]; October 28, 1998.
65 *ibid.*, s.1201(a).

This prohibition language is not limited to circumvention for purposes of infringement. However, a detailed list of exceptions is provided, which include reverse engineering of a lawfully obtained copy for the sole purpose of identifying and analyzing those elements of a program that are necessary to achieve interoperability between programs under particular circumstances,[66] and for certain permissible acts of encryption research.[67]

To "circumvent a technological measure" means to descramble a scrambled work, to decrypt an encrypted work, or otherwise to avoid, bypass, remove, deactivate or impair a technological measure, without the authority of the copyright owner. The DMCA provides that a technological measure effectively protects a right of a copyright owner, for purposes of the Act, if the measure, in the ordinary course of its operation, prevents, restricts, or otherwise limits the exercise of a right of a copyright owner under the title. In *Universal City Studios, Inc. v. Reimerdes*, the court pointed out that the legislative history of the DMCA makes clear that a technological measure "effectively controls access" to a copyrighted work if its *function* is to control access.[68] The intention was not to protect only successful or efficacious means of controlling accesss, as the defendants had argued. Such an interpretation would offer protection where none is needed and withhold protection where it is essential.

In summary, besides the anti-circumvention bans on the act of circumventing an access control device, the DMCA also bans access control circumvention devices, and copyright protection circumvention devices.[69] Therefore, a digital watermark or digital signature that constitutes an access control device is protected against acts of circumvention.

WCT, Article 12 Protects Rights Management Information

7–18 Turning now to Article 12 of the WCT, it will be observed that Article 12 is concerned specifically with remedies against knowingly removing or altering without authority "electronic rights management information" associated with a work, where:

> "[R]ights management information" means information which identifies the work, the author of the work, the owner of any right in the work, or information about the terms and conditions of use of the work, and any numbers or codes that represent such information, when any of these items of information is attached to a copy of a work or appears in connection with the communication of a work to the public.[70]

Remedies are to be provided against the distribution, importing for distribution, broadcasting or communicating to the public, without authority, works or copies of works knowing that electronic rights management information has been removed or altered without authority.[71] This obligation is not specific to any particular type of work.[72]

E.U. Implementation of WCT, Article 12

7–19 Notwithstanding the dependence of protection for technological measures such as digital watermarks or signatures on access- and use-controlling capability under Article 6 of the E.U. Directive, protection is available pursuant to Article 7, which implements

[66] *ibid.*, s.1201(f).
[67] *ibid.*, s.1201(g).
[68] 111 F.Suppl.2d 294 at 318 (S.D.N.Y. 2000).
[69] See Katz, *op. cit.*
[70] WCT, Art.12(2).
[71] WCT, Art. 12(1).
[72] See *Nimmer on Copyright* (Mathew Bender, New York, 1999), Chap. 12A, p. 91.

Article 12 of the WCT. Article 7 requires Member States to provide for adequate legal protection against any person performing without authority, the acts of (a) removal or alteration of any electronic rights-management information; and (b) the distribution, importation for distribution, broadcasting, communication or making available to the public, of copies of works or other subject matter protected under the Directive.[73]

Thus, to the extent that a technological measure comprises rights management information, protection is granted. The protection is operative where a person knows, or has reasonable grounds to know, that his acts induce, enable, or facilitate an infringement of any copyright or any rights related to copyright.[74] The expression "rights-management information", as used in the Directive, includes, among other things, any information provided by rightholders which identifies the work or other subject matter or information about the terms and conditions of use of the work or other subject matter, the right holder and any numbers or codes that represent such information.[75]

United States Implementation of WCT, Article 12

Section 1202 of the DMCA prohibits the provision of false copyright management information (CMI).[76] The definition of CMI includes the title and other identification of the work, the author, the owner, terms and conditions for use and identifying numbers or symbols referring to such information.[77] Furthermore, no person may, without the authority of the copyright owner or the law, intentionally remove or alter CMI, or distribute or import for distribution CMI, knowing that the CMI has been removed or altered without authority of the copyright owner or the law.[78] Also prohibited are the distribution, import for distribution or public performances of works, knowing that the CMI has been removed or altered without authority of the copyright owner or the law.[79] **7–20**

The legislative history of section 1202 of the DMCA states that the section is required to prohibit the intentional providing of false copyright information, such as the title of a work or the name of its author, with the intent to induce, enable, facilitate, or conceal infringement. It also prohibits the deliberate deleting or altering of copyright management information.[80] The legislative history also notes that copyright management information will assist in tracking and monitoring uses of copyrighted works, as well as licensing of rights and indicating attribution, creation and ownership.[81] Thus even a simple watermark that merely acts as a "marker" which can be used to track use of a copyright work appears to qualify for protection under section 1202, provided it contains information complying with the statutory definition of CMI.[82]

Summary and Conclusion

This chapter has suggested that certification marks, as currently conceived under United Kingdom trade mark law, do not appear to be adapted for certification of the authenticity of digital content. The function of a certification mark is to indicate **7–21**

[73] See n. 56, above. Amended Proposal, COM (1999) 250 final [1999] O.J. C180/6, Art. 7.1.
[74] *ibid.*
[75] *ibid.*, Art. 7.2.
[76] DMCA, s.1202(a).
[77] DMCA, s.1202(c).
[78] DMCA, s.1202(b).
[79] *ibid.*
[80] See *Nimmer on Copyright* (Mathew Bender, New York, 1999), Chap. 12A, p. 89.
[81] *ibid.*
[82] DMCA, s.1202(c).

certification to objective standards of particular characteristics such as geographical origin, material, mode of manufacture, quality or accuracy. However, the authenticity of a digital product is not a question of vouching for compliance of physical characteristics to physical or objective standards. Instead, the essential difference between unauthentic and authentic digital products resides in the legal status of the copy.

The digital authentication right put forward in this chapter provides expressly for the application of a proprietor's digital mark to products as a means of securing their authenticity. While the means may be new, the practice of authenticating products by mark reaches far back into history. As described in Chapter 1, above, marks have been affixed to goods by their makers as attestations of authenticity, for regulatory purposes, since medieval times at least. The marking of products was then closely controlled by the guilds, to protect themselves against unauthorised, counterfeit and sub-standard goods. In more recent times, the United Kingdom Trade Marks Act 1905, besides instituting a registrable certification mark,[83] defined a trade mark as a mark used or proposed to be used upon or in connection with goods for the purpose of indicating that they are the goods of the proprietor of such trade mark by virtue of manufacture, selection, *certification*, dealing with or offering for sale [emphasis added].[84] Certifying the authenticity of one's own product through marking is a time-honoured tradition.

In the digital era there is need to widen the concept of product, as used in connection with product certification, to encompass digital products which require authentication. Digital products comprise digital representations of information that are protected by copyright. Such products can be "marked" in digital space, such that the mark is not necessarily readable by human observers but is nevertheless machines-readable. At the machine-readable level, marks can be embedded in the digital content so as to resist counterfeiting, and indicate and protect authenticity by identifying the work, the author, or the right holder in a unique way that is imperceptible to humans.

The digital authentication mark can function as a "sentry", controlling access to a product and regulating its reproduction. However, it is normally only a question of time before a given watermark is "cracked" or circumvented by resourceful interlopers. Probably the strongest form of digital authentication and protection technology presently available is PKI cryptography. Until recently, access to the more sophisticated and strongest forms of cryptography has been subject to stringent governmental controls, notably on the part of the United States government, which has zealously controlled export of the technology. These controls have recently been lifted to a significant degree and there is room for guarded optimism among right holders that advanced encryption will now facilitate protection of digital products to a level of security hitherto unknown.[85]

[83] Trade Marks Act 1905, s.62.

[84] Trade Marks Act 1905, s.3.

[85] On January 12, 2000, the U.S. Department of Commerce Bureau of Export Regulation issued new regulations removing certain limitations on the export of U.S. encryption technology. See *Cryptography and Liberty 2000: An International Survey of Encryption Policy, Country Reports*, at website of the Electronic Privacy Information Center, Washington D.C. (www2.epic.org/reports/crypto2000/countries.html). See also T.E. Black, "Taking Account of the World As it Will Be: The Shifting Course of U.S. Encryption Policy" 53 Federal Communications Law Journal, 289 (2001).

Appendix A
COOPERS' MARKS

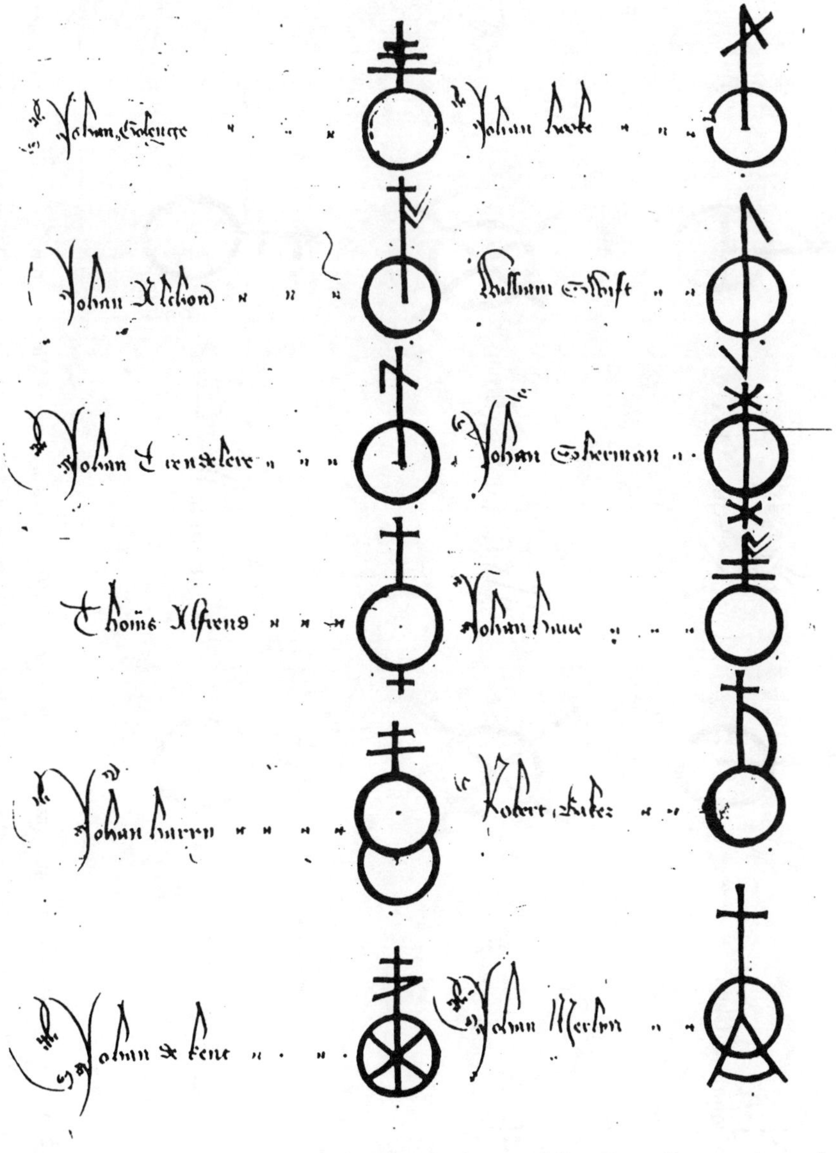

Figure 1. The first 12 entries made on the register of London Coopers' marks at the London Guildhall in 1420.

Figure 2. A selection of London Coopers' marks registered in 1420. The marks are arranged in three rows to highlight the similarities between the marks in each row.

The marks in Figures 1 and 2, were recorded following an ordinance of 1420, issued by the Mayor, Richard Whittington, and the Court of Aldermen, that every Cooper within the liberty of London should have his own iron mark or sign for marking barrels and kilderkins and have the same entered on record. Pursuant to the above ordinance the Coopers residing within the franchise of the City were to present their marks, made of iron, to the court within 14 days, to be there recorded.

Reproduced with kind permission of the Corporation of London Records Office. These marks are recorded in the City's Letter Book I at fos 246 and 247.

Appendix B
PRACTICE AMENDMENT CIRCULAR 2/01

Section 3 and Section 5 practice in relation to applications made to register a mark as both a trade mark and a Collective Mark, or as both a trade mark and Certification Mark

Background

The Trade Marks Act 1994 allows for three different types of marks serving different functions in the marketplace.

An ordinary trade mark distinguishes the origin of goods or services and serves to identify the manufacturer, producer or provider of those particular goods or services.

A collective mark indicates commercial origin of goods or services, but as collective marks they indicate origin in members of an association rather than origin in one party.

A certification mark does not indicate origin. The message conveyed by a certification mark, when it is applied to goods or used in connection with services, is that the goods or services have been examined, tested, inspected, or in some way certified by an independent organization who is not their producer, by methods determined by the certifier/owner to indicate or guarantee a specific characteristic or quality.

When applying to register a certification mark, the nature of the proprietor's business must be considered as it is a requirement of Schedule 2, Paragraph 4 of the Act that:

> "A certification mark shall not be registered if the proprietor carries on a business involving the supply of goods or services of the kind certified."

This paragraph is explicit—the proprietor of a certification mark shall not trade in the relevant goods or services.

When applying to register a collective mark, that status of the proprietor must be considered as it is a requirement of Section 49 of the Act that:

> "A collective mark is a mark distinguishing the goods or services of members of the association which is the proprietor of the mark from those of other undertakings."

This paragraph is explicit—the collective mark will be owned by an association (on behalf of its members) and will indicate origin in the members of the association rather than origin in one party.

It follows that an application to register an identical mark (or so nearly alike as to constitute essentially the same mark) as a certification mark (or as a collective mark) and as an ordinary trade mark, for the same goods or services should be regarded as prima facie evidence that the mark cannot serve the function specified for it in the Act.

Practice where the marks and goods/services are the same

If applications in the same ownership are made to register an identical (or essentially the same) mark as both a collective mark (or certification mark) and as an ordinary trade mark (or vice versa) for the same goods/services, objections should be taken to the later filed application under Section 3 (1)(a) and Section 3 (3)(a) and/or (b). If the later mark is a collective mark an objection should also be taken under Section 49. If it is a certification mark there should also be an objection under Section 50 and under Schedule 2, Paragraph 4.

An objection should be raised under Section 3 (1)(a) as the mark would be incapable of distinguishing goods and/or services of a particular trader from members of an association (if it is a collective mark) or from certified goods or services (if a certification mark).

The filing of an identical mark, or essentially the same mark, as both a trade mark and collective mark for the same goods/services would be contrary to Schedule 1, Paragraph 2 which states:

> "In relation to a collective mark the reference in Section 1 (1) (signs of which a trade mark may consist) to distinguishing goods or services of one undertaking from those of other undertakings shall be construed or interpreted as a reference to distinguishing goods or services of members of the association which is the proprietor of the mark from those of other undertakings."

and hence Section 3 (1)(a).

The filing of an identical mark, or essentially the same mark, as both a trade mark and a certification mark for the same goods and/or services would be contrary to Schedule 2, Paragraph 2 which states:

> "In relation to a certification mark the reference in Section 1 (1) (signs of which a trade mark may consist) to distinguishing goods or services of one undertaking from those of other undertakings shall be construed as a reference to distinguishing goods or services which are certified from those which are not."

and hence Section 3 (1)(a).

An objection should also be raised under Section 3 (3)(a) or (b) as a trade mark, collective mark or certification mark shall not be registered if it is contrary to public policy and/or of such a nature as to deceive the public (for instance as to the nature, quality or geographical origin of the goods or services).

The basic rule is that we should not register *identical* marks of different statuses for *identical* goods/services in any circumstances. Whether there is consent or they are in the same name is irrelevant because the Section 3 (3)(a) objection and (depending of the status of the later application) Section 3 (1)(a), Section 49 or Section 50 or Schedule 2, Paragraph 4 objection(s) are insurmountable.

Practice where the marks and/or goods/services are only similar

Where the marks are only similar, or the goods/services are only similar, there is no absolute bar to the registration of the later mark in the same ownership or, where there is consent, in different ownerships.

However, depending on the degree of similarity between the marks/goods or services, there may still be an objection under Section 3 (3)(a) or (b) to the later application.

If the goods/services are virtually the same there is likely to be an objection if one of the respective marks is a certification mark, eg. between "construction, building and repair services in Class 37" and "quality control services in the building industry in Class 42". This will give rise to an objection under Section 3 (3)(b).

Otherwise the later application may be allowed, but if the use of marks with different statuses causes confusion, this is a ground for revoking the certification or collective mark.

Appendix C
Practice Amendment Circular 13/00

Change of practice on "Retail Services"

The following will be published in Journals 6350, 6351 and 6352 on 18, 25 October and 1 November 2000.

Change of practice on "Retail Services"

1. The Registrar is changing her practice and will, in future, accept applications to register trade marks in respect of certain aspects of a "retail service."

Reasons for the change

2. The reasons for the change are that:—

i) The recitals to Council Directive 104/89 indicate that the purpose of the Directive is to approximate the trade mark laws of Member States; the harmonised laws are based upon a system of protection primarily founded on registration.

ii) The European Court of Justice has confirmed that the essential function of a trade mark is to guarantee to the consumer that the goods/services offered under a mark are under the control of a single undertaking which is responsible for their quality.

iii) Although this definition may not rule out the possibility of protection in cases of "dual branding" (ie the simultaneous use of two different brands on the same product—eg INTEL and TOSHIBA on a lap top computer) it is doubtful whether a retailer who does no more than bring together a wide variety of goods bearing the brands of other undertakings will be able to demonstrate the necessary connection with the goods so as to be able to properly register his mark for the goods he stocks.

iv) The retail sector in the UK contains many businesses with substantial goodwill based wholly or partly upon their activities as retailers. Retailers' names/signs serve to attract the public to one retailer as compared to another similar retailer. The names/ signs therefore appear to serve the function of a trade mark for the retailer's services, which essentially comprise the retailer's selection, range and convenient display of goods. It is inconsistent with the aims of the Directive for retailers' marks and the goodwill they represent to be protected only by non-trade mark laws which vary between Member States.

v) Whilst it is true that Article 50 of the Treaty of Rome defines services as those normally provided for remuneration, there is no corresponding entry in the Trade Mark Directive or the Act, and the European Court appears to have accepted that services which are paid for indirectly fall within the scope of the Treaty (see Coditel 1980 ECR 881 @ 889). It is well known that a retailer obtains remuneration indirectly through the retail "mark up" on goods.

vi) In principle, this appears little different from some other services for which it has long been possible to register trade marks (eg travel agents essentially act as retailers of travel and accommodation services and are remunerated through a fee equivalent to part of the cost of the holiday).

vii) The OHIM Second Board of Appeal has decided that, once properly defined, "retail services" can be the subject of a Community trade mark registration.

3. Whether a particular retail activity qualifies as a service will be a matter of fact and degree. For example, it is doubtful whether a factory shop outlet, which is situated on the factory premises, provides any service over and above a normal trade in the proprietor's own goods.

What will be accepted?

4. Although there is no relevant entry in Schedule 3 to the Trade Mark Rules 2000, the 7th edition of the International Classification of Goods and Services (Nice Classification) includes an explanatory note that Class 35 includes:

> "The bringing together, for the benefit of others, of a variety of goods (excluding the transportation thereof), enabling customers to conveniently view and purchase those goods."

There is no corresponding entry in the alphabetical list of services in Class 35 indicating that the wording in the explanatory note is a general indication rather than a specific description of a service. The Registrar will not object to this description of services in Class 35 provided that the nature of the retail service and (where this is not clear from the nature of the retail service) the market sector are also indicated. In the absence of such indications objections will be taken under section 34(2)—on the grounds that without an indication of the means of bringing goods together and displaying them, the description is too vague for registration—and section 3(6)—on the alternative ground that the wording of the explanatory note is too wide to be a proper description of any one retailer's services.

5. In the case of department stores, supermarkets, hypermarkets, convenience stores etc, the following specifications will be allowed in Class 35:

The bringing together, for the benefit of others, of a variety of goods, enabling customers to conveniently view and purchase those goods in a department store.

Or

The bringing together, for the benefit of others, of a variety of goods, enabling customers to conveniently view and purchase those goods in a supermarket.

6. In the case of specialist retail outlets, it will be necessary to specify the type of store by market sector, *e.g.*:

The bringing together, for the benefit of others, of a variety of goods, enabling customers to conveniently view and purchase those goods in a retail clothes store.

Or

The bringing together, for the benefit of others, of a variety of goods, enabling customers to conveniently view and purchase those goods in a retail off licence store.

Or

The bringing together, for the benefit of others, of a variety of goods, enabling customers to conveniently view and purchase those goods in a retail electrical store.

Or

The bringing together, for the benefit of others, of variety of goods, enabling customers to conveniently view and purchase those goods in a retail pharmacy.

Or

The bringing together, for the benefit of others, of a variety of goods, enabling customers to conveniently view and purchase those goods in a retail furniture store.

7. It is not appropriate to provide an exhaustive list of the goods brought together etc, because the specification should focus on the characteristics of the **service** provided. An indication of market sector is required but this is usually clear from the type of retail outlet specified.

Mail Order and Electronic shopping

8. The reasoning set out above suggests that it should be possible in some circumstances to register a trade mark in respect of the bringing together of goods through a catalogue or electronic shopping media. It is doubtful whether promoting one's own goods in a brochure or on an internet site provides any service. The Registrar will accept applications to register trade marks in respect of services comprising the bringing together of a variety of goods of other traders in a catalogue or through an electronic media, for the benefit of others.

9. As with retail store type registrations, some indication of the field of activity is necessary to avoid objections on the grounds that the descriptions are too broad and/or too vague. The Registrar will nevertheless accept specifications in Class 35 for:

The bringing together, for the benefit of others, of a variety of goods, through a television shopping channel, enabling customers to conveniently view and purchase those goods by means of telecommunications.

It is recognised that television shopping channels (like department stores) bring together a very wide and changing range of goods.

10. In other cases, eg catalogues, internet shopping, computer shopping, electronic shopping, online shopping, e-commerce etc, the mode of operation may not itself be sufficient to reveal the scope of the service and it will normally be necessary to specify the field of activity in order to avoid an objection under section 3(6). For example:

The bringing together, for the benefit of others, of a variety of goods, enabling customers to conveniently view and purchase those goods from a clothing and accessories catalogue by mail order or by means of telecommunications.

Or in the case of where a broader indication is justified, for example, when such services are provided in relation to a miscellaneous goods catalogue:

The bringing together, for the benefit of others, of a variety of goods, enabling customers to conveniently view and purchase those goods from a general merchandise catalogue by mail order or by means of telecommunications.

Similarly, in respect of services provided by a specialist e-commerce retailer through the internet, the following type of specification might be appropriate in the case of, for example, a sports goods supplier:

The bringing together, for the benefit of others, of a variety of goods, enabling customers to conveniently view and purchase those goods from an internet web site specialising in the marketing of sports wear and equipment.

Or if the e-tailer markets a wide range of miscellaneous goods, the following may be justified:

The bringing together, for the benefit of others, of a variety of goods, enabling customers to conveniently view and purchase those goods from a general merchandise internet web site.

Wholesale

11. The same general practice will apply to providers of wholesale services. The Registrar will accept:

> **The bringing together, for the benefit of others, of a variety of goods, enabling customers to conveniently view and purchase those goods in a wholesale outlet.**

What won't be accepted

12. For reasons stated under paragraph 4 above, the statement "the bringing together, for the benefit of others, of a variety of goods, enabling customers to conveniently view and purchase those goods", will not be accepted without further qualification.

13. In the case of Dee Corporation plc and Others Trade Mark Application [1990] RPC page 168, Falconer J said in relation to "retail services":

> *"Moreover, that definition is too indefinite to provide an identifiable specification of the service or services for a registration so that any person could know whether he would infringe or not".*

Therefore, the following terms are considered too vague and/or too broad and are unable to serve as adequately defined statements of services:

Retail services;

Retail store services;

Retailing;

Department store services;

Shops;

Factory shops [shops on factory premises];

Shopkeeping;

Merchandising;

Distributorship;

Supply or provision of goods;

Sales services;

Direct selling;

Mail order;

Mail order catalogue services

Catalogue services;

Television shopping;

Electronic shopping;

Internet shopping;

Computer shopping;

Online shopping;

E-commerce;

E-tailing.

This list is not exhaustive.

14. Objections will be taken against applications which include the above and similar terms under the following parts of the statute:

i) Section 34(2) of the Act—because the terms are too vague for classification;

ii) Rule 8 of the Trade Mark Rules 2000—because the application includes services that are too indefinite and as a consequence could relate to more than one class.

iii) Section 3(6) of the Act—because the terms are too broad in their scope.

As indicated by the examples shown in the preceding paragraphs of this notice, many of the above terms, if appropriately qualified, may be incorporated into specifications which are capable of providing sufficiently clear statements of services.

Search of the Register

15. The Registrar's provisional view is that, prima facie, there will only be a likelihood of confusion between a retailer's mark and a trade mark for related goods in (usually some combination of) the following circumstances:

i) where the retail service in question specialises in bringing together the type of goods for which a conflicting mark is registered in a goods class;

ii) where it is common practice in the trade for retail businesses of the type in question to produce a relevant range of "own brand" products;

iii) where the earlier trade mark has a highly distinctive character, either per se or because of the use made of it.

16. The reputation of the earlier trade mark and (unless it is obvious) the practices of the trade will only be taken into account on the basis of evidence in opposition/invalidation proceedings.

17. The Registrar will conduct a search for earlier trade marks as follows:

i) Applications for the "bringing together of a variety of goods etc" in department stores, convenience store, supermarket, newsagents or on a television shopping channel:
Only Class 35 will be searched in order to identify conflicting marks for the same or similar services.

ii) Applications which specify the type of specialist store that "bring together the goods" (or specialist catalogues etc), a search will normally be made into the main class or classes covering the principal goods brought together by the retailer. For example, in the case of:

The bringing together, for the benefit of others, of a variety of goods, enabling customers to conveniently view and purchase those goods in a retail clothes store.

Class 25 will be searched and the Registrar will consider whether to refuse protection for the later trade mark *ex officio*.

18. A similar approach will be followed if the later trade mark is proposed to be registered in respect of:

The bringing together, for the benefit of others, of a variety of goods, enabling customers to conveniently view and purchase those goods from a clothing and accessories catalogue by mail order or by means of telecommunications.

19. Whether an objection under section 5 is raised as a result of the search will depend upon the matters identified at paragraph 15 above, and the degree of similarity between the respective marks (which will normally have to be higher than would be the case if the respective marks were to be registered for the goods themselves).

20. A revised cross search list will be produced as soon as possible drawing upon the experience gained from examining the 600+ applications already before the Office. Once this is done, applications to register trade marks for certain goods may be subject to a search for similar services in Class 35.

Absolute grounds of refusal

21. Retail stores are commonly named after their geographical location. They will therefore be classified as a local service and applications to register geographical place names as trade marks for retail stores will normally be objected to if the place concerned has a population over 5000.

Provisional nature of guidance

22. The acceptance of retail marks in Class 35 marks a major departure from previous UK practice. This guidance represents the Registrar's current view of the matter, but it may change in the light of further experience or because of decisions subsequently taken in opposition or invalidation proceedings before the Office or the Courts.

Index